Such Agreeable Savages

An Englishwoman's Excursions
to the Gulf of Mexico &
Republic of Texas, 1842-1846

By Mrs. Matilda Charlotte Houstoun
with annotations by Michelle M. Haas

Copano Bay Press
2011

This annotated edition of Mrs. Houstoun's writings on Texas and the Gulf region includes the relevant portions from both of her North American travelogues: *Texas and the Gulf of Mexico* (first published in 1844) and *Hesperos* (published in 1850). Her collected observations of Texas appear together for the first time in this edition.

TABLE OF CONTENTS

A Sketch of Mrs. Houstoun

The refined and sometimes sarcastic author of this early narrative of Texas travel was born Matilda Charlotte Jesse in Staffordshire, England two centuries ago. There she was christened on August 16, 1811. The daughter of noted naturalist and well-known author Edward Jesse, Matilda was exposed to the luminaries of English arts and letters of the day from an early age.

At the age of sixteen, Miss Jesse became engaged to Reverend George Lionel Fraser. Despite (or perhaps because of) this early marriage she was very critical, in both of her travelogues, of the "young age" at which North American women were marrying. Widowed in 1833, her life of travel and adventure would soon begin with her second husband, British army captain William Houstoun. Married in 1840, they embarked for the Caribbean and Gulf of Mexico in September 1842 aboard their well-armed and well-appointed private yacht, *Dolphin.* Though she mentions traveling for the sake of her health, and though newspaper accounts demonstrate that Captain Houstoun referred to her as "an invalid," she appears to have endured the rigors of long sea voyages and tropical climates quite well. After returning to England in May of 1843, Mrs. Houstoun compiled her first book—a 2-volume set published in 1844 by Murray: *Texas and the Gulf of Mexico; or Yachting in the New World.*

Not much time would pass before the Houstouns would grace Texan and American shores again. After a holiday across Europe, they returned in April of 1845, touring parts of Canada and New England, visiting Cincinnati and steaming down the Mississippi to New Orleans. They revisited Texas, as well, with brief stays at Galveston, Morgan's New Washington and the home of Dr. Ashbel Smith on Galveston Bay in the winter of 1845-46. Five years would elapse before this second round of travels would find its way into print. In 1850, her new travelogue appeared as the 2-volume *Hesperos; or, Travels in the West.* In those intervening years, Captain Houstoun spent a considerable amount of his money in leasing some 80,000 acres in County Mayo for purposes of becoming a livestock farmer at the height of the Irish famine. The adventurous couple spent two decades in Ireland and, naturally, Mrs. Houstoun chronicled it in a book in 1879.

Contemporary reviews of her travel writings, though positive regarding her writing abilities, were not always so kind with regard to her research sensibilities. In the 1855 edition of *Woman's Record*, Mrs. Houstoun is described as being less than particular about her sources of information, being "as well satisfied with the lazy gossip of a low-bred rustic she meets in a steamboat, as if she had conversed with Washington Irving." As students of how our forebears lived in Texas, we are certainly as interested in the comments of such "low-bred rustics" as we are in those made by the statesmen of the day, with whom the Houstouns also kept company. That said, Mrs. Houstoun's writings are not free from inaccuracies and inconsistencies. Upon these hiccups in her recording of our history was borne this annotated edition of the Englishwoman's writings about Texas and the Gulf.

During their years in Ireland, Matilda Houstoun began her career as a novelist. Between 1862 and 1891, she would produce more than a dozen works of fiction, a triple volume semi-autobiographical novel and several biographical works. It seems death was the only circumstance that would quiet her pen. Her career ended in June of 1892. She died quietly at home in Pimlico.

EDITOR'S NOTE:
"...DURING THE WINTER OF 1844..."

As history publishers, we sometimes have occasion to improve upon a Texas classic by adding an index or adding new complementary material. Rarely, though, do we have an opportunity to correct an error that has enjoyed an illustrious 167-year career. Mrs. Houstoun's work provided such an opportunity.

In the opening paragraphs of *Texas and the Gulf of Mexico*, Mrs. Houstoun states that they departed England on September 13, 1843. But the events she described as occurring in Texas during her first trip, combined with hints provided in her second book, made it all sound slightly out of tune. We consulted other sources. They all concurred. And surely everyone from Streeter to the Library of Congress and every scholarly article and journal entry citing her books couldn't be wrong, could they? It turns out that they were. Virtually every interested party since 1844 used her erroneous dates. Why? Because she said, *in print*, that she departed in 1843! And we all know that books never lie.

The Houstouns left England on September 13, 1842. They arrived in New Orleans on December 6, 1842 and reached Galveston, for the first time, twelve days later. They made their final departure from Texas for England on March 31, 1843. Their mode of travel in a gun-toting luxury yacht caused quite a stir in New Orleans and Galveston. Thus, there are numerous newspaper accounts documenting the arrival of the *Dolphin* in 1842. William Bollaert made note of the arrival of his fellow countrymen in his important diary.

I initially thought that this must have been an error on her publisher's part. I felt sure she was aware of her dates of travel...and publishers, editors and printers *do* make mistakes. Once the plates were cast and the book went to print, poor Mrs. Houstoun wouldn't have had any way to correct such an error. What's a gal to do? Many years later, however, in an 1881 work, she sticks to her 1843-44 dates. In this book, *A Woman's Memories of World-Known Men*, she recalls a meeting with Henry Clay at New Orleans (which occurred in 1843) and states the year incorrectly..."during the winter of 1844."

I cannot name or speculate upon the reasons why Mrs. Houstoun wasn't more forthcoming about the dates of her travels. Much of her travel writing was reconstructed from letters mailed home to friends in England. Each of those letters, if not dated in the letter itself, must have carried either a manuscript postmark or a stamped postmark indicating the date. Perhaps she wasn't good with numbers. Perhaps she, like most of us, was stressed and running low on memory. Perhaps she drank a bit. Perhaps whatever the ailment was that sent her abroad for her health presented some impairment. Or perhaps she altered the dates intentionally. She and her husband were in Texas during two very interesting spots in our history. They kept company with and traveled with intimates of Sam Houston and Anson Jones, and the presidents themselves. I'd love to know the reason for the discrepancy, but for now, I can only correct it in print and make her contribution to our history make a bit more sense.

To this end, this edition is annotated. Interspersed within the text are bracketed notes that seek to put Matilda Houstoun's observations in the context of the bigger picture of Texas history. Corrections are made in this manner, as well, barring the infamous date discrepancy. That was changed outright.

-Michelle M. Haas, Managing Editor
Windy Hill

Aboard the *Dolphin*

The Houstouns crossed the Atlantic in style and their crossing set tongues to wagging in the Republic of Texas, then engaging the Mexicans on behalf of the Yucatan. It was widely rumored for some months that Captain Houstoun journeyed to Texas with the intention of joining the Texian navy. This myth was debunked in the December 10, 1842 number of the New Orleans *Daily Tropic*, which also gave a description of the *Dolphin*.

———— The Yacht Dolphin ————

We had the pleasure of visiting this beautiful yacht yesterday, and we are indebted to the gentlemanly owner and captain, Mr. Hueston, for the attention which he paid us. He and his family are merely travelling for pleasure, and the report he was to enter the Texian service is entirely unfounded. He visits Texas for the purpose of amusing himself in hunting buffaloes, and gazing upon the green bosomed prairies that spread themselves like oceans over the mighty West—His wife, who is an invalid, accompanies him, and her health, we are glad to learn, has been much improved by this beautiful mode of travelling. The captain told us that several of his friends in England are about to visit this country in a similar manner, and the descriptions of tourists who have witnessed the hunting of the buffalo and such game, have made the sportsmen on the other side of the water almost crazy, so eager is their desire to enjoy the excitement of prairie life.

His vessel is fitted up for pleasure, and her crew amount to only fourteen men. The state rooms of the captain's family and the dining room fill one-half of the yacht, and the furniture is of the most comfortable kind. A beautiful library, and a small armament of guns and pistols grace the dining room. Among other things, we were shown a rifle of a very particular description, manufactured, we believe, in England, and it is certainly the greatest improvement in firearms that has been made for some time. The yacht is pierced for twelve guns, and we know not which to admire the most—the taut, ship like appearance of everything on deck, or the domestic, family-like comfort of the cabins. The captain has merely visited New Orleans for the purpose of looking at the city, and will remain here only a few days.

CHAPTER I

DEPARTURE FROM BLACKWALL ⚓ SEA SICKNESS ⚓ THE SCHOONER-YACHT *DOLPHIN* ⚓ NANCY, THE BLACK WOMAN

Who has not seen and admired the remarkable and interesting view from the windows of the Trafalgar Hotel at Blackwall? It was on a bright afternoon early in September that I was seated in one of its cheerful rooms looking out on the broad river, and the busy steamers passing to and fro. It was my last evening before leaving England. We were about, if I may so express it, to take up our abode for the next twelve months on the bosom of the Ocean; our intention being to cross the Atlantic, and to visit a large part of the American Continent.

I always feel, before setting out on a long land journey, something approaching to depression of spirits; but on this occasion the entire novelty of the expedition prevented the attack, and my pleasurable anticipations were almost unalloyed. It was a voyage undertaken principally in search of health for me, and I was bound to be pleased with the arrangements made for my comfort. The sun had nearly set when I walked to the West India Dock, in which the *Dolphin* was lying. I could scarcely make her out in the dusky twilight, and this was my first introduction to my future home. The yacht had been often described to me, and yet I was surprised at the size of her cabins, and the extreme comfort of her internal arrangements.

I was met by the Master and the Doctor, and on going below found a most enjoyable state cabin, quantities of books, and in short every enjoyment which a reasonable woman could require. My own cabin was large, with two sofas, the bed being a swinging cot, which was taken down in the daytime. My first night on board was spent in the docks, as we intended to leave them at daybreak. No ships, I believe, ever sail when they ought to do so, or rather at the time originally fixed for their departure; and to this rule, ours was no exception. The middle of August was the time when we had intended to have taken our leave of England, but so many alterations and improvements had been required for the vessel, that the 13th of September had arrived before we were in readiness to leave Blackwall.

The schooner-yacht *Dolphin* is two hundred and nineteen tons burthen, drawing twelve feet of water, and measuring one hundred feet in length. She carries six guns, and her crew consisted of eleven men, one boy, a carpenter, cook and cook's mate. The other persons on board were the master and surgeon, the mate, steward and steward's mate, and my own maid. We had also with us a negress, a native of St. Thomas in the West Indies, who had been stewardess in one of the West India steamers, and who was to attend on me till my own maid became accustomed to the sea. We were in all four and twenty souls on board, and were bound for Madeira as our first resting place.

It was on the morning of the 13th of September 1842, that, after being hooked on to a steamer, we were tugged rapidly down the river. The weather was fine, as it generally is in the beginning of this most pleasant of months in the English climate. The morning air was clear, bright, and bracing, and ere we reached Gravesend a fresh breeze sprung up from the westward, which was just what we wanted. Immediately all sail was made, and having dismissed our little steamer, the *Dolphin* was soon scudding along, at the rate of ten knots an hour. Before dark we were off Dover, and had put our pilot into his boat.

We were becalmed a whole day off the Isle of Wight. This was tedious enough certainly, but still it was pleasant to look a little longer on the land we were leaving for so long a period, and I could not help thinking, as I gazed on the lovely island, how doubtful it was, that in my wanderings to the far West, I should see any to compare with it. But with all my romantic admiration for the shores of England, I confess I was not sorry when towards evening a breeze sprung up, taking advantage of which we crowded sail, and soon lost sight of the coast. Our delayed departure was the cause of considerable inconvenience to us, for on the 21st the moon changed and, as we had been led to expect, there arose a gale of wind that certainly surprised me.

I did not consider myself quite a freshwater sailor. I had frequently undertaken short voyages before, had yachted in the Mediterranean, and in the Channel, and steamed in various directions near home, but the Bay of Biscay was new to me. Nothing that I had ever before encountered had at all prepared me for what we were to undergo. It was a short pitching sea, with a head wind, called in the log book, "strong breezes and squally," but which I thought at the time were tremendous gales. Sails were reefed constantly, while occasionally a barque or schooner scudded past us, too much engaged in attending to her own safety to take any notice of us. I was at first surprised at the calmness and composure of the ship's crew, entertaining as I did a private opinion of my own that we were in imminent peril. I kept my fears to myself, however, and learnt to know better in time.

How ill and miserable many of our party looked when the wind first began to freshen! Till now, the sea had been calm as a summer lake, but we had at last to bid adieu to all the pleasurable sensations of fine weather sailing. The very dogs looked wretched, and instead of gambolling about, and enjoying in common with ourselves the novelty of the scene, they flung themselves heavily down, against the side, and when disturbed again by the violent motion of the ship, rolled uneasily and restlessly along the deck in search of some safer berth. The poor doctor was I think the greatest sufferer. It was really melancholy to see him, doubled up under the bulwarks, and obliged, if he attempted to move, to stick to everything that came in his way, like a leech. He bore his troubles with exemplary patience, as indeed we all did, and like everything else, they came to an end at last. I was happy enough not to suffer myself, but my maid was a wretched prey to the distressing malady of sea-sickness. I believe there never yet existed a lady's maid who was not, though I have never yet been able, either from physical or natural causes, to decide satisfactorily why it should be so. Here I must take the opportunity to remark, for the benefit of the world in general and bad sailors in particular, that the most popular dish at this time was curry. It seemed to answer the purposes both of food and medicine.

On September 22, fresh gales, and squally, with rain, two reefs in topsail, mainsail triced up, and very heavy swell. A fearful night succeeded to this stormy day—a night not to be forgotten, at least by me, for in the course of it, an event occurred which stamped its horrors on my imagination.

The wind being adverse, we were constantly obliged to "wear ship," and when this operation was going forward, great care was required, and every precaution taken to prevent such articles of furniture, etc, from getting adrift as were not lashed to the deck, or otherwise rendered immovable. When we were not prepared for the natural consequences of tacking, the tremendous lurches of the vessel set everything, to say nothing of ourselves, rolling about in mad confusion.

Towards the morning of the 23rd, when the uproar was at its height—sails changing, men rushing along the deck, the wind veering about in all directions and the consequent evolutions in full operation—my maid staggered into my cabin, pale as a ghost, and wringing her hands, "Oh ma'am, the captain says, we are going to turn over!" This was really an awful piece of information, conveyed too so suddenly. It tallied, moreover, with my own silent fears, and I confess that, at first, I fully shared in the panic.

A minute's reflection, and the still more consoling fact that we continued to remain afloat, showed me the absurdity of fear. After all, the whole affair arose from the kind attention on the part of the master, who before giving the order to "bout ship" had sent to apprise me of his intention, that I might not be taken by surprise. The message had, however, gone from mate to boatswain, boatswain to steward, etc, till, like all things conveyed through many hands, it became distorted, and by the time it reached my ears, had arrived at the appalling announcement that we were going to the bottom.

One good result we perceived from the gale, disagreeable and frightful enough as it was. It cured everyone on board of sea-sickness. I accounted for this by supposing it was the effect of the counter-irritation system and that the overpowering evil of mental anxiety removed the lesser one of corporeal uneasiness.

Some little time before Madeira appeared in sight, the weather moderated, and we all began to cheer up. The dogs shook themselves and lay down in the sun to dry. The idlers put on a thin semi-nautical costume, and Nancy, the black woman, who had been, however, anything but useful during the gales, came upon deck to warm herself. In fine weather, she was to be seen standing on the steps of the companion ladder, listening to the rough jokes of the sailors, with her shining black face just above the hatchway. She was evidently a favourite with the men, and I was often amused to see her standing there, showing every white tooth in her head, as she grinned a repartee to her merry tormentors. Nancy was a wit in her way, and, though not in her first youth, was certainly something of a coquette, and decidedly vain of her remaining attractions. I can see her now sitting on her stockingless heels in the forepart of the vessel, with her red cotton handkerchief tied over her head, chattering faster than any magpie. This was Nancy when the sea was calm. When the wind blew, the case was widely different, and though born and bred a slave, she thought she had as good a right to indulge in sickness and idleness as her neighbours.

The air had daily flit warmer as we proceeded southward, and the power of the sun by the time we saw Madeira, was almost too great to be pleasant. I felt glad to be spared the chilling changes of an English winter. The great merit of the climate of the Madeiras, consists, I believe, in its freedom from these great sources of suffering and illness to delicate and pulmonary constitutions. It is said that while the winter is twenty degrees warmer than in London, the summer is only seven warmer. Thus the extremes of heat and cold are not nearly so violent as in England. The latitude of Lisbon appeared also charming, and were it not for the dirt and other small inconveniences, I suppose that Lisbon would be quite as desirable a residence for consumptive patients as Madeira. It has certainly the advantage of being nearer home.

As we neared the land, I felt that one of the worst stages of our voyage was over. The Bay of Biscay once passed in safety, the wide Atlantic has but few terrors, and I am sufficient enough a sailor to be aware of the great advantages of having plenty of sea-room, and no land near.

Chapter II

Madeira ⚓ Funchal ⚓
Sugar Cane ⚓ Invalids ⚓
Bad Conduct of Three of the Crew

I was much struck by the first view of Madeira. It rises up high, black and steep from the sea, and looks at a distance like a huge ruined wall. As you approach nearer, however, you perceive with spots of houses on the hill-sides, churches, temples, and abrupt ridges of mountains, on which seem literally suspended the most lovely gardens. All this, mingled with the green foliage and the almost tropical vegetation, is lovely in the extreme.

On September 26, we brought up in Funchal Roads, in twenty-two fathoms water. The weather was extremely hot, at least it appeared so to us, though this was the cool season at Madeira. I need say nothing of the cordial kindness, and unlimited hospitality of the merchants at Funchal. The fact of their liberality and good feeling to strangers is too well known to need a comment, and our reception furnished but an extra example of its truth.

A nearer view of Funchal is very amusing to a stranger. The shores are crowded with boats, and wild looking Portuguese gesticulating and quarrelling. The shape of the boats is remarkable, their sterns are so high and pointed. The rowers perform their office in an erect posture, and with their faces turned towards the fore part of their craft. Children of very tender years, bronzed by the sun into a deep copper colour, are swimming about in all directions, and quite in deep water. The surface of the sea is studded by little black shining heads. In short, the inhabitants generally appear to me to partake of an amphibious nature.

The houses of Funchal are mostly of a dazzling white, which has a very unpleasant effect on the eyes. The roofs are generally flat, but you likewise see many turrets and steeples. There is an English Episcopal Church, and an excellent resident minister. The English Library and Reading

Club are excellent. There is, too, a public ballroom, which is well attended. In the reading club I have just mentioned, the amusements of cards and billiards may also be enjoyed.

I have often been surprised at the fondness for dancing which prevails in hot climates. The inhabitants seem to enjoy this exercise the more, the higher the thermometer ranges. I was told that, in Funchal, during the hottest months, balls were carried on with unabated spirit till a late hour in the morning, and that country dances and Scotch reels were executed with a spirit of enterprise and perseverance unknown in our northern latitudes.

It is indeed a most beautiful, clear, and enlivening climate, but nevertheless, I was certainly astonished at the degree of vigour which the inhabitants seemed to retain. We went on shore in a Portuguese boat, and I had an opportunity of comparing, which I always do with peculiar satisfaction, the superior cleanliness, promptitude, skill, and composure of an English sailor over his class in every other country. A Portuguese man-of-war lay alongside of the *Dolphin,* and the comparison certainly was not in favour of the former. Such hallooing and such confusion I never heard, as came wafted to us from our neighbours. The officers possessed, I am sure, but little of the salutary authority necessary to keep sailors to their duty.

We were most kindly received by Mr. Temple, who is a resident at Funchal, and gladly remained a week in his comfortable house. We spent our time very pleasantly in wandering about the island, which, even at this advanced period of the year, presents much both of vegetation and scenery, well worthy of notice. The flowers are beautiful; such a profusion of geraniums, fuchsias, and heliotropes, with the glorious belladonna lily and bright oleander! It is a perfect wilderness of sweets and brilliant colours. The human part of the scenery is by no means in keeping with all this, for a more dirty, disorderly, uncivilized population it would be difficult to imagine. Of police there are none, and the noises and confusion in the streets, especially at night, are most disagreeable and effectually chase sleep away, at least from the eyes of a newcomer. Mr. Temple's house is situated close to the guardhouse and, as the sentries are by far the most noisy people in the place, the neighbourhood is not agreeable. One of their favourite amusements at night was imitating the noises and cries of different animals. They alternately crow like cocks, roar like bulls and gobble like fifty turkeys. Their imitations, I must say, were correct, but the effect was anything but pleasing. There appears to be but little religious feeling among them; indeed their priests seemed to be almost objects of contempt, and their places of worship to be nearly neglected.

The squalid poverty you everywhere meet with is pitiable and revolting. The children run about almost in a state of nudity, and are the ugliest little set of wretches, excepting, perhaps, the diminutive old women, I ever saw. The Portuguese inhabitants generally require but a small quantity of food, and that consists principally of fruits and Indian corn. They are, though most frequently short in stature, a very strong and hardy race, and their powers of enduring fatigue are great. Of the truth of this I had ample proof in my palanquin-bearers, who under a broiling sun, carried me at a sort of ambling pace to the tops of the highest hills, without appearing in the slightest degree exhausted. It is true that on arriving at the summits, they generally begged for a cup of wine at the houses of call, which are conveniently placed there. It is, however, to strangers only that they are in the habit of making the application.

The vineyards are very pretty and the vines are trained over wooden pillars, supporting a latticework of bamboo. The grapes are dried in the shade, which is said to give them a peculiar richness of flavour. The vine was first introduced in Madeira in the year 1420, and was brought from the Island of Crete.

The vintage is just over and numbers of peasants are busily employed in bringing down the newly-made wine from the vineyards in the hills. Some of the men have immense pigskins, filled with the red fluid, slung over their shoulders, while others are driving the pretty cream-coloured oxen into the town, laden in a similar manner. The vision of the pigskins is quite horrid—they are filled to their utmost extent, even to the legs, the mouth and nose being tied up. This appearance of being a real animal is rendered still more unpleasant by the blood-red stains on the hide of the creature. The drivers of the wagons, which are of a most simple and primitive form, are shrieking and bellowing all the while, by way of encouraging their beasts, and that with voices unequalled in the world, I should imagine, for shrillness and power.

The grapes from which the largest quantity of wine is made are small and extremely sweet; we have taken a large quantity of them on board, besides bananas, and various sorts of commons fruits. The grapes from which the Malmsey wine is made grow upon rocks, over which they are trained—they are not gathered till overripe.

Among the many fine views which a stranger at Madeira should not fail to visit, that of the Coural stands preeminent. The road to this beautiful spot is steep and stony. It is a valley completely enclosed by high abrupt hills, none of which are less than a thousand feet in height. The road lies alarmingly near the edge of the precipices, and is moreover extremely narrow. The horses are, however, so active and well trained, that no positive danger exists. A Portuguese runner generally accompanies your horse, encouraging him both by threats and caresses to proceed, and often not a little impeding his progress by hanging on at his tail. The horses are well shaped, though small, and particularly adapted to the nature of the country, and the roads.

The Mount Church, built on extremely high ground, a short distance from Funchal, cannot be passed unnoticed. The view of the town and roadstead from it is most beautiful and curious. There is a large convent, at which artificial flowers and other sorts of ornamental work can be procured, besides delicious liqueurs, which the nuns manufacture in great variety.

The most beautiful flowers and shrubs are found on the summits of the hills, and the whole appearance of the country is rich and luxuriant, far beyond my powers of description. The interior of the houses are as enjoyable as the gardens are beautiful; the rooms are large, high, and airy, and the floors during the hot season are spread with a fine matting. Very little furniture is admitted, and the breeze is allowed to circulate freely through the houses.

The dress of the gentlemen is as glaring as the colour of the houses, being white from head to foot—jacket of white linen, sailcloth boots and trousers of the same. A large palmetto hat completes the costume, which if not becoming, is well suited to the climate. I enjoyed my palanquin extremely. The motion is very easy, and sufficiently rapid, considering the great inequalities of the ground. I do not think that a horse could get over the ground quicker. It was some time before I hardened my heart to the supposed sufferings of the bearers, which after all were entirely imaginary. Englishmen would, I am sure, sink very soon under the exertion, besides the natural objection entertained by our countrymen to being used as beasts of burden.

The sugar cane grows in considerable quantities, and it was formerly the staple commodity of the island, but, not proving very productive as an article of commerce, its culture was abandoned for that of the vine. Coffee, likewise, though of a most superior kind, is grown but in small quantities. The coffee-trees are very handsome, and grow to a larger size than even in the West Indies or Cuba.

Vines are found growing at a very great height, some say nearly three thousand feet above the level of the sea; but, though even in these elevated situations they bear fruit, no wine can be made from it. The chestnuts are excellent, and in great profusion. There are a good many rabbits and wild hogs on the island, but goats and oxen are the most common, as well as the most useful animals of which it can boast. Here, for the first time, I tasted that most indispensable article of negro food—the sweet potato. I cannot say that I approved of it as an adjunct to meat, but roasted like a chestnut and eaten hot, it is very tolerable.

I confess that in spite of its bright sun and flowery hills, Madeira has left a melancholy impression on my mind. I met so many wasted invalids, pale hectic girls, and young men, struggling vainly against decay. Oh! that sad feat of the physician who can do no more, and "despairing of his fee tomorrow," sends his patient away to breathe his last in a foreign land! Poor wanderers! I saw their last resting-place. "After life's fitful fever they sleep well,"—as well as though they reposed under a grassy mound at home. And yet—I would wish to have those whom I had loved when living near to me in death. It is a fancy, and the wise would doubtless call it a weak one, but who can reason away a fancy, or dogmatise on the feelings of the heart? I have been assured that consumptive patients at Madeira lose, in the charm of scenery and under the influence of the climate, a sense of their danger, and the precariousness of their existence; that their spirits become raised, and that at the last they quietly sink to eternal rest with their sketch-books in their hands, and hopeful smiles upon their lips—I doubt it. Can they shut their eyes upon the hundreds of fellow sufferers whom they daily meet? Or forget wherefore they are there? It is a comfortable belief, however, for their friends at home.

But I am not yet done with Madeira. I must say something of its rain, and a little more of its sunshine. The former falls in great quantities during four months of the year—October, November, December, and January. The rain was described to me as descending in torrents, but greatly must the inhabitants enjoy the first refreshing and purifying drops, after the long spell of sunshine. The honey is delicious at Madeira. The bees have such flowers to revel amongst that it would be strange were it otherwise. The dress of the Portuguese inhabitants is extremely picturesque. It consists of a blue jacket covered with silver buttons, a little cap on one side of the head, about the size of a large saucer, a white or striped shirt, and very wide trousers.

The anchorage in Funchal Roads is anything but safe. More than once during our stay we were in doubt whether we should not be obliged to up-anchor and stand out to sea, although there was not more than half a gale of wind blowing at the time.

We secured a good stock of turkeys, besides ducks and fowls, and a very promising goat. The latter, however, fulfilled none of the promises made for her. Mariana, for that was her name, enjoyed the reputation of being one of the best of her kind on the island. Indeed her Portuguese owner, having exhausted his vocabulary of praise, wound it up by saying, that "she was fit to hang in a lady's ear." This, considering that she was about three feet high, and large in proportion, with a most formidable pair of horns, was saying a good deal. By the man's account she was a perfect annuity to him and we considered ourselves fortunate in securing her services.

Unluckily for us, Mariana was not "a good sailor," and from the first she refused her accustomed aliment, and would taste nothing, except occasional scraps of such food as one would imagine no sensible goat of any country would have touched. Brandy cherries and birch brooms she particularly relished. On one occasion, when in her awkwardness she upset the mustard-pot, (in hot weather we dined on deck) the contents were greedily devoured. So much for a Madeira goat, but as I could not willingly revert to her again, I will close her eventful history here. We bore with her caprices till we arrived at Jamaica, when we turned her into the Dockyard, under the protection of the Commodore, where I believe her to be at this moment. The little bullocks must be much better feeders, to judge from the excellence of the beef. The mutton is by no means so good.

Three of our men took the opportunity of our stay at Madeira to misconduct themselves sadly, so much so, as to require the assistance of the local authorities in bringing them to punishment. They were three of our finest men, and had hitherto conducted themselves well, at least to outward appearance. But the cheapness of the wine made it irresistible. One night they were more than commonly noisy in the forecastle, so the master sent to order them to be quiet and to put out the lights. This, the three men in question refused to do, and moreover grew so violent and unruly that it was found necessary to send for some Portuguese soldiers, from a schooner lying nearly alongside, to assist in capturing the delinquents. They were desperate in their resistance, vowing death and destruction to all on board and daring the Doctor, who was armed to the teeth, and all the others in authority, to approach them. I happened to be on shore, and knew nothing of these occurrences till the following morning.

They were at length safely lodged in a miserable prison, on a small insulated rock called the Loo. Here, if anywhere, repentance was sure to come, and come it did, but all too late for two of the culprits. These men had made themselves so obnoxious to the rest of the crew, and were moreover such confirmed bad subjects, that all idea of compromise was out of the question. But with the other man the case was different. He was a favourite with his messmates, and there was evidence to prove that he had been led away by the rest, besides which, he had offended in a less degree. All things considered, we granted him a free pardon, while the others were left on the rock, to their solitude and their remorse.

Chapter III

Barbadoes ⚓ Expensive Provisions ⚓ Miss Betsey Austin

On the eighth day from our landing at Funchal, we were again in readiness for sea. It was a lovely summer evening, about seven o'clock, when the order was given to up-anchor and set sail for the West Indies. The windlass was manned, and as I listened to the jovial chorus of the crew, as they cheerily sung at their work, I could not help thinking of their late companions on the lone Loo Rock, and mentally comparing them to the captive knight of old, in Mrs. Hemans' beautiful ballad. It was, however, I fear, a sad waste of sentiment.

On the third day from leaving Madeira, we saw on the lee-bow the wonderful Peak of Teneriffe, and this at the immense distance of one hundred and forty miles! A curious aspect it wore, a high bank of white clouds seeming to extend itself half-way up to the heavens, and that small distinct peak of land crowning the whole.

Having been informed at Madeira that we should have a fresh northeast wind, which would infallibly and expeditiously waft us to Barbadoes, and also that having once set our sails, we should not have to shift them till we arrived there, we were not prepared for the long calm which followed. A repetition of the words "calm and fine," varied only by occasional changes to, "light airs and fine," is all I can find in the logbook for many days. As for the employment of the hands, it consisted in spreading and furling awnings, fitting and mending cutter sails, spinning yarn, and washing clothes. As for holy-stoning the decks, I set my face against that from the first. It is the worst description of nervous torture of which I ever heard, excepting perhaps, the infliction of the *squee gee*, which, as its name almost implies, sets every tooth in one's head on edge for a week. Brooms and swabs are bad enough, but to these I was obliged to submit.

This, certainly, was not a very animating life. Still, what with fishing for dolphins and bonetas, watching anxiously for wind, which sometimes came in the tantalizing shape of cats' paws, time slipped along, though the ship did not. I tasted one of the bonetas, which the sailors had cooked for themselves, and very tough and dry it was. A dolphin, which soon after followed its unwise example and allowed himself to be enticed on board, proved rather better. We dressed up our namesake with wine and other condiments, and he was pronounced to be "not bad." Still I greatly doubt if we should have allowed him even this scanty meed of praise, had a turbot or John Dory been within reach.

And now, having brought my readers into a dead calm, or, as I have learnt to say in America, a fix, I think it high time to apologise for inflicting upon them any fuller account of such a tedious time. Still, as a long continuance of calm weather at sea is an acknowledged trial both to the temper and spirits, I have thought it better to give some account of the manner in which we endured it, for the benefit of adventurous persons, who may hereafter be disposed to follow us and brave the dangers of the wide Atlantic in a yacht.

But to return to our voyage. The exceeding beauty of the stars and sky within the tropics has been often described, but had I not witnessed their nightly glory, my imagination never could have done them justice. A lonely ship in the wide ocean must ever, I think, be a source of poetical feeling, even to the coldest fancy. But the calm and quiet of the sensation is raised to a trusting and almost holy train of thought, when the heat of the day is over, and the blazing sun has gone down to his rest, you lie beneath that canopy studded with most brilliant stars, and feel with the poet, a longing "to tread that golden path of rays that seems to lead to some bright isle of rest."

One particularly quiet breezeless day, a shark gave us a good deal of employment and amusement. He was swimming about the ship for hours, with the pretty little pilot fish playing about his monstrous nose. Every sort of bait, from salt junk to tempting candles, was offered for his acceptance, and rejected. The monster evidently was not hungry, for though he smelt at them all, nothing would induce him to nibble at the baited hook. Once only they succeeded in hooking him, but he very soon broke away. Towards the evening, however, he grew more sociable, and condescended to eat some biscuit which I threw to him over the side. He was an enormous creature, at least ten feet in length. There was something very unpleasant in the idea of this horrid "creature following in our wake," and though I did not share in the sailors' superstition of their being harbingers of death, I looked at him with great distaste, feeling that he was thirsting for our blood.

We saw flying-fish in great numbers. They flew on board at night, being attracted by the light, and were found in the morning on deck and in the chains. I ate them for breakfast, and found them delicious; like a herring in flavour and consistency, but more delicate.

While copying my journal in England, on a positively winter's day in the month of June—dark, drizzling, and cheerless—how strange it appears that I ever could have disliked the sun, in the way I did in the tropics. How often, in the morning, did I then find myself exclaiming against its scorching rays. At six o'clock, and often even at an earlier hour, I was on deck, driven up by the intolerable heat of the cabin, which being below the surface of the water, was necessarily hotter than it was above. It was contrary to all orders to spread the awning, before the decks were swabbed up, so I had ample leisure for complaint. There was that terrible sun again; not a cloud above or around, but one wide canopy of blue over our heads. Nothing to break the line of the horizon and the azure sea, shining as crystal, with its long wearying swell. Yes! There was the perpetual sun glaring on us through the long day, and still more fiercely in the fervid noon. The winds were asleep, and the ship rolled heavily with her creaking masts and idly-flapping sails. One day was so like another, that sometimes weariness almost took the place of hope: "When will it end?" I used to exclaim, "When will there be a cloud?" It put me in mind of Coleridge's beautiful description of a calm, in the "Ancient Mariner." And truly the schooner did look "like a painted ship upon a painted sea."

On the 31st, light breezes, hardly more than cats' paws, but they gave us hope. The lookout man reported a sail on the lee-bow. All eyes were strained to catch a view of the vessel, as she gradually neared us. She proved to be a small brig, and hoisted English colours. She commenced making signals and our master, deciding that she wished to speak us, slightly altered our course to facilitate this. Her only reason for nearing us appeared to be to ascertain our longitude. Having done this (for we chalked it on the outside of the bulwark) she proceeded on her way. The sight of this ship was quite an event and gave us matter of discussion for the rest of the day. If I had followed my inclinations I should have entered into conversation with her, so eagerly did I long for the sight of fresh objects and I felt quite surprised at the apathy with which she passed us by.

During all this time the heat was intense, the thermometer ranged from 88 to 96 under the awning, and there was no wind to refresh us. The only manner in which I could procure a breath of air, was by spreading a mattress on the deck, between the ports, which were left open. It was fortunate that the yacht contained a large supply of water as, from the unexpected length of the passage and the intense heat, an unusual quantity was daily consumed. Had the calm lasted much longer, however, we might have had a rationing of water. As it was, indeed, our fresh provisions began to run short, and turkeys and fowls were anxiously counted over and cared for.

There was much difficulty, after a time, in finding employment for the ship's company. As it is well known that the only method of keeping sailors out of mischief and free from grumbling is never to let them be idle, all kinds of work were resorted to.

The men, in fact, were seldom left in repose. They were always either spinning yarn, making mats, scraping cables, cleaning guns, or occupied in some task of a similar nature. We did not quite follow the example of American ships, in which it is said of the sailors, that "Six days they labour, and do all that they are able, and on the seventh, holystone the docks and scrape the cable."

Sunday, of course, was a day of rest and idleness. On that day the men, clad in their light clean dresses, after attending prayers on deck, lay listlessly about the forecastle. The best, and those most religiously inclined (and sailors are often so, in spite of their reckless manners) were seen reading their Prayer Books, or some sober book from the ship's library. Others were poring over old scraps of newspapers or letters, which from their long-folded creases, were evidently the much and long-prized missives of their wives, or friends in distant England.

Thus, Sunday passed away, but on weekdays the evenings were cheered by a fiddler, and enlivened by song. Music, such as "charmed the spirits of the deep," was heard from the forecastle, and in absence of better and more refined strains, shortened our silent way. One of the performers, the steward's mate, who boasted of having been "on the stage" at an earlier period of his life, had a beautiful voice, and really sung very tolerably. Sailor's ditties are very mournful things, not at all like the joyous choruses I had imagined them to be. I often longed to give them some new and more lively airs to vary their monotonous concerts.

Still, though we scarcely appeared to move, we certainly progressed a little, for after a most tedious passage of thirty days, I was told we were within a hundred miles of Barbadoes. This was indeed most welcome intelligence, as we intended to make that island. On the afternoon of this day, when at least eighty miles from any land, a hawk was perceived flying round the ship. How glad I was to see him! Poor thing! He was very tired, as well he might be, after his long aerial journey. After performing a few feeble evolutions, and alighting occasionally on different parts of the rigging, he settled on the foreyard-arm, and being quite exhausted, was easily taken. The creature did not live through the night. He was a kestrel and a very fine one. In consideration of its long flight, and out of gratitude to it as having been the first harbinger of land, we thought his skin worthy of being preserved, for the purpose of stuffing, and it was put into the menagerie accordingly.

At six o'clock in the morning of the 2nd of November, we were within a very few miles of the land. Barbadoes is a very low island, and does not strike one with any feeling of either wonder or admiration. You see a few white-looking houses on the slight elevations. The sight of tropical trees, coconut, palms, etc, must always be interesting to one who sees them for the first time. About eight o'clock we made Bridgetown, and at ten a.m. brought up in Carlisle Bay, in seven fathom water.

Nancy, the negress, gave me, immediately on our arrival, fresh proof that nervous fancies are not confined to fine or even white ladies. Immediately after we had come to an anchor, her conduct was most remarkable. She commenced running wildly about the deck, evidently under the influence of some nervous panic. Everyone she met, she informed with striking marks of dismay on her countenance, that she must be near her end, for that she had a loud and terrific sound in her ears, which she was persuaded was the result of some fatal malady. The men only laughed at her, and at length she appealed to me for advice and consolation. I was too merciful to keep her longer in suspense, and told her what everyone in the ship might have done, had they not enjoyed her tribulation. I told her that the noise she thought to be exclusively her own, proceeded from myriads of frogs and grasshoppers, which we all distinctly heard, though at a considerable distance from the land.

The first interesting object which claimed our attention was an English man-of-war, the *Imaum*. She had arrived a few hours before us, and was lying at anchor. We had taken up our position close to her and, on comparing notes, we found that her passage from Madeira had been as long as our own.

I became almost persuaded, by this new example of delay, of the truth of what I had previously suspected—that the existence of trade winds is a vulgar error, a sort of travellers' wonder. It was a constant demand of the doctor's, "Where is the trade wind?" and a standing joke on board, that it had gone out of its course to annoy us. It was some consolation to find that we had companions in misfortune, and to be quite sure that the winds of heaven, and not the little *Dolphin*, had been at fault.

We were soon surrounded by boats, filled with individuals of every shade of black, brown, and yellow. The black ladies, dressed in white, and adorned with the most brilliant colours, glass-bead necklaces, with gaudy handkerchiefs tied round their heads, were chattering and laughing, bargaining and coquetting, but still comporting themselves with a dignity, and an air of grandeur, which showed them duly conscious of their claim to respect, in being "true 'Badian born." I began to believe that, as they themselves assert, "you must go to Barbadoes to learn manners." I was very much amused by these freed bondswomen. They came upon the quarter-deck without any ceremony, walked down into the cabin, and made themselves quite at home.

The negroes brought alongside such fruits as the island afforded, and they were poor enough. Having heard much in praise of the West India fruits, I was disappointed in those I saw. There were bad oranges, worse grapes and no pines, at which we felt ourselves much aggrieved. Shaddocks, guavas, coconuts, and bananas—all indifferent. Still, notwithstanding the want of flavour of their contents, the fruit baskets were immediately emptied by our men, who seemed greatly to enjoy the sour oranges and tasteless coconuts. An immense quantity of grass was also purchased by them, for the purpose of making hats. These hats, which they make with much ingenuity, I expected would be both light and cool; they however turned out to be neither. They sew the plaits so closely together, that all such purpose is defeated. As an addition to the original weight, many sailors put on a covering of canvass and paint it thickly over.

After inquiring the prices of various necessaries, we made the discovery (too late) that we had come to the wrong island for supplies. Everything we required was both indifferent and expensive. Barbadoes, I was told, imports almost everything from Tobago and Martinique, and it was to St. Pierre, the capital of the latter island, that we ought to have betaken ourselves. Beef and mutton are tenpence a pound at Bridgetown, and water, of which we required a considerable supply, a dollar a cask. Turtles are brought from Tobago, cattle from the Costa firma, and fruit and vegetables from Antigua and Martinique. Still, it is well known, that the island of Barbadoes affords provisions of many sorts which are raised on its own soil. Unfortunately for us, they were not the kinds we required. I believe the exports of sugar average about 300,000 cwts. annually.

Barbadoes is said to be one of the healthiest of the West India Islands. Nevertheless, in spite of the prevalent opinion, I confess that the country gave me the idea of being anything but salubrious, principally from its lowness, and also from the immense number of frogs and grasshoppers, which we heard throwing out their various notes in all directions. This alone gives an idea of marshiness and dampness, which precludes that of health. Barbadoes was one of the first, if not the very first, of the Caribbean Islands colonized by the English. For several years during the early part of the seventeenth century, the Earl of Carlisle was hereditary proprietor of the island, by virtue of a grant obtained from James the First. After the Restoration, it became the property of the Crown. The coloured population seem to me to be tolerably well off, and not very idle.

We went on shore in the cool of the evening, having appointed a carriage to be in waiting for us at the landing. And such a carriage and horses! It was wonderful, from their appearance, how they contrived to go at all, but go they did, and at a tremendous pace. In vain I implored the negro driver to rein in his steeds. I believe he was revenging himself upon them for the previous drivings he had himself undergone in his own proper person, for he flogged away most unmercifully.

Bridgetown is a long straggling town. There are no striking-looking buildings in it, but the streets are in general broad, and the houses white; there is a disagreeable smell of coconut oil, but otherwise the city gives you a pleasant impression of freshness and cleanliness, particularly when compared with Funchal, the last town we had seen. There are several churches and chapels, and a cathedral, besides several buildings for charitable purposes. The population of Bridgetown is about twenty-two thousand. On leaving the town and the pretty gardens which surround it, our road lay for several miles through an extremely flat country. There is very little wood on the island—some mahogany, coconut trees, and palms, and also a good many shrubs—but the country is in general very bare. The flowers, however, are beautiful. The datura scented the evening air, and fuchsias and heliotropes drooped over the garden walls.

Oxen are more used as beasts of burden than horses, but the meat is not good. We were told, that at the proper season there is plenty of shooting, consisting of plover, teal, wild duck, etc. Aloes are very much cultivated, to judge from the number of plants to be seen on the sides of the roads. The ginger is not reckoned so good as that grown in Jamaica. There is a great deal of land still uncultivated. Towards the north, the country becomes much higher, and is comparatively cold. This part is known by the appropriate name of Scotland, and it must be a welcome change to the scorched inhabitants of the south, to refresh themselves occasionally by inhaling its invigorating breezes. Rum is very dear in Barbadoes, at least good rum, such as English sailors like. The proportion of black and coloured people to white is about six to one, of which by far the greatest number are black.

The barracks are large, convenient, and airy. We returned by a different road from the one by which we left the capital, and after driving through a considerable portion of the town, we visited the parade-ground, where the band of the 92nd regiment was playing for the amusement of some half-dozen coloured people, on foot, who were looking on. I noticed one or two ladies on horseback, and Colonel McDonald, who accompanied them, told us, for our satisfaction, that the season had been, and was particularly healthy. The men, however, looked, I thought weakened and worn. We then pursued our drive as far as the Government House. Here I was rather entertained at our black charioteer, who, pointing out to our notice a large building surrounded by iron railings, and guarded by a sentry, informed us that it was the "Queen's House, all kep' fine, furnish, ready for de Queen hersef, when she come to see 'Badian people." He seemed to entertain no doubt of the Queen's intention of crossing the Atlantic, and evidently was rather surprised that her Majesty had not taken an earlier opportunity of visiting this interesting portion of her subjects.

Still, after all there was to be seen at Bridgetown, I should be almost inclined to think, from the oft-repeated question which was addressed to me afterwards, "Did you see Betsey Austin?" that that worthy lady is the principal attraction of the place. Betsey, or Miss Betsey Austin, as she is called, is a person of considerable importance, who keeps the principal hotel at Bridgetown. She has a large acquaintance amongst naval men, and is justly celebrated in Captain Marryatt's delightful novel *Peter Simple*. She assured us she owed much of her present prosperity to the work in question, and seemed duly grateful to the author. "He berry nice man, Captain Marryatt." Betsey may have her little faults, and who has not, but she must have a kindly heart in her capacious person from all I have heard. Miss Caroline Lee, her sister, is mistress of another hotel in the town, and makes better preserves of all kinds than anyone else in the island. We took in a large supply of livestock, such as turtles, turkeys, guinea fowls and ducks.

Two of our sailors became embroiled in a quarrel at one of the spirit shops at Bridgetown. One of them, the carpenter, after a hard fight, passed a night in prison. I do not believe they were much in fault, as the coloured population of Barbadoes is notorious for seeking quarrels with English sailors. The sailors, as is well known, have no particular objection to a row at any time. On lecturing the carpenter, who was a Scotchman, for the folly of his conduct which had consigned him to the hands of the police, and caused him to spend a night in prison, he replied, "If I had been myself, it's no the dozen of them should have ta'en me."

CHAPTER IV

JAMAICA ⚓ PORT ROYAL ⚓ CREOLES ⚓
THE COLOURED POPULATION ⚓ GHOSTS

On November 4, we left Carlisle Bay at 5 o'clock p.m. The *Imaum,* a line-of-battle ship, had weighed her anchor five hours previously, and we hoped to have the "pleasure of her company" on the way, a sail being at all times a welcome sight at sea.

November 5—Shortened sail to a squall, took in a reef in main-sail, double-reefed fore-trysail.

November 6—Strong winds, thunder and lightning, treble reefed foresail. How impossible it is in words to give an idea of the grandeur, the fearful magnificence of a storm at sea! What a variety are there of stirring and deafening sounds, filling the mind with mingled feelings of admiration and awe! There is the shrill treble of the wind, whistling its fractious way through the rigging, joined with the never-ceasing roar of the foaming and angry sea, while the deep bass of the gradually nearing thunder is heard distinct above it all. The sea is one wild chaos of mountains —mountains never for one instant still; now receiving us deep into a fearful hollow, from which it seems as though we never could rise again; and now carrying us over their summits, only to be dashed with greater fury into the raging abyss below. And how manfully the little schooner rides over the frantic waves! How lightly she rises again, and how carelessly she dashes the water from her bows as she passes on, unharmed, over the troubled waters! If a heavier sea than usual breaks and you hear the dull heavy blow against her side, there is a tremble, a quiver, as though the poor little thing were stricken to the heart. It is, however, but for a moment, and the little *Dolphin* is bounding on again as proudly as before.

It would be a cold heart, I think, that would not feel an absolute affection for a ship that has carried one in safety through perils such as these. She seems so like a thing of life, and I am sure I have parted with many a so-called friend with infinitely less regret than I shall experience when I look my last on our safe and happy little schooner.

Two nights before we arrived at Jamaica, the lightning was most vivid. The sky seemed to open, and to have changed its ordinary hues for a covering of flame—while every moment, on this brilliant ground, the red zigzag forks darted out their angry tongues of fire like some fierce and goaded animal. For hours I gazed on this most magnificent sight. I could not make up my mind to go below, though the rain began to pour in torrents. No one who has not witnessed a storm of thunder and lightning in tropical climates, can form an idea of the mingled beauty, and terror of the effect. For all the world I would not have missed the sight, terrific and awe-inspiring as it was.

Towards night the tempest was at its height and the sound of the contending elements, as if roaring for their prey, deadened the voice of man. Suddenly, a noise more stunning than the rest struck upon the ear. It was the electric fluid against the mainmast. The sound it made was like that of two hands clapping, but five hundred times as loud. Our mast was only saved from destruction, and with it, doubtless, our own lives, by the circumstance of the rigging being wet, and acting as a conductor, by which means the lightning was conveyed over the side into the sea.

One of the most remarkable occurrences during the storm was one which affected my own person. At the same time that the mast was struck, I felt a warm and most peculiar sensation down my hand, and immediately mentioned the circumstance. For many hours afterwards, a deep red mark, about six inches in length, and one in breadth, was plainly to be seen in the place where I had felt the heat, and what I should describe as almost pain. As I was standing in the direction in which the lightning passed, it is to be supposed that I received at the same time the slightest possible shock. The escape we all had from this worst of dangers was great and providential indeed. In a small vessel, once on fire, with a large quantity of gunpowder on board, our destruction must have been inevitable, had not the Power which had sustained us so long among the dangers of the deep stretched forth a hand of deliverance over us.

During the night, the gale continued with unabated fury. To sleep was impossible, and as I lay in my cot, rocking from side to side and longing for daylight, I heard a strange and unfamiliar sound outside my cabin door. On going out to ascertain from whence it proceeded, I found some flying-fish, which had come down the companion-ladder with the wind and spray, flapping their delicate wings on the oil-cloth. It was a strange situation for flying-fish to find themselves in!

The *Imaum* was near us during the gale, and at night we occasionally burnt blue-lights, which to me was very cheering.

November 8—Squally, with heavy rain. Under treble-reefed topsails.

November 9—We were rounding Morant Point. Oh! what a swell was there. How we were thrown about. For the first and only time the cook requested a diminution of the daily number of dishes, and the sound of breaking crockery was heard playing its destructive accompaniment to the sound of the storm.

A lighthouse, which was not mentioned in any of the nautical books, caused some surprise to those on board who had been in the West Indies before. This lighthouse, which was an iron one and one hundred feet high, had, we afterwards found, been sent out not long before from England.

During the whole of the 10th, the highlands of Jamaica were in sight. We passed over the ancient town of Port Royal, which now lies "full fathom five" buried beneath the sea. Soon after noon of the 11th, we entered the harbour of its successor of the same name. We went in without a pilot, in a gale of wind, and going at the rate of twelve knots an hour. The *Dolphin*, as usual, behaved beautifully, answering to her helm, and dashing through the troubled waters in most perfect style. The rain was pouring down in torrents, such rain as is seldom seen except within the tropics. In these latitudes, it seems not so much to descend in drops, but in a positive sheet of water. The best of Mackintoshes are no protection from its violence; they are wet through in five minutes. An experienced resident in this climate recommended a thick blanket as the best dress in which to encounter these storms.

The town of Port Royal owes its origin to General Brague, in the year 1657. He first discovered its advantages as a military position. Its safe and splendid harbour and the opportunities it afforded for commerce very soon raised it to a pitch of wealth and prosperity, unsurpassed by any other of our West India possessions. Its greatest source of wealth, however, seems to have been owing to the plunder deposited there by the buccaneers. Gold, silver, jewels, laces, and all the riches of the Spanish possessions in America, were constantly brought there. It would be impossible to form any idea of the immense value of the spoils. Port Royal reached its highest pitch of prosperity about 1692, and it is from that year that its gradual decay may be dated. A tremendous earthquake overthrew, and buried beneath the waves, all the principal streets of the once flourishing city of Port Royal. Thousands perished through this awful calamity, and the waves of the restless sea rolled over the once splendid church and handsome buildings of the doomed city. There are some who declare that the steeple of the principal church may still be seen many fathoms under water in a calm day.

It was melancholy to reflect on the frightful loss of life, and of the numbers of human beings whose bones were strewn about the bottom of the harbour, in which we were now securely floating. The sharks swim carelessly over heaps of treasure, and mounds of gold. I have often wondered why some of our speculators who, in other parts of the world employ their energies in fishing for treasure, have not endeavoured to rescue some of these buried riches from the bottom of the deep.

The glory and prosperity of Port Royal seem to have departed forever. Scarcely had the remaining inhabitants recovered from their panic after the quake and restored a few of the streets to something of their former state, when the ill-fated town was again destroyed by fire. Two hurricanes, one in 1722, and another in 1744, successively razed it to the ground.

Jamaica has always been famous as the resort of pirates. Among the places of historical interest, as regards these adventurers, Cow Bay stands pre-eminent. It was there that, in the year 1681, an engagement was fought between the Governor, Sir Henry Morgan, and Everson, the Dutch pirate. The force of the latter consisted of but two ships, one of which was taken, and the pirate killed. The other vessel escaped. The crew of the one which was taken were desperate and fought bravely for their lives. Those who were not killed in action were executed on the shore. All the men were English. Some years after this occurrence, the neighbourhood of Port Royal was visited by a whole fleet of pirates, who then infested these seas. The barbarities they committed along the coast, upon the harmless and inoffensive inhabitants who were so unfortunate as to fall within their reach, are described as dreadful, and for miles around, the pirates desolated the country by fire and sword.

There is certainly great beauty in the surrounding country, but Port Royal itself is as ugly as a town can well be. Immediately after our arrival, our kind friend, Commodore Byng, sent to invite us to make his house our home during our stay in the island. The offer was gladly accepted, and we were soon landed at the dockyard, under a scorching sun. No sooner had we left the yacht than the sailors, one and all, threw off their clothes and plunged into the water. The master, of course, ordered them instantly on board again. Their escape from the jaws of the innumerable sharks which here infest the water, was almost miraculous. The thoughtlessness of sailors is really wonderful.

The Commodore's house is most comfortable. Never shall I forget the delightful relief it afforded, after undergoing the intense heat of the sun's rays, as they pierced through the insufficient barrier of our quarter-deck awning. On shore, we enjoyed exceedingly the green jalousies through which the sea-breeze blew refreshingly, and then the delicious iced water, and the luxurious sofas and rocking-chairs! I repeat, the change was most delightful.

The day after our arrival a sad tragedy occurred, at least it was a tragedy to me. My beautiful young Newfoundland dog, Wallace, who fetched and carried as no dog ever did before, and whose spirits and good-humour rendered him a favourite wherever he went, swam on shore in high health and spirits. But while bounding about in the exuberance of delight at having escaped from the confinement of the ship, he suddenly fell down in a fit, having, as we supposed, received a sunstroke. His sufferings, poor fellow, were soon over, and he was buried in a corner of the dockyard. I grieved for him at the time, and greatly missed his honest greeting when I returned on board.

The view from the Commodore's house is interesting. Coconut trees waved their hearse-like tops to the breeze close to its walls, and within a stone's throw lay the old *Magnificent.* Further off, we descried the delicate masts of our own little *Dolphin,* while the flag of the good ship *Imaum* was floating in the distance. The opposite land was clearly to be discerned. Up and down, before the house, paced the black sentry, calling the hours as they came round, and the bells of the various ships echoed his cry.

The house, like most of those in tropical climates, is raised from the ground on high pillars. This mode of architecture not only renders the apartments much cooler, but preserves those who inhabit them, in some measure, from the attacks of insects and reptiles. Every expedient measure is resorted to for protection from the bites of the detestable mosquitoes; notwithstanding which, in common with all newcomers, I found them most annoying. It is not so much the actual pain of the sting, at the time, as the aggravation of it afterwards, that is so trying. And in this climate, where the slightest scratch often becomes a serious affair, the irritation produced by a mosquito bite is often attended with bad, and even dangerous results. Two of our men were in the hospital for some time, in consequence of the venomous bites of these vicious little creatures.

We had been much surprised at the dearness of everything at Barbadoes but we were more astonished, from the same cause, at Port Royal. Mutton, bad and dry, tenpence a pound; a turkey, 1 pound 5 shillings; and a small bottle of milk, 1 shilling and sixpence. Eggs are sixpence each and all other necessaries of life in proportion.

The residents told us it was impossible to open one's mouth, for the purpose of eating for under a dollar, and we found no great difficulty in believing them. Sugar is much dearer than in England, and I need not add, much worse, as it is well known that the refining process of the best is carried on in the "old country."

Jamaica, to my idea, presents the melancholy picture of a land whose prosperity has passed away. Indolence is, I think, the principal characteristic of the inhabitants of this island at the present day, but it does not appear that one hundred and fifty years ago they were much more inclined to exertion than they are now. You see people of every hue—Creoles or natives, whites, blacks, and Indians; the latter with varieties of the species. There is a regular rule here by which to discover and to class the different castes, and to ascertain the exact proportion of black blood which runs in the veins of each. I could not understand, without taking more trouble than I thought the subject worthy of, the complicated classification, which is almost reduced to a science here; but it is of importance, to judge from the pains bestowed upon it.

The Creole is generally handsome, and well made, but from indolence and other causes, they are apt to become corpulent. They are said to be irritable, but generous and kind-hearted, and their love of expense and show is great. Now, however, they possess, generally speaking, but very little of the means necessary to enable them to indulge in their favourite tastes and pursuits. That the Creoles have been losers to a large amount by the abolition of the slave trade, there can be no doubt; and but little, that the prosperity of the island generally, its trade and resources, have gradually declined. I think it also more than questionable, whether the slaves themselves have found a greater aggregate of happiness since their freedom was declared. They wander about now in rags and destitution. Idleness is their occupation, and drunkenness their striking vice.

There is a look of hopeless indolence about the coloured population, which I did not remark in any of the other countries we visited. At Barbadoes, there appears to be some cleanliness and some self-respect, which is visible in their manners, and in their attention to dress, and the adornment of their persons. Here, on the contrary, they seem thoroughly degraded. On my first arrival, finding walking and even riding on horseback, too great an exertion in such a climate, I inquired of a lady who was paying me a visit, and who had been some time in the country, whether there were not palanquins for the use of individuals, who, like myself, were unaccustomed to the climate? She shook her head, "There is not a man in the island," was the reply, "who would consent to degrade himself by becoming a palanquin-bearer!" And these people but yesterday were slaves! What they might be, had liberty been bestowed upon them gradually, and in a more judicious manner, I cannot say. But I have often thought that, had each man been allowed to work out his liberation, the boon would have appeared more valuable, as we rarely prize that which has caused us no difficulty in the attainment. A still more important result would have been, that a second nature, the well-known fruits of habit, would have been acquired. Certainly their present condition is not so good, as not to make any other very desirable.

After writing all this, it has occurred to me, that the same thing has been said before, and much better than I can say it. It is truth, I believe, which is always something in this false generation. Speaking about truth, I may say it, no subject has ever afforded a stronger proof of the depth at which this virtue lies buried, than that of slavery. That there were some who abused their power over the negroes there can, I fear, be no doubt. At the same time it is equally true, that the rare instances of oppression were greatly magnified by the morbid sensibilities and sickly sentimentalities of well-meaning abolitionists.

I was made so very comfortable at the house of the hospitable Commodore, that I can say nothing, by experience, of the discomforts attending a residence on the island. The Governor, Lord Elgin, with whom we had the pleasure of being previously acquainted, gave us the kindest invitation to pay him a few days' visit at his residence among the hills. I did not feel equal to the journey, which must be performed on horseback, and commenced at five in the morning in order to avoid the heat of the sun, but I greatly regretted not being able to see more of the interior of the island.

Our first excursion was to Spanish Town. The route to Port Henderson from Port Royal is by water; it is about six miles from the latter place. It is very much to be deplored that the religious edifices, erected by the Spaniards here, should have been so little respected by the English, who succeeded them. Whether from fanatical fury, or other causes, they have been mostly destroyed, or suffered to fall into gradual decay. Spanish Town is irregularly built, and, partly perhaps from the glare of the white houses, appeared to me still more oppressive than Port Royal.

The town is built on rather high ground, sloping towards the shore. As there is no marshy land between it and the sea, the refreshing sea-breeze blows healthily over the town. Spanish Town is long and narrow, and its buildings may extend to about a mile in length. There is a church and a chapel. The former is handsome; the pews, pulpit, etc, are of cedar, and the aisles are paved with marble. The chapel stands near the Governor's house; and not far off is the guard-house, where a party of regular soldiers are always on duty. The Queen's house occupies one side of a large square. It was built in 1762, and is one of the finest of the kind in the West Indies. The length of the façade is two hundred feet, and it is of most beautiful freestone, which in this clear air and smokeless climate, retains its whiteness throughout all time.

The Hall of Audience is a fine well-proportioned saloon, about seventy-five by thirty feet. Some part of this immense building is appropriated to public dinners, balls, etc. The Assembly Chamber, or Common House, is about eighty feet in length, by forty in breadth. There is a raised platform at one end, which is lined with seats for members. The chair of the Speaker is raised a little higher than the rest. Here, among the legislative assembly, are to be seen both black and white faces. The former direct, with the white inhabitants, the affairs of the island, and I am told that among them are one or two intelligent men.

It will, indeed, be a work of time and difficulty to restore Jamaica to anything like its former prosperity, to correct the abuses which have crept into its government, and to restore confidence among all classes. The state of things is, however, improving, and may it continue to do so. Lord Elgin is exerting himself to further these desirable ends. The universal popularity and esteem with which he is regarded, as well as the prospect of success, must cheer him while he devotes his talents and energies in this formerly almost hopeless cause.

The hospital stands at the east end of the town, near the river. The situation appeared to me to be ill-chosen for the purposes of health. Great care, however, is taken of the sick, and large sums of money are granted in order to defray the expenses of their support, and the cost of medical aid.

The market of Spanish Town is well supplied with fish, and black crabs, which are really delicious, and with tolerable poultry, milk, fruits, vegetables, etc. I have compared the prices of some of the necessaries of life before the abolition of slavery, with what they are at present, and I find them now very much higher, in many cases, nearly two-thirds.

Turtle has not changed much in price. We found it the cheapest food, as it is also the best, in Jamaica, and we ate it in all shapes—cutlets, roasted, grilled, and made into soups—till we were quite tired of it

There is a fine range of hills, north, and northwest of the town. Among these, are the pens, or villas of the rich inhabitants, who go there occasionally to enjoy health and coolness. The country is most beautiful and there are fine chalybeate springs in every direction. The road from Spanish Town to Port Henderson is excellent, but most disagreeably dusty. We could only go out after the sun was set, owing to the intense heat, and the twilight is so short in low latitudes that it was generally dark long before we returned to the yacht.

It was a favourite excursion of mine that of visiting Kingston after sunset, and by water. The view of the town from the sea is very fine. The distance from Port Royal is about six miles, through what are called the Shallows. For a considerable part of the way, the passage is so narrow, in consequence of the mangroves, which literally grow out of the water, that there is scarcely room for the oars of the boatmen. The scene is singular and pretty, and after the scorching heat of the day, the cool evening air was delight-fully refreshing. Oysters adhere in great numbers to the mangroves.

Kingston stands in an amphitheater of hills, and has full enjoyment both of the land and sea-breeze. The shape of the celebrated Blue Mountains is so varied and capricious, that one can hardly help fancying it the result of those fear-ful earthquakes, with which these countries have often been visited. The savannahs, or plains at the bottom of them, are charming. The mountains are in many parts covered with the thickest foliage. The prickly pear grows in great quantities, and there being but few paths, and those made in the Indian fashion (for single file,) it is by no means safe to trust yourself in the forests without a guide.

The houses at Kingston are much superior to those at Spanish Town. The soil on which the former town is built is partly gravel, but, owing in great measure to the torrents of water which descend from the high country, it is surrounded by a vast accumulation of mud. The effluvia arising from this, and from the oozy nature of the soil is terrible. The water, too, here is bad and unwholesome. In short, it is a dreadful place, and you can hardly go through the streets without being assailed by visions, or ideas of plague, pestilence, and sudden death.

We were in the habit of seeing occasionally here, a poor depressed, weary, young man who had made up his mind that he should have the fever, and must inevitably die. I never saw anyone so depressed by the idea of death. His very face had grown yellow by anticipation, and yet he was in good health, and manifested no other symptoms of decay. Every day he brought us some fresh story of illness or fever. And as his face was growing visibly longer, day by day, it must be that by this time, if alarm has not hurried him into the Port Royal burying ground, he is surely a perfect sight to look upon.

The market is near the water side, and is well supplied especially with vegetables, such as lettuces, cucumbers, French beans, artichokes, celery, peas, beans, etc, all brought from the mountains. I was told that in the season, there are delicious strawberries, grapes, melons, mulberries, etc. The apples are excellent and so, I have no doubt, are all the other fruits, as the climate among the hills varies from actual cold to temperate. A marketboat goes daily to Port Royal and back.

The birds of Jamaica are very various and beautiful. I must say *a propos* of birds, that one of the most disagreeable sights I ever witnessed was a row of that horrid description of vultures, called scavengers. They were resting on a wall, gorged with their disgusting meal, their eyes closed, and their heads sunk between their shoulders. These unpleasant creatures are protected by the government, and there is a very heavy penalty incurred by killing one of them. They are very useful, devouring carrion and preventing the accumulation of offal. Were it not for the scavengers, putrid and other fevers, would be still more prevalent than they are at present. Our doctor was very anxious to shoot one, and we with difficulty dissuaded him.

It is strange, that in a climate like this, greater care is not taken to cleanse the streets and to ventilate the apartments of the houses. I am told that in the lodging-houses the rooms are so close and confined that it is impossible to breathe in them freely. The over-filled cemeteries being in the heart of the living population is another great instance of imprudence. They have such dismal names too for some of their streets and houses, "Dead Man's Hole," for instance. Enough to kill a nervous person, directly he sets his foot in it. The quarters of the soldiers have been removed from Kingston to a higher ground on the hills. Thus some amelioration in the lot of these poor fellows has been effected. The latter position is so much higher, that it has been found, already, an improvement in their lot.

There is a tolerable theatre at Kingston, which however, is not very well attended by the inhabitants, though occasionally an Italian Company comes from Havanna for a month or two. There are several houses in the town where sugar is refined, and which, I was told, were worth seeing, but I confess I did not feel very enterprising in this climate.

Good rum is very high-priced, and the same quality, which, in England, can be purchased at three shillings a gallon, cannot here be procured at less than nine. The reason for this is that the rum is sent to England, where it undergoes some improving process, and that on its return to Jamaica, its price is increased to this large amount by colonial dues, charge of freight, etc. The rum of the country, before it takes a voyage to England, is execrable. I could not avoid hearing frequent complaints on this subject, from those charged—to use an American phrase—with liquoring the ship's company, and the latter certainly did not seem to approve of the quality of the liquor.

But to return to Kingston. The moon had risen when we returned from our excursion. As its brilliant disk rose over the distant blue mountains, revealing their bold outlines and shedding a subdued light over the tranquil sea, a more beautiful effect, or one more worthy of some great painter's hand, could scarcely be imagined. And yet, over this calm scene, the angel of death was hovering! Strange, that so lovely a land should he the stronghold of disease, the burial-place of the young, the healthy, and the gay! But so it is! Today strong in health, and fresh in spirit; tomorrow, numbered among the dead.

In no country that I ever heard of, is superstition more rife than it is in Jamaica. Even Ireland, that land of fancy and wild imaginings, can boast but few national ghosts and interesting revenants compared with those which are said to flourish on this island. They have their "duffies," a most unpleasant species of ghost, answering to the Irish "banshee," who are said to wander about in numbers proportioned to the deaths which take place. In sickly seasons, it is said, they may be seen to any amount. Of course, in common with all national ghosts that ever were heard of, they prefer the burial-ground as their place of resort. By all accounts, they are fearful things, those duffies. And, as national ghosts, they have a decided claim to respect and consideration.

The burial-ground of Port Royal is just outside the town, and is a most congenial spot for their unholy revels. It is strewed with human bones of all sorts and dimensions. Here they are said to hover over the silent graves, dancing about in wild glee, and sometimes even venturing beyond the limits of the graveyard, to pay nocturnal visits to their former friends. There are several coconut trees in and about the burial-ground. Their tops wave about, not at all unlike the plumes of a hearse, and add greatly to the gloom of the place. The ghost of a certain merchant, who died some time ago in Jamaica, is said to mount nightly to the top of one or other of these coconut trees and, after taking a deliberate survey of the country, descends and makes his way into the town. At the time of his death, several persons owed him money to a considerable amount; in particular, one rather influential person, against whom he appears to entertain a bitter grudge. The duffy of the dead merchant frequently, in the dead of the night, "when all around are sleeping," enters the house of his quondam friend, and pummels his corpulent sides till he roars for mercy. I was seriously informed by a respectable lodging-house keeper, whose house had formerly been a hospital, that on moonlight nights, I might see troops of its former inhabitants, those who had died within the walls, walking leisurely up and down the verandah and looking complacently in upon its present occupants.

No fear of these nightly visitors seemed to be felt by anyone. On the contrary, they were evidently considered as a sort of domestic animal, whom, however, it would be injudicious to disturb.

It may be mentioned, that there are many superstitions peculiar to the negroes, upon whose fears and credulity it is easy, but very barbarous, to work.

The sea-breeze at Port Royal blows with considerable violence. On one occasion, I recollect a heavy decanter, full of wine, being literally blown off the table by the strength of the wind, as it blustered through the Commodore's house. The wind is considered here so healthy, and so reviving in its effects, that it is universally called "the doctor." I found his measures, however, rather too violent to be agreeable, and always fancied I felt the heat more, after he had ceased to blow upon me, or rather, in the intervals between his puffs. I found, also, that many people agreed with me, in disliking his diurnal visits.

The time was now fast drawing near when we were to take our leave of our pleasant quarters. In spite, however, of tropical heat, mosquitoes, and white ants, it required a great effort to make up our minds to bid adieu to our kind and hospitable host.

A few days before our departure, the Commodore, with several officers of the *Imaum*, Captain Bruce, etc, gave us the pleasure of their company at dinner on board the *Dolphin*. It was their farewell visit. The principal event which marked the party was that the Commodore's servant fell into the sea, while attempting to get into the barge. He rose immediately, and was speedily picked up; happily with the usual number of limbs, for he had a narrow escape from the sharks. Necessary business connected with the yacht had already detained us a considerable time. New sails had to be fitted, and awnings repaired, besides many other arrangements of which I do not know the nature. We had also to replace our two sailors who were left at Madeira. This we found no difficulty in doing; the two new hands were men-of-war's men, and called "very smart." The steward's mate had also taken to drinking and idling, and was discharged. He was the "tragedian," and made his appearance, during our stay, on the boards of the Kingston Theatre. A substitute for him was not easily procured, but we succeeded at last and were declared in readiness for sea.

We were to weigh anchor at five o'clock in the morning, and consequently decided to sleep on board the last night. Adieus are always painful, whether addressed to place or people. I never leave a house, which in all probability I never shall see again, without a heavy heart, and the last minute always comes too soon. After bestowing our last words, and last good wishes on our host, we shook hands with the best and most warmhearted of negresses, Sally Adams. This pattern for housekeepers to single gentlemen has filled the like office at Port Royal time out of mind, but only as an amateur. She is a sick-nurse at the Hospital, and friend and assistant-general to all who require her aid. It is handed down traditionally, that Sally Adams performed these kind offices in the time of Admiral Rodney; and I am not at all sure that she does not entertain a personal recollection of the unfortunate Vice-Admiral Hosier.

Nancy, the negress, who had proved herself, in stormy weather, anything but an acquisition to our ship's company, we despatched in a steamer to her native island, St. Thomas'. She was not a good specimen of her country. Though by no means wanting in intellect, she possessed the worst quality of the fool—cunning. I have often, through my cabin-door, heard her boasting of her ingenuity in deceiving a former mistress, or rather owner, who, by her own account, treated her with the greatest kindness. "I made believe pain in side, no work, then missus come and nurse, and rub side, and do all work herself." I was not sorry when she left us. Her extreme ugliness really disfigured the ship.

At eight o'clock in the evening we took a final leave of our kind friends, and prepared ourselves for the noises and rockings, which make one every moment mentally acknowledge the truth of the saying, that, "a ship is a thing you never can be quiet in."

The *Lightning* man-of-war steamer left Port Royal for Haiti, with prisoners, at the time of our departure from Jamaica. After remaining a day or two at St. Domingo, she was expected to leave that island for Havanna, to which city we were also bound. I had indulged the hope of again having a consort to sail with us, as there is something to me very satisfactory in the idea of having a friend near, on the wide waters. I have been often told, that in case of danger, there is seldom any chance of their being of any use, yet the very sight of them is cheering.

Having been merely fastened to a buoy, we were soon underway the next morning. Again, and most probably for the last time, I gazed on the beautiful scenery and luxuriant vegetation of this most lovely of the West India Islands. The Blue Mountains, half hid among the clouds, and the dark hills rising from the sea, were glorious to witness.

Since we left Jamaica, sad changes have taken place. The excellent Bishop, whom we left doing good, and "given to hospitality," has fallen a victim to the climate; while Lady Elgin, the young, the beautiful, and the good, has also been laid low. The Assembly at Jamaica have voted eight hundred pounds to be expended in the erection of a tablet to the memory of the lamented Lady Elgin, as a mark of the respect in which she was universally held.

If the remaining friends and relations of those that are thus prematurely laid in the grave can find a consolation in their bereavement, it must be in the sympathy of the many who knew and appreciated the virtues of the dead; and in the belief, that in another world, the virtues of the departed have secured them, through faith in their Redeemer, an eternity of happiness and peace.

Rest, then, weary wanderer, here,
Be still—for sacred ground is near;
Here 'neath a simple tablet lying,
The lov'd in life, the blest when dying,
Waits, in this dark and still abode,
A summons to attend her God!
A peaceful halo fills the air,
And tells that faith is sleeping there.
The young, the highborn, sleeps below,
For her, the tears of thousands flow.
Then, wanderer through this world of care,
Breathe o'er this spot a silent prayer;
Pray for the desolate and poor,
Who ne'er were driven from her door,
Pray that the rich who here abide
May imitate so fair a guide:
May they, like her, with open hand,
Spread gladness through a grateful land;
Winning, on earth, a people's love;
An angel's glorious lot above!

Chapter V
Cape Corrientes ⚓ The Mississippi ⚓ Balize ⚓
Rifle Shooting ⚓ Catfish ⚓ River Scenery

November 22—Light airs and fine. Five o'clock received the pilot on board—passed Portuguese shoal—ten o'clock discharged pilot.—Ten p.m. Beautiful moon, light night, running six knots passed Portland Point and Pedro Bluffs.

November 26—This morning we made the Island of Cuba and as we supposed Cape San Antonio. The land was very low and rocky, with here and there a few pines. Our books of directions mentioned the great resemblance between Cape Corrientes and Cape San Antonio, and also how often they were mistaken for one another. As the weather was cloudy, and, owing to the currents, as we were not over sure of our exact position, we kept a good offing and soon after discovered Cape San Antonio well to the westward. The land we had first made was Cape Corrientes. We had also a proof of the accuracy of our charts; the wrecks of two vessels being observable on the shore about three miles to the west of Cape Corrientes, where they had run up high and dry, fancying they were well past the westernmost point of Cuba. No sooner had we rounded Cape San Antonio, than we found our change of course entailed upon us a dead foul wind. We were also no longer under the shelter of the island. It was blowing very hard and the strong wind, in opposition to the current, produced a most unpleasant kind of sea. We were under single-reefed mainsail and forestud-sail, and double-reefed fore-trysail. Midnight—heavy squalls, attended with thunder, rain and lightning. There are few things more provoking after having undergone discomfort and fear, and after having fancied oneself a perfect heroine, than to be told that it was a mere nothing, blowing rather fresh, etc. I often felt quite mortified at having my illusions destroyed in this rough manner.

November 27—Double reefed fore-trysail—three sails in sight. In the afternoon moderate gales, midnight, squally.

This was all disagreeable enough, so we called a council, or in Indian language, a Palaver, and determined to give up Havanna for the present and to bear up for New Orleans. The change was delightful. We had the wind with us and skipped along beautifully at seven, eight, and nine knots an hour, a few double reefs, but nothing to signify.

November 30—Fresh breezes and fine, sounded, no bottom, at thirty-five fathom. In the afternoon, double reefs again in mainsail.

December 1—Sounded, forty-five fathom, mud, altered course and set square sail. Three o'clock p.m. received a pilot on board. Saw a lighthouse on starboard bow; at five o'clock we brought up off Balize in three fathom water, furled sails, cleared decks and set the watch. And this was the Mississippi! The giant river of which I had heard so much! It really was very disappointing—mud, and reeds, and floating logs, yellow fever, dampness and desolation! I believe there are about two hundred souls in this wretched little village of Balize, at least fifty of them are pilots. They go very far out to sea and their boats, though not handsome, are well built and safe.

The chief officer of the customs, and the great man of the place, came on board immediately and was most kind in his offers of assistance. He had shooting "first rate" for my husband, and a ball with a drum and tambour to enliven the ladies, i.e. my maid and myself! By his account, game is very plentiful here at all seasons of the year—snipes in abundance, and thousands of wild ducks; and a short way up the river, plenty of deer, quail, gray squirrel and woodcock. Fish, to our surprise, is rather a scarce commodity here. The sort most frequently caught is called the catfish, of which, by the bye, our new acquaintance told us rather a remarkable anecdote. "Well sir," he began, "this is queer what I'm going to tell you, but it's a fact, that a friend of mine had a pointer dog marked with very particular spots, and this pointer had seven first-rate pups, all marked the same. Well sir, my friend he didn't want the pups, so he just threw them slick into the Mississippi. He was raised, my friend was, up north a way, and he threw the pups in good two hundred miles from here, he did. Well sir, it might be a couple of days after this I was a fishing, and I caught as fine a catfish as ever you saw, and in its inside what might you think I found? Just my friend's pointer pups, two of them was dead surely, but the rest was only a little hungry!—and that's a fact! by this and by that."

This singular personage was very proud of his skill in rifle-shooting, and sent us evidences of his skill, in the shape of some delicious wild ducks shot that morning. He had come off conqueror in a well-contested match with Alligator, the famous Indian chief, and, what was of much greater importance to him, he had likewise proved his superiority as a sportsman over an "English nobleman!" He forgot the name of this "distinguished individual," as he called him. By his account the "nobleman" was travelling for pleasure (a circumstance in itself always sufficiently surprising to a Yankee mind) and finding himself at Balize, challenged our informant to a rifle-match. The peer boasted of being a first-rate shot. He had won the cup at Manchester, by his skill with the rifle, and in short "he would show the American what shooting was."

"Well," said the narrator, "his Lordship dressed himself in a smart new bright green velvet hunting coat, with mother-of-pearl buttons as big as a dollar. Why I tell you, that coat was enough to have skeered all the ducks away from the river from this to eternity. Well, sir, he put on the coat, and then he stood up to fire, without a thought of keeping himself out of sight of the birds, and then away he popped, and a splendid gun he had too, quite first-rate. Well sir, I shot twenty-two ducks out of twenty-three shots; a man with us shot ten out of twelve, while my Lord he never brought down a bird. I guess he was surprised a little—I wish I didn't obliviate his name, but I do—and that's a fact."

Our friend was really very useful to us, as he was a good specimen of a genuine Yankee: kind-hearted and hospitable to a degree; rather given to drawing the longbow but, as a sportsman, and a very good one, he must stand excused. His son was a very pleasant-mannered boy, a midshipman in the United States Navy. The two, together, supplied us plentifully with game, which we were not sorry to procure, as we intended sailing up the river to New Orleans, a mode of voyaging, which, with contrary winds, frequently occupies a considerable length of time. The distance is about one hundred and five miles.

It is not very easy to procure provisions of any sort at Balize. Beef is brought from the city (New Orleans) only in sufficient quantities to supply the wants of the pilots and their families, and is very high priced, namely, one shilling and threepence a pound. Fowls and eggs are still scarcer; no poultry is reared in the neighbourhood. Milk was not to be had at any price but we were told that there was a widow lady up the river, who had milch cows, and might possibly be induced to part with some of their produce. With this hope I was obliged to be contented, though, not having enjoyed the luxury of milk in my tea since leaving Jamaica, I confess I was rather disappointed in having to wait still longer for what we are accustomed to consider an indispensable article of diet.

December 2—Weighed anchor, and made sail up the river with a fair wind, moderate and fine. It is always customary to "take steam" up the Mississippi, so our determination of sailing caused great astonishment, but it was so much more agreeable and independent a course, that we had no hesitation in adopting it. The noise of the high-pressure engines, which are almost invariably used, is very disagreeable. You have not even the advantage of coming quickly to the end of your voyage, as the steamer generally takes several vessels in tow, and consequently, her steam is not of sufficient power and you do not average more than three or four knots an hour.

After losing sight of the harbour, you see nothing on either side of the river for several miles but the same low reedy banks. Banks, however, they cannot be called, as there is not the slightest perceptible elevation. You meet with innumerable snags and floating logs, which give a very desolate, ruinous look to the surface of the water. On ascending a few rattlings, one of the crew said he could see the sea over the tops of the low trees. There are several passes out of the river, and between them extend these swampy forests.

Occasionally we passed, or met a large raft, floating up or down the stream. These rafts have generally a little hut built on them, in which there is a fire, and the men who have charge of these floating islands, are very often seen comfortably cooking their dinner; the muddy water all the while rippling over their wooden island, and finding its way out again as quietly as it came in.

Too much cannot be said of the extreme muddiness and ugliness of this celebrated river, a few miles from its mouth. Its fogs "whip" those of our Thames. By the bye, the Yankees use the verb, "to whip," invariably where we say "to beat." For instance, when we first entered the river, as we lay at anchor, a little schooner passed us, and without any previous greeting, the master hailed us through his speaking trumpet, with the modest remark, "Well stranger, I guess I could whip you pretty considerable, I could." And by way, as he evidently considered making good his boast, he proceeded, taking advantage of our situation, to sail round us in a most triumphant manner. The Americans are great boasters—I cannot with any regard to truth, say they are not—and they are particularly glad to whip the English when they can. At the same time the vaunt is generally made in the spirit of good humour and honest rivalship, and if taken in the same way, would never lead, as is too generally the case, to quarrels and heartburnings.

By degrees the scenery improves and the woods are thicker. Still the timber is not of large growth, though the late autumn colours of the leaves rendered them very varied and beautiful. The most common tree is the sycamore, not quite the same as ours of the same name, but nearly so. The brilliant crimson of its seed-pods, contrasted finely with the brown and changing leaves. As we advanced up the

river the trees were of a more considerable size, and there
was much more variety in their foliage. Ilex and the live oak
are very frequent. There is a peculiarity in the appearance
of the woods, owing to the trees being almost universally
covered with the long drooping Spanish moss. This para-
sitical plant hangs from every branch and twig, descending
in long weeping clusters. These dependants often grow to
the length of six or eight feet, and are of a grayish colour.
They give a sombre hue to the forests and render their appearance somewhat monotonous. The shores increased in
beauty as we proceeded, being diversified with splendid
magnolias and cottonwood trees. Occasionally we saw
extensive clearings, on which were temporary wooden
houses erected near the riverside. They are occupied by
the wood-cutters, who are employed in felling and stack-
ing the wood for the innumerable steamers which work up
and down the river. These insatiable monsters of the deep
(the Mississippi is said to have no bottom) will soon effect
the almost total destruction of those characteristic forests.
They are fast disappearing under the hands of the busy
"go-ahead" steamboat companies.

We had a fine breeze all day, and though there was much
trimming of sails and beating up reaches, we found the
logbook spoke well of our progress. We asked a Yankee
fisherman, after we came to an anchor, how far we were
from New Orleans, and his reply was "Well, I expect it
will be sixty miles about from the city." This was a very
good day's work, particularly as we were working against
a current running from four to five miles an hour, and
encouraged us to persevere. All day we had been hailed
every hour by some steamer or other. The *Webster*, the
President, or the *Henry Clay*, with the oft repeated, "Well,
I guess you want to take steam up to the City?" "No,"
"no," " no," we had answered till we were tired.

Now, all was comparatively still. The huge river was
composing itself to rest after its labours. There was occasionally a murmuring sound from the adjacent shore, as
if some drowsy insects were humming their latest evening

song. Now and then the light paddle of a canoe went ripple, ripple past. Here we lay, our two lights gleaming through the evening mist, our sails furled, all hands below save the solitary lookout man. Yes, here we lay on the broad bosom of the giant Mississippi. What rest it was after the stormy nights to which we had so long been accustomed.

During the night the fog became very thick, and we were kept rather in a state of alarm from the number of steamers, which were constantly passing us. By the American law you are obliged to have two lights constantly burning at the masthead at night. Should any vessel, not showing the required number, be run against on the river by another ship, the former will not be entitled to any remuneration for damage sustained in the concussion.

December 3—The morning was damp, chilly and foggy, but before nine o'clock the sun had cleared away the mist, and we were again underway. As we progressed, the clearings became more frequent and greater signs of civilization were apparent. There was the more finished cottage, with its little garden crowded with orange trees, and most of them had in addition a small patch of Indian corn. The oranges are small, but grew very thickly. They are sweet and eatable, though not to be compared to any which come to England. The weather was very chilly; the thermometer on deck at noon in the sun, stood at 54°, which to us, so lately arrived from the scorching heat of the West Indies, was really cold; but notwithstanding this, we found the mosquitoes very troublesome.

All this day we had quite sufficient amusement in watching the birds, which were displaying their bright colours in the variously tinted woods. They really were beautiful, and we were quite near enough to the shore to distinguish their colours, and generally speaking, their species. There was the mockingbird with its elegant shape but rather dingy plumage, jays and woodpeckers of every hue, and the gaudy Virginia nightingale in great numbers. We saw also wild ducks and flocks of wild swans and geese, the latter of which were extremely shy and wild. Of course every travel-

ler in America is prepared by previous description to admire
the autumn foliage of these "pathless woods." There is,
however, a richness and variety in them—the bright and
almost dazzling crimson shaded into rich golden yellow,
and intermingled with the brightest evergreens—which is
perfectly indescribable. If a painter were to attempt depict-
ing them to the life, he would be called "as mad as Turner,"
and truly no mortal hand could image forth such scenes as
these.

In this, our second day's pilgrimage, I noticed several
smart houses, the residences of sugar growers, whose
manufactories were always near at hand. Rather further
removed were the log huts of the slaves. We saw the latter
in great numbers, both male and female, working in the
clearings. They seemed very cheerful, and we often heard
them laugh merrily as we passed by. After all that I have
been told of the sufferings of these people, it quite glad-
dened my heart to hear them. We made this day but little
progress towards "the City," there being scarcely any wind.
Eighteen miles, however, were better than nothing, and as
we were not pressed for time, we still refused the offer of
our friends in the steam-tugs.

At four o'clock p.m., the breeze died away entirely, and
we came to an anchor in seven fathom water. In the evening, after dinner, we rowed to the shore, our object being
to procure a little milk, and seeing some cows in a neigh-
bouring clearing, we did not quite despair of success. The
river here is about a mile wide. We had, therefore, some
little distance to row, and the current was running very
strong. We did not take any of the men with us, as they had
been so much employed all day in tacking, trimming sails,
etc. On reaching the shore, the doctor alone landed. We
waited a long time, so long that the mosquitoes tired with
worrying us went to rest, and the mighty fog, which I had
hoped to escape, covered us over like a curtain. At length
there came the welcome sound of approaching footsteps,
and our companion accompanied by three men made his
appearance. He had literally been unable to escape before,

so warm had been his welcome from these rude sons of the forest. They were profuse in their offers of assistance, and I believe would really have given us anything they possessed. From the lady who kept the cows, we procured a small bottle of milk, for which we paid two bits—about one shilling. They likewise brought me some fresh eggs, which were quite a luxury.

The question now was "How to find the *Dolphin*?" There is nothing so bewildering as a thick fog, and by the time we had rowed, as we thought, to the middle of the stream, we found ourselves completely puzzled, both as to our own whereabouts and that of the schooner. The steamers were puffing up and down, thick and fast, giving us but little note of their approach. Indeed, were they ever so near, from the extreme density of the fog, there was every chance of our steering precisely the wrong way. Our only guide was our knowledge that the two lights of the *Dolphin* were to be looked for under the north star. We were at length enabled to catch a glimpse of her, as the fog hung low over the water, and our guiding star brought us to our home in safety. In less than an hour I found myself to my infinite relief in my floating home playing "Hail Columbia" with variations; an appropriate compliment to the "great City," we were approaching.

December 4—Alas! No wind, another lingering day. But the weather was warmer, and the birds were singing so gaily that they reminded me of an English day in June. There was now no variety in the scenery. We came to an anchor early in the afternoon, having made about ten miles! After dinner we rowed in the gig for some time along the banks, and landed several times in the hope of procuring fresh provisions. Meeting with no success, we returned on board laden with orange branches covered with fruit. All night the fog was very thick and the mosquitoes most annoying.

CHAPTER VI
NEW ORLEANS ⚓ TEXAN COMMODORE ⚓
ST. CHARLES HOTEL ⚓ MANNERS & CUSTOMS ⚓
YELLOW FEVER ⚓ EDUCATION

December 5—Only fifteen miles from the city. Its towers, and the dome of the St. Charles's Hotel, distinctly to be seen! All rather tired with the monotony of our fresh water voyage. A dead calm till two o'clock, p.m. It was dusk before we reached New Orleans. The first view of the town from the river is very striking; I think I never saw, in any other, so long and continuous a line of large, and even grand-looking buildings. The innumerable lights which gleamed from the houses and public buildings, and which were reflected on the river, were to us, so long unused to the cheerful aspect of a large and bustling city, a most welcome sight.

December 6—If New Orleans appeared delightful to us by the light of its gas-lamps, what did it not do when seen in the face of day! It was the busiest scene! Such forests of masts! Such flaunting colours and flags, of every hue and of every country! Really, as the Yankees say, "Orleens may stump the univarse for a city." Five tiers of shipping in the harbour! This is their busiest time for taking in cargo.

There is a beautiful corvette lying near us with a long low hull, and raking masts; at the mainmast is flying a small flag, with one star on its brilliant white ground. It is the star of the young Republic of Texas. "Boat alongside!" "Side ropes!" It is the gig of the Texan Commodore. He had sent a lieutenant from the *San Jacinto*, with many kind offers of assistance and civility. In about an hour Mr. Houstoun returned the visit, and brought the Commodore back with him.

The latter gave us a good deal of information as to the state of the Texan country, and some news from the army. His countrymen and the Mexicans are continuing a desultory warfare, and with but little present prospect of coming to an amicable settlement. One thing which the Commodore told us gave us a good deal of disappointment. We found that our plan of going to Aransas could not be put into execution. From all we had heard, the country about that river is the finest in Texas, and affords the best sports, there being wild animals in great variety. Unfortunately, the *Dolphin*, he assured us, drew too much water for the bar at the mouth of Aransas harbour, and lying outside is by no means safe.

The *San Jacinto*, though of eight hundred tons, drew but ten feet; she was fully armed and equipped. All the Commodore wanted for was money, and that seemed very scarce with him just then. Had he but possessed that necessary article, he "would go to sea, take the *Montezuma* and *Guadaloupe*, and whip the Mexicans all round!" And so he very likely would, for he enjoys the reputation of being a good officer, and a very fighting one. Mr. Houstoun went on shore with the Commodore, and was introduced to the British Consul. During his absence a great many boats came alongside. What could we be, a miniature man-of-war, with our guns run out at the port-holes, and our white stripe? No one knew. But we heard afterwards, that our expected advent had been announced in a New Orleans newspaper, and in that we were described as an armed vessel, going to fight for the cause of freedom, i.e. to take the part of the Yucatanese. Truly, though I wish them every success, I hope I may never hear the voices of our six-pounders in their behalf.

[*EDITOR'S NOTE: The schooner* San Jacinto *was wrecked during a storm off the Cayos Arcas in late October 1840, so Mrs. Houstoun certainly didn't encounter her in New Orleans in 1842. It is probable that the ship with the displacement and draught that the author describes seeing in conjunction with her visit with Commodore Moore was the flagship* Austin. *Moore was in New Orleans with the* Austin *and the remains of his declining fleet. The epic battle between Commodore Moore and President Houston was underway, and Moore was stuck at New Orleans awaiting access to $120,000+ in funds appropriated to the navy by* *regular and special sessions of the Sixth Congress. Just days before his meeting with the Houstouns, Moore penned a letter from the* Austin *to Acting Secretary of War & Marine, M. C. Hamilton, suggesting that he'd be delighted to obey orders to sail against Mexico in support of Yucatán if he had two nickels to rub together. He couldn't even obey orders to return to Galveston, for want of money and men to get the vessels there. In just a few weeks, by act of another special session of Congress, the Texas Navy would be legally disbanded, although the Houston vs. Moore saga would continue well on into the next decade.]*

We found the mosquitoes most disagreeable; they were worse, if possible, than at Jamaica. But to make me some amends, I had such beautiful flowers! Jessamines of every kind; daphnes, roses, violets! Such a December bouquet and all growing in the open air! How refreshing they were, and how they reminded me of summer in distant England.

We made it a rule, in general, not to sleep out of our own house, but were tempted to break it here. Previous to our arrival, we had heard so much of the great Hotel of St. Charles, the immense extent of its accommodations, and the size of its apartments, that we decided upon spending a few days there, in order to see these wonders with our own eyes, and judge of them with our understandings.

The St. Charles's Hotel was built on speculation by the proprietor of the Astor House, at New York, and I believe the former to be, if possible, a still more prosperous undertaking than the Astor House. It contains within its walls accommodation for at least five hundred persons. We landed in the gig about twelve o'clock, and such a scene of business and bustle never before met my eyes! The Strand, or Levee, as it is called, is crowded by busy-looking men, passing in all directions. Evidently their heads are full of business. Speculations and "operations," in course or in perspective, fill up every thought and feeling. No one looks at you, or delays for a moment his walk or his conversation for trivial causes. Indeed, I am inclined to believe, that were a mad dog at their heels, it would make but little impression upon their absorbed faculties. Black slaves, laughing, joking, swearing, and hallooing, are rolling along the sugar-casks, or tumbling over the bales of cotton. Sailors of merchant vessels, the only idlers in this busy scene, are lounging about, with their pipes in their mouths, and their hands in their pockets.

It is a most animated, and to a stranger, most amusing sight; but with all this bustling and noise, there is no confusion, and I saw no disorderly persons about. Who are those gaily-dressed men sitting astride upon cotton bales, and looking so composed, while discussing some serious question with each other? You can judge nothing from their countenances. They are so well schooled and tutored, that no one would imagine an important mercantile negotiation was in progress. That gentleman mounted on a molasses-cask, whistling, cutting up a stick, as if for the bare life (but in reality to prevent his countenance from betraying his feelings) is doing business with the man who is balancing himself on an empty barrel near him. The latter, with the eternal quid in the corner of his mouth, is clearly looking out "for the giraffe," or taking care to not get taken, and, after a while, he rises with great coolness, with "Well, Sir, I calculate there's a something of a string-halt in the bargain; it's a horrid sight of money, Sir, you're asking, and as I'm in a tarnation hurry to liquor, I'll just put it off till next fall."

I need hardly say that this shrewd gentleman was recalled, and a bargain concluded. The process of liquoring is gone through several times before a bargain is struck. This, the first specimen I saw of Americans, in their own country, struck me forcibly. It showed me that those who, in dress, appearance, etc, are decidedly the gentlemen of the land, are so devoted to money making, as evidently to have neither time, nor many ideas to waste on other subjects. It convinced me that, though the contemplation of America as a nation and at a distance, may, and indeed must be interesting, the investigation and survey of the people who compose that nation, must soon become wearying and monotonous. One may be amused for a time at the shrewdness with which they make their bargains, at the acuteness of their remarks, and the originality of their expressions. But once convinced, as I speedily became, that their every action proceeds from a love of amassing wealth, you cease to become interested in individuals whose conduct and whose pleasures are swayed by such an ignoble cause.

The Americans are accounted, and I believe justly so, a moral people, but even this merit is, I think, not so great a one in their case as it is among other nations. Their love of wealth being all-powerful, and being gratified only by the strictest attention to business, it follows, necessarily, that the habits of their lives generally become quiet and restrained.

You seldom see an American lady accompanied in her walks, rides, or drives (except on Sundays) by a gentleman. It would be a waste of time, and consequently a useless expenditure of money, to indulge in the gentle and refining society of the female sex. Young, delicate, and pretty women are met unprotected, clad in the gayest colours. I believe they are not denied any of the innocent enjoyments procured by dress and female society, and they may be seen pacing the streets, from store to store, and from boarding-house to boarding-house, shopping, and paying visits. This custom of young married women not having a home of their own, but inhabiting those nests of gossip called boarding-houses, seems to me injudicious and reprehensible. The young American wife (and they marry when almost children) is thus left all day without the society of her husband, or the protection of his presence. Her conversation is limited to the vicious details of scandal, or the insipid twaddle of dress, and in a place where all have a right to enter, the good and the well-disposed woman must frequently come in contact with many, who, had she possessed a home of her own, would never have been admitted to her presence.

There were a variety of carriages standing for hire on the Levee. Their cleanliness, the excellence and ease of their springs, to say nothing of the well-appointed appearance of most of the drivers, would put to shame the hired vehicles in most of the capitals of Europe. We chose an open carriage, though the weather was extremely cold, for we were curious to see as much as we could of this interesting city.

I remarked how closely those whom I met or passed resembled each other. It is difficult to mistake a Yankee for the inhabitant or native of any other country. They are almost all closely shaven, not a vestige of beard or whisker is left, and then their garments are all so precisely the same! I felt I should never be able to distinguish one man from another. I could not at first comprehend why all the male inhabitants looked so precisely like figures made on the same model, but my lengthened drive through the streets enlightened me. Outside a great many of the "notion" stores, I saw just such figures hanging up—coat, *pantalon a sous pied*—in short, the whole outward man. There was this difference, and be it remarked, it is an essential one— the latter were men of straw. Such cannot be said of the wealthy merchants of New Orleans. The fact is this, there are no working tailors at New Orleans, and every article of dress comes ready-made from the Northern States. There are merchant tailors in plenty, and if the traveller in New Orleans is in want of a suit of clothes, he must, if of the masculine sex, betake himself to one of these gentlemen, and he will be forthwith fitted with anything he may happen to want. "Pants" are daily announced, as a cargo just arrived "from New York;" the latter city evidently has the responsibility of setting the fashions to the elegants of the other cities of the Union. These garments being all of the same colour and fashion, fully accounts for the similarity of the appearance of the inhabitants.

Everyone in America (and I include even New Orleans, where the admixture of French blood and the southern clime would doubtless cause an appearance of gaiety, if it can be looked for anywhere in the States)—everyone in America, I say, looks grave, serious, and reflective. There is none of the sportive, light-hearted manner visible among the French, and occasionally among our own countrymen. Their very amusements, and they are few, are partaken of without any show of relaxation or pleasure. Why is this? Because business pursues them into the very heart of their enjoyments; because, in fact, it *is* their enjoyment, and business is certainly not a lively thing. It neither opens the heart, nor expands the countenance.

De Tocqueville says: "I believe the seriousness of the Americans arises partly from their pride. In democratic countries, even poor men entertain a lofty notion of their personal importance: they look upon themselves with complacency, and are apt to suppose that others are looking at them too. With this disposition, they watch their language and their actions with care, and do not lay themselves open to betray their deficiencies; to preserve their dignity, they think it necessary to preserve their gravity."

If the Americans are the proud, sensitive people that De Tocqueville asserts them to be, how is it that this pride is wholly and solely personal? How is it that it does not make them feel more acutely as a nation, and induce them to bestow a little of the anxiety they display for themselves as individuals, on the honour and name of the country of which they affect to be so vain.

The fact is, that, like many other proud, or I should say, vain people, it is the very sense of their public deficiencies, and the knowledge that their want of national faith is held up as a scorn and a warning among the nations of the earth, that induces them to wrap themselves up in this dignified (?) gravity, and in a cold and repellent demeanour. An American does not even relax at his meals (to be sure, they occupy but a short space of time.) His attachment to his cares is greater than ours to our pleasures; and it is this, as I said before, that renders him so uninteresting a character.

The ladies cannot be uninteresting here; they are so pretty, so gentle, and so feminine-looking. I have said that they walk alone, and unprotected. At the same time, I ought to add, that so great is the respect in which ladies are held in

America, that such a course can rarely be attended by any disagreeable consequences. The taste which the American ladies display in their dress is questionable. It is true, their gowns, bonnets, caps, etc, all arrive from Paris, and I much question whether an American lady would condescend to wear anything which she even suspected was made by any other than Parisian fingers.

The natural conclusion to be drawn from this fact would be that the American ladies dress well. I, however, am far from thinking so. It is true, that each individual article is well made, and the fashion correct. How can it be otherwise, when expense is not regarded, and Braudrant's choicest showrooms are ransacked for the New World? Still the *tout ensemble* is not pleasing; the cap or bonnet, however pretty, is not put on well, and the colours are never tastefully mingled.

Ladies in America are too fond of glaring colours and, though their faces are lovely, they do not hold themselves well, and their figures are rarely good. I think I never saw so much beauty, or loveliness, so varied in its character, as I did in New Orleans. There was the fair English-American, with her slight stooping figure, far surpassing, in charm of feature, the beauties of the "Old Country." The Creole-brunette, with her springy form, and active, graceful walk, cannot be passed unnoticed; she looks very determined, however, and as if the strife of active and angry passions were often at war within her bosom. But lastly, and far more beautiful than either, I noticed the rich dark cheek of the Quadroon. The eloquent blood in her soft cheek speaks but too plainly of her despised descent. She seems to blush at the injustice of man, who visits upon her the sins of her fathers. The passerby arrogantly bids her stand aside, for he is holier than she. In bitter contempt, the women of the land shrink from her contact, and the large sleepy eye, half hid by its curled fringes, is hardly raised, as gracefully and humbly she passes them by. Poor thing! What wonder, if, feeling that she is neglected and oppressed, she should turn in the desolation of her heart to other ties. Deprived too frequently of the many consolations of kindred affection; a solitary link in the chain of human sympathies—brotherless, friendless, alone! Let those who have never known what solitude of the heart is, speak harshly of the errors of the despised Quadroon. I can but pity her.

All these and much more, I saw and noticed during my first long drive through the busy streets of New Orleans. There is indeed much to see, and much to remark upon, but close observation, after a time, becomes wearying, and I was not sorry to find myself arrived at the hotel. What a really magnificent building it is, with its immense façades; it quite strains ones eyes to catch a glimpse of its gigantic dome. The Americans certainly build remarkably fine looking edifices sometimes. I am not sure, however, that they are intended to last. Yankees are too apt to chalk out fine plans and commence splendid buildings, which after a time, and when only begun, they leave to Providence to finish.

"A new country is never too young for exertion—push on—keep moving—go ahead." This is the American's motto. They forget their youth, and consequent want of strength, in this very love of exertion, and fondness for attempt and "movin.'"

All this however does not apply to the St. Charles, which is finished, and is as good a specimen of a first-rate hotel as can be found anywhere. The establishment is conducted on a most liberal and splendid scale. The rooms for the *tables d'hote* are immense, and public eating goes on at all hours of the day. Longer time is spent at table by the Americans at New Orleans than in other parts of the Union, and greater attention is paid to the details of the cuisine. This may perhaps be accounted for by the admixture of French inhabitants, and consequent Gallic tastes and feelings.

The ladies have a *table d'hote* appropriated to them alone; I could not understand why they were to have this indulgence, if indulgence it can be called. I wondered at first why they could not wait till the hour of their husband's return from exchange, for their afternoon, and, what we consider, principal meal.

I found out during my stay, that eating was, to judge from the frequency of its recurrence, the favourite amusement of the ladies of New Orleans. They breakfasted at nine, then a luncheon was spread at eleven, dinner at four, tea at six, and supper at nine o'clock. At all these hours, a gong of tremendous power sounds clangingly through the hotel, summoning the fair boarders from their different apartments, to join in the social meal.

About one hundred ladies, I was told, sat down daily to these feminine repasts. I do not think that English women would submit to this, and great credit is due the fair Americans for the submission with which they give in to the wishes of their "lords." To be sure there is much in habit, and American women know, from their marriage day, the delights of living publicly in boarding houses, while they are altogether ignorant of the charms of a private life, the quiet delights of home, its necessary duties, and its chosen society.

It is the want of employment to fill up their long leisure hours (for though highly gifted and carefully educated, American ladies are not all studious and literary) which increases the number of their meals, fosters their love of dress, and creates the tendency to gossip.

The ladies here see but little of their husbands; it would be well were it otherwise. The influence of a wife is silent but great, and no women in any country are better formed to use their power with moderation and discretion, had they but the opportunity of exerting it. All day the husband is absent attending to his everlasting business, and developing habits and manners, which the few short moments he devotes to ladies' society are insufficient to counteract.

Still women take a high position in the United States. Their education is superior to that of the men, and their writings have in late years raised them to an elevated grade on the ladder of literary fame.

But I must return to the internal arrangements of this hotel, which, in fact, afford an excellent idea of the mode of life in this great capital of the Southern States. The evenings are occupied by music and dancing: the latter is a favourite amusement here, as I believe it to be generally in America. The ladies invite such gentlemen as they think agreeable, to take part in their amusements. Every evening till long past midnight, I was kept awake by the stirring and animated sounds occasioned by a "carpet dance," with its accompanying giggling, fiddling, and floor-shaking. Still, I was quite glad to hear them, for I had really felt for the monotonous lives led by the poor ladies, and had imagined the gentlemen capable of nothing but bargaining, liquoring and "shaving" (taking your neighbour at a disadvantage.) I was wrong, and so have many travellers in the States been before me. Most of the latter have neither remained long enough in the country to discover the truth, nor have they ever sufficiently thrown away the veil of prejudice, so as to enable them to see otherwise than "through a glass darkly."

Our private apartments were very comfortable, well carpeted, with excellent fires, luxurious furniture, and curtains of the richest blue damask. The only hotel to which I can at all compare it is that of Les Princes at Paris. I could almost have fancied myself in that region of luxury, good living, and civility—there are white helps of the male sex (our attendant was English) and seven excellent Parisian cooks; I need not add that the cuisine was as good as possible. My bedroom was delightful; such snow-white mosquito curtains, and endless rocking chairs and, really, had it not been for the appearance of the two former I should have found it hard to remember that I had not back-tracked the Atlantic.

An American breakfast (when it is good of its kind) is not to be surpassed in any other country; great variety of fish and fruit, preserves of every kind, and cakes of all sizes and descriptions. The buffalo-tongues are very praiseworthy, and so are the Philadelphia hams, which they assert (and I cannot deny) "whip the Westphalia by a long chalk." I thought their far-famed buckwheat cakes delicious. They are buttered and eaten when hot—but how unwholesome! Nothing but an American digestion could venture to indulge in them habitually.

The price of all these little enjoyments is rather high, in proportion to either Paris or London. For three rooms, food, lights, in short everything except wine included for my husband, myself, and my maid, the charge was seventeen dollars a day; but then it must be remembered that we "dieted" in private.

The day after our arrival, our new acquaintance Commodore Moore paid us a visit, accompanied by a General Euston. The former certainly did spin us some wonderful yarns, concerning the new country we were about to visit. It was all very amusing, and only made us the more determined to see and judge for ourselves. (The poor Commodore since those days has done many wonderful things, besides just saying them. I was quite sorry to read in a Texan paper, that he had been accused of piracy. He certainly appeared ready to do anything, as the schoolboys say, "from pitch and toss to manslaughter" for his country. General Euston has likewise, I regret to learn, paid the debt of nature, having been murdered—poor old gentleman—by a faction. These things appear more sad when one has known the parties, however slightly.)

[*EDITOR'S NOTE: Positively identifying "General Euston" was daunting, as no figure quite seemed to fit the profile as Mrs. Houstoun provided it. The most likely candidate, however, appears to be General Felix Huston, former commanding general of the Army of the Republic. He took up residence in New Orleans in 1840, after his tumultuous stint with the Texas Army. A friendship, or at very least a relationship based upon shared grievances against Sam Houston, seems plausible between Moore and Huston. Mrs. Houstoun's description of "Euston's" murder doesn't fit Huston, but her knowledge of this event may well have been simple misconstrued hearsay. Unfortunately for us, she doesn't at all reference her source of the news of the General's murder.*]

I did not see, in America, any of the offensive familiarity which is said to exist between masters and servants, or any of that objection on the part of the waiting class to attend as servants upon those whom the accident or acquisition of wealth had placed, for the time being, in a superior situation of life. In America no honest calling is degrading, each man aspiring at some future period to hold as important a place in the world as another. Thus, while fulfilling the duties of a servant, he certainly feels himself upon an equality with his present employer, who may (however important his present situation) have commenced life with as small an amount of the all-powerful cash as himself. This feeling and these aspirations, naturally prevent any of the lowliness, and indeed servility, which is often the characteristic of servants in aristocratic countries. It does more—it no doubt induces that certainty of equality which to us is so objectionable.

As sensible men, however, having entered into a temporary engagement and covenant to serve, and, therefore, to obey, they do not (at least those who wish to maintain a good reputation, and gratify their employers) indulge in useless vaunts of liberty and equality, but without servility, and with sufficient respect, do their duty during their voluntary engagement, as well, or better, than the servants of many other countries. The terms of service over, the former master may shake hands with, and converse in familiar terms with his quondam servant without fear of compromising his dignity, or coming in contact with language and habits inferior or different to his own. Some there must be whose disposition and frame of mind are dangerously affected by this state of things; who lose the sense of their temporary dependence in the broad sea of democratic and over-liberal opinions. But these instances, among a serious, methodical, and sensible people like the Americans, are rare, and by no means sufficient to controvert my opinion that (to use the words of the French writer, from whom I have previously quoted) "the relation of servants and masters is not disorganized." It is rather dangerous to take English servants to the United States. There are very few, comparatively speaking, whose attachment and good sense are proof against the tempting charms and delusions of nominal equality.

We had, fortunately, many opportunities during our stay of becoming acquainted with some of the most wealthy merchants of this wealthy city, and I did not fail to make every inquiry of them concerning its resources, its institutions and its capabilities as a rising commercial capital. The situation of New Orleans is one of almost unparalleled eligibility. It can command twenty thousand miles of river navigation; thus, indeed, having "water privileges" on a large scale. And then, with the sea, its navigation is perfectly easy, not only directly down the Mississippi, but by a canal and basin to the lake of Pontchartrain. Thus, its proximity to the ocean renders it almost a seaport town. The immense quantity of cotton with which the city is literally choked up, during that part of the year when the crop is brought in, would alone give one some faint idea of the extent of its commerce. During the time we were in the harbour, there could not have been much fewer than sixteen hundred commercial flat-bottomed boats busily engaged in it.

Louisiana, of which New Orleans is the capital, comprised, in the year 1538, Florida, Alabama, Mississippi, South Tennessee and Missouri. It received its name from the French King. In 1718, the city of New Orleans was founded. In 1732, the population amounted to five hundred whites and two thousand blacks. In 1812, Louisiana became one of the States of the Union. In this year, also, the first steamboat built on the Mississippi came down the river from Pittsburg to New Orleans. Soon after this, the war with England was concluded. But prior to this year, several new settlements had been made. Lands were colonized in Arkansas, but the principal settlements were at Dauphin Island, Pensacola, and Mobile. In the year 1727, the Jesuits and Ursuline nuns arrived from France, and many convents and religious edifices were erected. In

1730, the Council House and jail were built. During this year, the price of a negro was one hundred and twenty-six dollars, now it averages five hundred!

In 1769, the colony was ceded to Spain, and in the same year the yellow fever made its first appearance at New Orleans. The Cathedral, or Church of St. Louis, is one of the most interesting objects in the city, though, that suffered to fall almost into ruins. It was built about this period, by the Spaniards. The architecture, though beautiful, is said by connoisseurs to be neither pure nor regular. The grand entrance, consisting of a semicircular arched door, with two Tuscan columns on either side, is in the middle of the front part of the building, which is finely situated, in the centre of the Place d'Armes,

On looking over the annual lists of the amount of shipping in the harbour, in learning the value of their cargo and in comparing, one year with another, the census, and the revenue, one cannot but consider New Orleans as an unparalleled instance of the rapid increase of prosperity.

In the year 1802, two hundred and fifty-six vessels, of different kinds, entered the Mississippi. The population of the city, in 1810, was twenty-four thousand five hundred and fifty-two, having been trebled in seven years. As I before mentioned, the great epoch in the history of this rising city, took place in the year 1812, when the first steamboat entered its harbour. In 1834, the city was first lighted with gas. In 1830, the population, including blacks and whites, amounted to forty-nine thousand eight hundred and twenty-six. In ordinary years, the amount of deaths in New Orleans averages three thousand eight hundred. It is calculated that about one in fifty die of pulmonary consumption; and five hundred, at least, in passing through the acclimating process.

According to the official details in the record of the dead, during the year 1822, the largest number of deaths, in any one day, of yellow fever, was sixty; and of other casualties, eighty. During 1841, the highest number, from yellow fever, was forty-three; and the greatest mortality, sixty; thus satisfactorily showing, that the health of the city is improving.

The process of draining the immense morasses, which almost surround New Orleans, is attended with great difficulty, and proceeds but slowly. The greatest rise of the Mississippi takes place early in the summer, when the snows melt in the north and the hill country. When this rise takes place, the streets of New Orleans are three or four feet below the level of the river, and its inundations are sometimes of great service in cleansing and refreshing the city, during this season of heat and fever.

There are many charitable associations in New Orleans, and noble institutions for the relief of the sick and poor. The churches are handsome and numerous, and the prisons remarkably well conducted.

The markets are clean, and more than usually well supplied with every necessity of life. Fruit is in great abundance; apples, nuts of all kinds and sizes, from the cocoa to the pecan, and pineapples in profusion—the latter were introduced from the island of Cuba.

But to return to the public buildings. We greatly regretted having been at New Orleans after the burning of the St. Charles' Theatre. I believe it was almost unrivalled, even in Europe, for its size, comfort, and the splendour of its decorations. The cotton presses on the Levee are well worth seeing, as are also the Merchants' Exchange, and the Banks. The City Exchange is also very handsome.

Fires are very frequent at New Orleans, partly owing to the large proportion of wood used in erecting the houses. The fire arrangements are admirable.

Their system of national education cannot be too highly praised. There is a compelled tax of one per cent on all appraised property. For this, everyone receives instruction for his children, be they ever so numerous. This education comprises every branch of knowledge, and every sort of accomplishment. The masters themselves are people of acknowledged worth and consideration, and receive large salaries. On Washington's birthday, thousands of these young citizens were paraded through the streets, their teachers or governors at their head. They were on their way to church, to fete the memory of their national hero.

I noticed one extremely pretty and lady-like person at the head of one of the lines of girls. She was very young and held down her head, as if rather an unwilling sharer in the exhibition. On inquiry, I found she was the wife of a military man with a small income. She possessed great musical talent and had been appointed-singing mistress, with a salary of two hundred pounds per annum. To an European, and especially to an Englishman, this admixture of the classes of society, seems at first both strange and ill-advised. But he should recollect, that there is not, as with us, a broad line of demarcation to separate the rich or the well-born, from the poor and low. Each has a right to mingle with each, and it is not the degradation of poverty, but of vice and incapacity, which keeps one man below another. I am aware, though no politician, that in thickly-populated countries, and in governments such as ours, this system of education could not be carried out. But in the States, where there is plenty of space for each man to run his career, without jostling his neighbour, where courage, perseverance, and talent are sure to be rewarded with success, it is assuredly sound policy to raise as many useful citizens, and as few ignorant and unprincipled ones as possible.

The whole character of the city, particularly of that part which is called the French quarter, is very indicative of its Gallic origin. The names of the streets are principally French, with generally an English translation beneath, such as, Rue des Grands Homines (Great Men Street,) Rue des Morales (Moral Street,) etc. There are few good roads, as I found to my particular inconvenience, being shaken and jolted in a manner perfectly indescribable. The streets are wretchedly paved, but the carriages are good, and the springs on which they are hung, particularly safe and easy.

Nothing can exceed the civility of the storekeepers. It is true, they will not put themselves much out of their way, but then a refusal or an excuse is made with politeness, and you are not pressed and urged to purchase, as you so often are in European shops. A stranger also should recollect that the value he sets upon his dollar is very different from the estimation in which it is held here. He must learn to regard it as a sixpence, and part with it as such.

Dollars are not scarce at New Orleans. As a proof of this, I will mention a trifling affair which occurred, I remember, soon after our arrival. One of our party went into a watch-maker's store, to purchase a glass for a watch. After a short delay, a gentleman emerged from an inner room, with his mouth filled, not only with the eternal quid, but with no small portion of his dinner besides. On hearing the demand, he very coolly replied, "Well now, as I'm eating my dinner, if you're going right up and down town, s'pose you call again, and see if I've done, and then we'll put a glass in that watch." His surprised customer took up his property, and slightly hinted that he would go to another store for his glass. No attempt was made to detain him—the dollar was no more to the New Orleans trader, as I said before, than a sixpence.

We had now been a fortnight at anchor in the Mississippi, and, like true sailors, were longing for a change and variety. On the 13th of December, therefore, it was with cheerful hearts, that the men manned the windlass and prepared for sea. How I enjoyed their impromptu songs! The words were rough, and the airs were still more so. Still, as I heard the fine voice of the boatswain, leading off with:

> *The saucy schooner off she go,*
> *Merrily on to Texas ho!*

I was quite exhilarated, and felt as if no future tempests could lessen my love either for the ship or its element.

Chapter VII

December 13—Left New Orleans, and made sail down the river. Wind and current both in our favour. Brought up at six o'clock in nine fathom water; cold but fine.

December 14—Working down the river; moderate breezes and fine. At five o'clock, p.m., anchored in eight fathom water, with fifteen fathom cable.

December 15—Towards the close of this day we found ourselves near the southwest pass out of the river, and truly rejoiced we were, for we were quite tired of mud, and snags, and longed for the blue water of the deep sea.

December 16—Fresh breezes, and a bright sun, the weather was rather cold, but the freshness of the air coming over the sea was delightful, and we were all enjoying in anticipation, the delights of the wild country to which we were bound.

December 17—Strong breezes, and cloudy. The *Dolphin* seems delighted to be in her own element again, freshwater evidently does not agree with her. She is going nine and ten knots an hour, and there is scarcely any motion, the wind is so fair. The land of Texas is very low, and the guidebooks mention three trees, the only ones on the island of Galveston, as a landmark. For these signs of vegetation we were anxiously looking on the morning of the second day from our leaving the river. In the meanwhile, a man was kept almost constantly in the chains sounding for bottom. This precaution is I believe highly necessary in this part of the Gulf. Late in the evening we sounded in ten fathom water.

December 18—Sounding all the morning—ten fathom, then eight—seven—and five, in quick succession. This did not seem to me very agreeable, from the lowness of the island, and the circumstance of the wind blowing on shore.

There was a very thick sea-mist too, and we could scarcely see the length of the ship ahead. From time to time the fog however rolled suddenly away, and during one of these intervals, the man at the masthead sung out "land on the weather bow."

This was at eleven o'clock, a.m. The wind had freshened considerably, and there was a disagreeable drizzling rain falling, when at a distance of three or four miles from Galveston we shortened sail, and at noon distinctly made out the town of Galveston. I beg its pardon, as I am aware that "city" is the correct term for so important a place.

The fog and mist had by this time considerably lessened in density, and we could distinguish a few gray-looking houses, a church or two, and some masts of vessels, but the latter were neither numerous nor imposing. Allowance must be made for this poorness of appearance, when we remember that we saw all these things through an incessant rain, which made them, and indeed the whole prospect, look cheerless and forlorn.

Before our arrival we had heard much of the dangers attending an entrance into the harbour. The small depth of water on its bar had always been held up to us in *terrorem*, and as a reason for avoiding this part of the coast in the *Dolphin* altogether. All these recollections made us naturally anxious for the appearance of the pilot, for whom we made a signal immediately after shortening sail. As he did not make his appearance, we stood off again and waited with some degree of impatience, in hopes of seeing his boat leave the shore.

We spent at least three hours in this manner, shortening the time as well as we could in abusing all the government authorities indiscriminately, and pilots in particular. At length, however, to our great relief, a large steamer, the *New York*, which we had observed some time previously occupied in getting up her steam, was seen coming towards us. Her high-pressure engine was puffing and blowing, like some huge elephant out of breath, and her deck covered with curious passengers.

When she had arrived within speaking-trumpet distance, the captain hailed us through this instrument, which is still in general use in American ships, and gave us the welcome information that he had a pilot on board. We were delighted, as we now saw some chance of coming to an anchor that day. The prospect of spending another night standing off and on was by no means agreeable.

Before taking leave of us, the captain, in a true Yankee spirit of "making an operation," offered to tow us over the bar. This was on his own account, and for this piece of civility and trifling assistance, the performance of which would have occupied him half an hour, he demanded the moderate sum of one hundred dollars! Of course the offer was declined; however, as it was made civilly, hats were mutually raised in token of amity, and the *New York* puffed back to her station in the harbour.

We had now received the pilot on board. He was an Englishman, and a good sailor, as well as a safe and experienced pilot. There is at present a great want of these useful individuals at Galveston, and also—as our own pilot informed us—an insufficiency of buoys. A few rotten barrels are placed here and there, often in wrong places, and, not seldom, are removed by accident or malice.

A strong northerly wind had prevailed for some days, and a considerable quantity of water had in consequence been blown out of the harbour. The bar was thus even less covered than usual, and it became necessary to trip the vessel. This operation consists in running the guns forward, and shifting the ballast; thus she was put on an even keel, and the chances of her bumping (as it is called) on the bar are considerably lessened. The crossing this formidable impediment was a moment of great excitement. The lead was thrown into the sea without intermission; it was "by the mark four"—"quarter less three"—"by the mark two"—"quarter less two," called out rapidly one after another, by the man in the chains.

Now was the trying moment. Even the pilot looked anxious, and we every moment expected to feel the bottom.

After the suspense of a minute, or indeed less, the pilot drew a long breath, and exclaimed "all safe, Sir, now." The guns were run aft again with all despatch, and we were steering straight into the harbour.

After crossing the bar, there is an extremely narrow channel through which vessels must necessarily pass before they can arrive at a safe anchorage. In this channel we felt the bottom, or rather side, but it is of soft mud, and there is no danger in the contact.

In another half hour we found ourselves safely anchored in Galveston harbour, within a hundred and fifty yards of the strand, in four fathoms water. After dinner we were agreeably surprised by a visit from Captain Elliott, her Britannic Majesty's Charge d'Affaires in this republic. We had heard, much to our regret, that Captain Elliott was at Washington, the present seat of government, and had such been the case, we should have lost much useful information, as regards the republic, and infinite amusement and enjoyment personally.

Previously to my arrival I confess to having known but little of Texas, its position, its resources, or its extent. It is just possible that my ignorance in this respect may be shared by others, and if so, some account of the republic may not be unwelcome.

Texas is bounded on the north, by the Red River, on the south by the Gulf of Mexico, on the east by the Sabine River and Louisiana, and on the west by the Rio Grande del Norte. Comprised within these limits is an area of nearly five hundred thousand square miles. It has more than three hundred miles of territory bordering on the Gulf of Mexico, its coast lying nearly N.W. and S.E. Supposing Texas to have an average breadth of between three to four hundred miles, and extending in a northwesterly direction for about seven hundred, its surface may be said to present an inclined plane gradually descending towards the sea. Towards the northwest is an elevated range of hills, spurs of the Rocky Mountains from whence several rivers take their source, flowing towards the Gulf of Mexico, in a direction nearly parallel to each other, and about sixty miles apart.

Texas has three divisions of country differing from each other to a remarkable extent, not only as regards its surface and soil, but also its climate. These are termed respectively, by its inhabitants, the Low, the Rolling, and the Hilly Country. The first of these, bordering upon the Gulf of Mexico, and along the whole line of coast, is a perfectly level low tract extending about sixty or seventy miles. To these lowlands, which are certainly not healthy but wonderfully rich and productive, succeed the beautifully undulating Rolling Prairies. Nothing can surpass this portion of Texas in natural attractions. Its ever-verdant prairies resemble our most beautiful parks. Magnificent clumps of timber are scattered over its surface, and its valleys are watered by quick-running limpid streams. The third division comprises the high, broken, mountainous tract more to the north, at a distance of three or four hundred miles from the sea-coast. Here are said to be table-lands, with a soil scarcely inferior to the former divisions, and fully equal to either of the others in beauty and climate. This country, as also the entire tract to the northward, has not yet been sufficiently explored to form any very accurate judgment of its merits.

The principal rivers, commencing from the eastward, are the Sabine and the Neches, both flowing into the Sabine Lake, out of which there is a narrow inlet to the Gulf, with a bar across the channel, having only six feet of water. This is the only mud-bar on the coast, as those of all the harbours westward are of hard sand. The Trinity flows into Galveston Bay. The Brazos flows directly into the Gulf, with a most dangerous bar at its embouchure, having not more than five or six feet of water.

The Colorado flows into the Bay of Matagorda, which, like the Bay of Galveston, and almost all the other bays on this coast, is only separated from the Gulf of Mexico by a narrow strip of land rarely more than a mile or two in breadth. The bay is nearly forty miles in length, and has

a bar at its entrance with seven feet of water. The Guadaloupe, St. Antonio, and Neches, are inferior in size to
those I have previously mentioned, but, like them, flow
into similar long narrow bays, separated from the sea by
a sandy ridge of a mile or more in breadth. The Bay of
Aransas, which receives the Guadaloupe and San Antonio
Rivers, is connected with the sea by an extremely narrow
channel, with six feet and a half of water over its bar. The
Rio Grande del Norte, forming the western boundary of
Texas, rises in the Rocky Mountains. It is said not to be
navigable, on account of its rapids, till within two hundred
miles of the sea, near the town of Loredo. It is described as
a noble stream, three or four hundred yards wide, and of
considerable depth.

The Republic of Texas most undoubtedly owes its origin
to Moses Austin, who first conceived the plan of establishing a considerable colony in that country. This was
eventually effected by his son, Stephen Austin, assisted by
Mr. Williams; both Americans by birth, and men of distinguished talent and enterprise. With the latter we had the
good fortune to become acquainted in Texas, and had to
thank him for a great deal of valuable information regarding
the country and its history. Previous to the year 1821, the
central part of Texas appears to have been only frequented
by roving bands of Indians. There were a few settlements
on its eastern frontier, bordering upon Louisiana; and the
Mexicans, to the amount of four or five thousand, were
established in the neighbourhood of San Antonio de Bexar,
and Goliad, or La Bahia.

Moses Austin received his original grant in the year
1820, when Mexico was under the rule of Spain, and died
soon after in the United States, whilst preparing to put his
plans for colonization into effect. Soon after his father's
death, Stephen Austin started with a small body of settlers
from New Orleans. After arriving in Texas and carefully
exploring the country, he selected, as the lands most desirable, a tract of country lying between the Brazos and the
Colorado rivers, at about seventy miles distance from the

sea. After a short period, he again returned to the United States and made arrangements for colonizing on a more extended scale.

In the meantime, Mexico had finally succeeded in throwing off the yoke of Spain. On Austin's return, therefore, to his colony, in 1822, what was his mortification to find that, before he could proceed with the distribution of lands, it would be necessary for him to proceed to Mexico, to solicit from the new government a confirmation of the grant made to his father! It was at this period, and whilst the Congress were debating upon Austin's petition, and also other applications of a similar nature, that Iturbide overthrew the existing government, and proclaimed himself Emperor.

Austin had no difficulty in obtaining the object of his visit. Mexico has always been too weak to govern her distant provinces. At this period, being utterly unable to protect her settlers in Texas, and indeed, her own frontiers, from the ravages of hostile Indians, she was only too glad to avail herself of any offers made by foreigners to colonize and settle in the rich plains of Texas. This seems to have continued to be the prevailing feeling of the successive governments in Mexico, from 1822 till the year 1830. In that interval, almost the whole of Texas was granted to different individuals, who were called impresarios, or contractors. The contract was that they were to introduce into the country, and settle, a stipulated number of families in order to be entitled to the land granted by government. To return, however, to Stephen Austin.

Scarcely had Iturbide granted his petition, when the Emperor was himself dethroned by Santa Anna, who immediately annulled all grants of land made by his predecessor in power. Thus, Austin had again to solicit from the Cortes a confirmation of his former grant. This he at last succeeded in obtaining, and soon after returned to Texas. There he had to struggle with a variety of difficulties. His infant colony, now consisting of about three hundred families, was to be governed without any controlling power, unless we except the moral influence which his superior

mental qualities enabled him to exercise over the rude settlers. The population was now rapidly increasing. In the
year 1825, nearly the whole of Texas had been granted
away to impresarios, and in 1830, we find that settlements
had sprung up in every part of the country.

CHAPTER VIII

EARLY COLONIZATION & POLITICS ⚓
TEXAS DECLARATION OF INDEPENDENCE ⚓

No country has been more calumniated and misrepresented than Texas. She has been called the Alsatia of the United States; and again, the "pestiferous swamps of Texas," "pillaged from the too confiding Mexicans," etc. The greater part of these misstatements, that have appeared in England, concerning Texas, are said to have been circulated by the Mexican bond-holders, and others interested in the prosperity of Mexico. The Mexican debt to British bond-holders amounts to nearly ten millions sterling, and Santa Anna, in the year 1837, either despairing of ever recovering Texas or hoping to acquire powerful allies in the Mexican bond-holders, made over to that body lands in Texas to the extent of forty million acres, as further security for the principal and interest of their bonds. These lands were to be specially hypothecated, until the total extinction of the bonds, and the government engaged to give complete possession to the guaranteed lands. This transaction is altogether so strange and ridiculous, as to be scarcely credible.

The Americans, however, have been far more bitter in their attacks upon the unoffending Republic. The Southern States were doubtless influenced in their conduct by jealousy of the far superior soil and climate of Texas, and her probable commercial advantages. The Northern States of America, on the other hand, are ranged against the Republic on account of the existence of slavery in the country, and from a feeling that the interests of Texas are thereby connected with the slaveholding States of the Union, and thus increase their power.

It appears to me, that few people have ever had more just cause than the Texans for throwing off an oppressive yoke, and separating themselves from a nation, which had so long proved its incapacity even for self-government. Previous to Texas declaring her independence, the Mexican Republic had been constantly a prey to internal dissensions. Civil war, in all its horrors, had desolated the country. Her political institutions had been changed, or overthrown, according to the interest or caprice of each successive military chief of the country. The rule of these political leaders was invariably marked by bloodshed, cruelty and oppression, and the country was in a constant state of anarchy and revolution.

I shall now endeavour to show the political position of Texas during the first years of her colonization, and afterwards to describe the events which were the more immediate cause of her declaration of independence.

Under the constitution of 1824, Mexico was a confederated Republic, somewhat similar to the United States, having a President, Vice-President, Senate, and a House of Representatives, as a central government. Each State had, however, its separate independent government. The Mexican government, as I have before mentioned, having found itself obliged, for its own security, to encourage colonization in Texas, declared by a decree of the Mexican Congress, dated 7th May, 1824:

"That Texas is to be annexed to the Mexican province of Cohahuila, until it is of sufficient importance to form a separate State, when it is to become an independent State of the Mexican Republic, equal to the other States of which the same is composed, free, sovereign, and independent, in whatever exclusively relates to its internal government and administration."

This decree was declared " inviolable," and the act says, "can never be reformed."

It was then, on the faith of this decree, that new settlers were constantly arriving in Texas, from all countries. This state of things continued till the year 1830, when the hitherto increasing prosperity of the country received its first check.

Bustamente, an adventurer, who by intrigue or bloodshed, had contrived to possess himself of the first office in the Mexican Republic, prohibited the further ingress of foreigners, and issued several decrees inimical to the interests of Texas. The Mexican government, apparently jealous of its rising influence and prosperity, seems now to have made several enactments, at variance with the constitution of 1824. To effect these, it was necessary to introduce a considerable force of Mexican soldiers into the country. Thus, it eventually ended in Texas being placed almost entirely under military rule. It would be difficult to give an adequate idea of the numerous acts of injustice and oppression to which the settlers were subjected at this period. They were at length driven to resistance, and the military commandants, or governors, were soon forced out of the country, and with them the whole of the Mexican troops.

The oppressive rule of Bustamente was, fortunately, brought to a conclusion in the year 1832. His object had been to establish a central government, instead of the federal constitution, but finding himself unable to cope with the superior mental powers and military conduct of Santa Anna, he resigned his office in favour of General Pedraza, and early in 1833, Santa Anna was proclaimed President.

The Texans, having now had sufficient experience of the bad effects arising from their being under the administration of the State of Cohahuila, resolved to petition the Supreme Government for a separation of the provinces, and demanded that Texas should be granted an independent state government, in conformity with the federal compact, and Act of Congress, of 1824.

The memorial set forth, that Texas was virtually without any government at all; that the language of the people was different; that Cohahuila and Texas were altogether dissimilar in soil, climate, and natural productions; that owing to the numerical inequality of their respective representatives, the enactment of laws beneficial to Texas could only emanate from the "generous courtesy" of her constitutional partner, and that legislative advantages to the one might, from incompatibility of interests, be ruinous to the other.

Protection from Indian depredations, they declared to be of vital importance to Texas, which protection Cohahuila was unable to render. The Indians in their immediate neighbourhood had been denied justice, which would be granted by independent Texas. Finally, Texas possessed the necessary elements for a state government, and for her attachment to the federal constitution and to the republic, the Texans pledged their lives and honours.

Stephen Austin was the person selected by the people to proceed to Mexico, and to submit their petition for the consideration of the Cortes. Austin, after waiting nearly a year in the capital, and being able to gain no reply to the petition with which he had been charged, wrote to the authorities in Texas, recommending them at once to organize a State, *de facto*, without waiting for the decision of Congress.

This was considered by the government as a treasonable proceeding and shortly afterwards Austin was arrested at Saltillo whilst on his return to Texas. Being brought back to the capital, he was imprisoned in the dungeons of the Inquisition for upwards of a year. He did not return to Texas till more than two years had elapsed from the date of his departure, and not until Santa Anna had overthrown the federal constitution of the Republic. He established in its place a Central Consolidated Government rendering him wholly independent of the States of the Confederacy, and thus, in fact, becoming military dictator of Mexico.

Several of the States were of course opposed to this change. Some, indeed, resorted to arms, but were unable to resist the power of the dictator. The constitutional authorities of Cohahuila and Texas assembled at Monclova, and solemnly protested against this change of government. They were, however, driven from office by a military force under General Cos. The government was then dissolved, and the Governor, and other members of the State legislature, were imprisoned. Thus, the central government was established—in opposition to the will of the States and of the people—by the forcible and unconstitutional destruction of the social compact which they had sworn to support. It was at this juncture that Austin was released. Santa Anna,becoming alarmed at the public meetings and various demonstrations of opposition in Texas, determined on sending Austin back to his country as a mediator.

At a public meeting, soon after his return to Texas, he made the following speech, giving very fully his opinions of the state of affairs, and also recommending such measures as he thought advisable to be pursued. "I left Texas," said Mr. Austin, "in April, 1833, as the public agent of the people, for the purpose of applying for the admission of this country into the Mexican confederation, as a state separate from Cohahuila. This application was based upon the constitutional and vested rights of Texas, and was sustained by me in the city of Mexico to the utmost of my abilities. No honourable means were spared to effect the objects of my mission, and to oppose the forming of Texas into a territory, which was attempted. I rigidly adhered to the instructions and wishes of my constituents, so far as they were communicated to me. My efforts to serve Texas involved me in the labyrinth of Mexican politics! I was arrested, and have suffered a long persecution and imprisonment.

"I consider it to be my duty to give an account of these events to my constituents, and will, therefore, at this time, merely observe that I have never, in any manner, agreed to anything, or admitted anything, that would compromise the constitutional or vested rights of Texas. These rights belong to the people, and can only be surrendered by them.

"I fully hoped to have found Texas at peace, and in tranquillity, but regret I find it in commotion; all disorganized, all in anarchy, and threatened with immediate hostilities. This state of things is deeply to be lamented; it is a great misfortune, but it is one which has not been produced by any acts of the people of this country. On the contrary, it is the natural and inevitable consequence of the revolution that has spread all over Mexico, and of the imprudent and impolitic measures, both of the general and state governments, with regard to Texas. The people here are not to blame, and cannot be justly censured. They are farmers, cultivators of the soil, and are pacific from interest, from occupation and from inclination. They have uniformly endeavoured to sustain the constitution and the public peace, and have never deviated from their duty as Mexican citizens.

"If any acts of imprudence have been committed by individuals, they evidently resulted from the revolutionary state of the whole nation, the imprudent and censurable conduct of the state authorities, and the total want of a local government in Texas.

"It is, indeed, a source of surprise and creditable congratulation, that so few acts of this description have occurred under the peculiar circumstances of the times. It is, however, to be remembered, that acts of this nature were not the acts of the people, nor is Texas responsible for them. They were, as I before observed, the natural consequences of the revolutionary state of the Mexican nation; and Texas certainly did not originate that revolution; neither have the people, as a people, participated in it. The consciences and hands of the Texans are free from censure, and clean.

"The revolution in Mexico is drawing to a close. The object is, to change the form of government, destroy the federal constitution of 1824, and establish a central or consolidated government. The states are to be converted into provinces.

"Whether the people of Texas ought or ought not to agree with this change, and relinquish all or a part of their constitutional and vested rights, under the constitution of 1824, is a question of the most vital importance; one that calls for the deliberate consideration of the people, and can only be decided by them, fairly convened for the purpose.

"As a citizen of Texas, I have a right to an opinion on so important a matter. I have no other right, and pretend to no other. In the report which I consider it my duty to make to my constituents, I intend to give my views on the present situation of the country, and especially as to the constitutional and natural rights of Texas, and will, therefore, at this time, merely touch this subject.

"Under the Spanish government, Texas was a separate and distinct province. As such it had a separate and distinct local organization. It was one of the unities that composed the general mass of the nation, and as such participated in the war of the revolution, and was represented in the constituent Congress of Mexico, that formed the constitution of 1824. This constituent Congress, so far from destroying this unity, expressly recognised and confirmed it by the law of May 7, 1824, which united Texas with Cohahuila, provisionally, under the especial guarantee of being made a state of the Mexican confederation, as soon as it possessed the necessary elements.

"That law, and the federal constitution, gave to Texas a specific political existence, and vested in its inhabitants special and defined rights, which can only be relinquished by the people of Texas, acting for themselves, as a unity, and not as a part of Cohahuila, for the reason that the union with Cohahuila was limited, and only gave power to the state of Cohahuila and Texas to govern Texas for the time being, but always subject to the vested rights of Texas. The State, therefore, cannot relinquish those vested rights, by agreeing to the change of government, or by any other act, unless expressly authorized by the people of Texas to do so; neither can the general government of Mexico legally deprive Texas of them, without the consent of the people. These are my opinions.

"An important question now presents itself to the people of this country. The federal constitution of 1824 is about to be destroyed, and a central government established; and the people will soon be called upon to say whether they agree to this change or not. This matter requires the most calm discussion, the most mature deliberation, and the most perfect union. How is this to be had? I see but one way, and that is by a general consultation of the people, by means of delegates elected for the purpose, with full powers to give such an answer, in the name of Texas, to this question, as they may deem best, and to adopt such measures as the tranquillity and salvation of the country may require.

"It is my duty to state, that General Santa Anna verbally and expressly authorized me to say to the people of Texas, that he was their friend, that he wished for their prosperity, and would do all he could to promote it; and that in the new constitution, he would use his influence to give to the people of Texas a special organization, suited to their education, habits, and situation.

"Several of the most influential and intelligent men in Mexico, and especially the Minister of Relations and War, expressed themselves in the same manner. These declarations afford another and a more urgent necessity for a general consultation, of all Texas, in order to inform the general government, and especially General Santa Anna, what kind of organization will suit the education, habits and situation of this people.

"It is also proper for me to state, that in all my conversations with the President and Ministers, and men of influence, I advised that no troops should be sent to Texas, and no cruisers along the coast. I gave it as my decided opinion, that the inevitable consequence of sending an armed force to this country, would be war. I stated that there was a sound and correct moral principle in the people of Texas, that was abundantly sufficient to restrain, or put down, all turbulent and seditious movements, but that this moral principle could not, and would not, unite with any armed force sent against this country. On the contrary, it would resist and repel it, and ought to do so.

"This point presents another strong reason why the people of Texas should meet in general consultation. This country is now in anarchy, threatened with hostilities; armed vessels are capturing all they can catch on the coast, and acts of piracy are said to be committed under cover of the Mexican flag. Can this state of things exist without precipitating the country into a war? I think it cannot; and, therefore, believe, that it is our bounden and solemn duty, as Mexicans and as Texans, to represent the evils that are likely to result from this mistaken and most impolitic policy in the military movements.

"My friends, I can truly say, that no one has been, or is now, more anxious than myself to keep trouble away from this country. No one has been, or now is, more faithful to his duty as a Mexican citizen, and no one has personally sacrificed, or suffered more in the discharge of this duty. I have uniformly been opposed to have anything to do with the family political quarrels of the Mexicans.

"Texas needs peace, and a local government; its inhabitants are farmers, and they need a calm and a quiet life. But how can I, or anyone, remain indifferent, when our rights, our all, appear to be in jeopardy; and when it is our duty, as well as our obligation, as good Mexican citizens, to express our opinions on the present state of things, and to represent our situation to the government? It is impossible. The crisis is such, as to bring it home to the judgment of every man, that something must be done, and that without delay. The question will, perhaps, be asked, what are we to do? I have already indicated my opinion. Let all personalities, or divisions, or excitements, or passion, or violence, be banished from among us. Let a general consultation of the people of Texas be convened as speedily as possible to be composed of the best and most calm, and intelligent and firm men in the country; and let them decide what representations ought to be made to the general government, and what ought to be done in future."

I have copied at full length the sentiments and opinions of Austin, which he expressed on his return from Mexico because his opinion on this important subject had great weight with all parties. The character of Austin stood high, as an unprejudiced observer, a just man, and a disinterested member of the state. Even the Mexicans, though they had uniformly oppressed and persecuted him, in the main, did justice to his unbending principles of honour and integrity. The account given, on the authority of such a man as Austin, of the motives and grievances which influenced the colonists, should, I think go far in refutation of the many unjust, and ill-founded charges that have been made against the Texan people.

Though repeatedly stigmatized, as owing their origin to ruffians and runaway rogues from every part of the world, we find the new settlers influenced in their struggles for freedom by feelings of which more civilized and longer established countries might be justly proud.

The colonists certainly were inclined to treat the opinions of Austin with deference, and to be guided by his judgment. It is probable that, had Mexico, at this crisis, adopted conciliating measures and acted with common justice towards the colony, the progress of disaffection and revolt would have been arrested, and Texas would have been retained as one of the States of the confederacy.

How long, however, it would have continued so, it is not for me to determine. It is not probable that a country formed of such independent spirits would have remained under any yoke, particularly that of a state where the language and habits were so essentially different from their own, and whose capital was distant from their frontier at least twelve hundred miles.

CHAPTER IX

TEXAS WAR FOR INDEPENDENCE ⚓
CRUELTY OF SANTA ANNA ⚓ BATTLE OF SAN JACINTO

In conformity with the advice of Austin, committees of safety and vigilance were now formed, and resolutions passed, to insist on their rights, under the federal constitution of 1824. Troops were organized and every preparation made to resist the Mexican forces, which were expected to be sent against them. In these anticipations they were not disappointed. General Cos soon after arrived at Copano, and marched thence to Bexar.

The first meeting of the hostile troops was at Gonzales. The Mexicans, in an attack upon the town, were repulsed with great bravery, and suffered considerable loss, both in killed and wounded. Shortly after this, a more important victory was gained, in the capture of the town and garrison of Goliad, containing a great quantity of military stores, besides three hundred stand of arms and two brass cannon. This was followed by the election of General Austin, as Commander-in-Chief of the Texan army. The new leader, under the banner of the Mexican federal constitution, immediately marched upon Bexar, a town strongly garrisoned by the Mexican troops under General Cos.

After several engagements in the neighbourhood, which invariably resulted in favour of the colonists, the town of Bexar was stormed by a party of three hundred volunteers. The Mexicans behaved with determined bravery, but were unable to withstand the fury of their assailants. Upwards of three hundred had fallen before the unerring rifles of the Texans, and on the fourth day the garrison agreed to capitulate.

General Cos and his party were allowed to return into Mexico with their arms and private property, under their parole of honour that they would never again assist in any way, to oppose the re-establishment of the federal constitution of 1824. The Texans, by the achievement, gained possession of a large quantity of military stores, including nineteen pieces of ordnance and two swivel guns, several hundred stand of arms, and abundance of ammunition.

The country was now freed for the present from Mexican troops, and a general convention of delegates, from the different municipalities of Texas, was forthwith held at San Filipe de Austin. On the 3rd of November, 1835, a state government was organized for Texas, and their motives and principles proclaimed in the following manifesto:

"Declaration of the people of Texas in general convention assembled.

"Whereas, General Antonio Lopez de Santa Anna, and other military chieftains, have, by force of arms, overthrown the federal institutions of Mexico, and dissolved the social compact which existed between Texas and the other members of the Mexican confederacy; now, the good people of Texas, availing themselves of their natural rights, solemnly declare—

"First—That they have taken up arms in defence of their rights and liberties, which are threatened by the encroachments of military despots, and in defence of the republican principles of the federal constitution of Mexico.

"Second—That Texas is no longer morally or civilly bound by the compact of Union; yet stimulated by the generosity and sympathy common to a free people, they offer their support and assistance to such of the members of the Mexican Confederacy, as will take up arms against military despotism.

"Third—That they do not acknowledge that the present authorities of the nominal Mexican Republic have the right to govern within the limits of Texas.

"Fourth—That they will not cease to carry on war against the said authorities, whilst their troops are within the limits of Texas.

"Fifth—That they hold it to be their right, during the disorganization of the Federal System, and the reign of despotism, to withdraw from the Union, to establish an independent government, or to adopt such measures as they may deem best calculated to protect their rights and liberties; but that they will continue faithful to the Mexican Government, so long as that nation is governed by the constitution and laws that were formed for the government of the political association.

"Sixth—That Texas is responsible for the expenses of her armies now in the field.

"Seventh—That the public faith of Texas is pledged for the payment of any debts contracted by her agents.

"Eighth—That she will reward by donations in land, all who volunteer their services in her present struggle, and receive them as citizens.

"These Declarations we solemnly avow to the world, and call God to witness their truth and sincerity, and invoke defeat and disgrace upon our heads should we prove guilty of duplicity.

B. T. Archer, President"

The struggle for independence had now fairly commenced. Two months had scarcely elapsed after the departure of General Cos, when almost all the military resources of Mexico were brought against Texas, directed by Santa Anna in person. This invasion seems to have occurred at a most unfortunate period for the settlers. Austin, with several others of their most influential men, had been sent as Commissioners to the United States, to seek assistance from those who might be expected to sympathize in the cause of independence, and another party had marched towards Matamoros on the Mexican frontier.

The town of San Antonio de Bexar was thus left defenceless. Its garrison of one hundred and forty men were obliged to take refuge in the fort of the Alamo on the opposite side of the river. Here they defended themselves for a fortnight against a force amounting to four thousand men. The Mexicans though frequently repulsed, at length succeeded in taking the place by storm, and the whole of its garrison were put to the sword. After the final struggle, there were left but seven men, and these were refused quarter. It is also asserted that such were the feelings of exasperation evinced by the Mexicans from the determined resistance made by the Texans, that the bodies of the dead were subjected to every sort of indignity. The obstinate courage of the Texans is said to have caused them a loss of nearly fifteen hundred men, and no treatment was thought sufficiently bad for their conquered foes, living or dead.

Thus fell the Alamo after a defence highly creditable to Texan bravery and military skill. Shortly after this period, the invaders obtained another advantage over Colonel Fannin and a body of three hundred men. In this instance the Mexicans behaved with almost unparalleled treachery and cruelty. Santa Anna came up with Colonel Fannin and his little army, as they were retreating before the superior numbers of the Mexicans. The Texan Colonel, notwithstanding the disparity of numbers, engaged the enemy and fought with desperation till darkness put an end to the conflict. Four or five hundred of the enemy had fallen before the deadly aim of the Texans, who now entrenched themselves in the prairie, resolved to sell their lives as dearly as possible. During the night, however, the Mexicans received a reinforcement, and Colonel Fannin determined to surrender, provided he could obtain an honourable capitulation. The propositions made by Colonel Fannin were accepted by Santa Anna, and terms of capitulation were then signed and formally interchanged.

According to these terms, the Texans were to surrender, and to give up their arms, on condition of their lives being spared, and their being allowed to retire into the United States. No sooner, though, were they in his power than Santa Anna, regardless of faith and honour, ordered them all to be massacred, under circumstances of aggravated cruelty.

On the 11th of March a convention assembled at Washington, had declared Texas a "free, sovereign and independent republic." A constitution was framed, and an executive government appointed, to act until other elections should be made by the people. The provisional government retired to Galveston Island, where they remained until the conclusion of the war.

The Texans were now thoroughly exasperated by the cruelty and want of faith they had experienced at the hands of the Mexicans, and fortunately for them, Santa Anna found at length a rival more than his match in General Houston. The Texan army under his command was now posted on the Colorado River, and amounted to about twelve hundred men. The enemy, having received considerable reinforcements, occupied the river both above and below him. General Houston, apprehensive of being surrounded, deemed it advisable to retire to the Brazos, which he crossed on the 12th of April. He led his troops to Buffalo Bayou, and down its right bank to within a short distance of its junction with the San Jacinto River.

The Mexican army soon approached, and occasional skirmishes took place during the day, until Santa Anna withdrew his troops to a position on the banks of the San Jacinto and there commenced a fortification about a mile distant from the Texan camp. Houston had ordered the bridge on the only road communicating with the Brazos to be destroyed, thus cutting off all possibility of the enemy's escape.

The Texans commenced the attack at half past three and a most sanguinary conflict ensued. The Colonists fought as men only do when they contend for life and freedom, and they were irresistible. I extract the following details from General Houston's report of the battle of San Jacinto: "About nine o'clock on the morning of the 21st, the enemy were reinforced by five hundred choice troops, under the command of General Cos increasing their effective force to upwards of fifteen hundred men, whilst our aggregate force for the field numbered only seven hundred and eighty-three.

"The conflict lasted about eighteen minutes from the time of close action until we were in possession of the enemy's encampment, taking one piece of cannon, four stand of colours, all their camp equipage, stores and baggage."

"The conflict in the breastwork lasted but a few moments; many of the troops encountered hand to hand, and not having the advantage of bayonets on our side, our rifle-men used their pieces as war-clubs breaking many of them off at the breach. The rout commenced at half-past four, and the pursuit by the main army continued until twilight."

"In the battle the enemy's loss was six hundred and thirty killed, among whom was one General Officer, four Colonels, two Lieutenant-Colonels, two Second Lieuten-ant-Colonels, seven Captains, one Cadet. Prisoners, seven hundred and thirty. President General Santa Anna, General Cos, four Colonels, Aids de Camp to General Santa Anna, and the Colonel of the Guerrero Battalion are included in the number. General Santa Anna was not taken until the 22nd, and General Cos yesterday, very few having escaped.

"About six hundred muskets, three hundred sabres, and two hundred pistols, have been collected since the action; several hundred mules and horses were taken, and nearly twelve thousand dollars in specie. For several days previous to the action our troops were engaged in forced marches, exposed to excessive rains, and the additional in convenience of extremely bad roads, badly supplied with rations and clothing, yet amid every difficulty they bore up with cheerfulness and fortitude, and performed their marches with spirit and alacrity—there was no murmuring."

An important blow was now given to the Mexican power in Texas. Be it remembered this decisive victory over the chosen troops of Mexico, was gained by a mere handful of raw undisciplined volunteers, armed with rifles alone, and suddenly drawn together from their agricultural pursuits to defend their liberty and independence.

CHAPTER X

⚓ SANTA ANNA AS PRISONER ⚓
END OF THE REVOLUTION ⚓ TEXAS CONSTITUTION

As has been already mentioned, the prisoners of importance taken on this occasion were Santa Anna the President, and General Cos. The former was captured on the day following that on which the engagement was fought. He was discovered disguised, and without any vestige of soldierly uniform, wandering alone, on the banks of Buffalo Bayou. This was indeed a sudden and most overwhelming change; a terrible turn in the wheel of fortune. He was secured without difficulty, as he had retained no arms in his sudden flight. It was perhaps fortunate for him that the party by whom he was taken were ignorant of his name and rank, as the people were beyond measure exasperated against him.

Santa Anna was conveyed without delay to the presence of General Houston, who, having been wounded in the ankle during the engagement, was lying underneath a tree. The head of the Texan General rested upon a rough pillow, his war-saddle being laid under his head. A blanket was spread beneath him, and this was his only couch. Santa Anna was led up to him, and boldly announced himself thus—"Soy Antonio Lopez de Santa Anna, Presidente de la Republica Mexicana, y General en Gefe del ejercito de operaciones."

Upon this introduction General Houston politely requested his prisoner to take a seat on a medicine-chest. To this he consented, but appearing rather faint and not a little agitated, the chest was opened for some remedy for these complaints. Having swallowed a considerable quantity of opium, the patient declared himself better, and found words to say to his captor, "You were born to no ordinary destiny; you have conquered the Napoleon of the West!" What vanity in this freebooting leader of a degraded and miserable people!

The President's own account of this interview with the Mexican General, when the latter was a prisoner, and entirely in Houston's power, is very characteristic of his own bold and decided nature. His deadly foe was in his hands, he had proved himself merciless and unworthy of faith, and had, by his own conduct, forfeited all claim to the consideration and forbearance due towards a prisoner of war.

The place of meeting was not one calculated to impress the Mexican with awe, or to give him an exalted idea either of the riches or power of his conqueror. But the dignity of Houston did not depend upon outward show, and he received his prisoner, as a great man should—without parade or any outward demonstration of triumph. In the course of the conversation which followed, Santa Anna, whether by design or otherwise, addressed his captor by the title of General, omitting the word President, and thus, according to Houston's view of the matter, tacitly denying his right to independence and authority. "I only looked at him, gentlemen," said the Texan President in his account of the audience. "I looked at him once, and he corrected the mistake; if he hadn't, you know, gentlemen, I should have closed the scene;" meaning, he should have at once signed his death warrant. The look must have been an expressive one indeed, and yet it may be doubted whether the Mexican was aware by how slender a hair the sword that hung over his head was suspended. Better, far better would it have been for his country had the President not allowed his kindness of heart to overcome his sense of justice. Had he ordered the execution of Santa Anna, much bloodshed would have been spared, and many evils prevented.

The political motives which influenced General Houston on this occasion are not known; but the liberation of Santa Anna was not effected without great difficulty, and much opposition. The majority of the people demanded his execution, as a just atonement for the blood of their fellow citizens, who, by his merciless and treacherous mode of warfare, had been so inhumanely sacrificed. After a time, however, a convention was agreed upon, and the Mexican general was set at liberty. His intention was to embark without loss of time for Vera Cruz. This, however, he soon found was not an easy matter to effect. The rage and animosity of the Texans against him had not, in any degree, subsided. The excitement was so great and universal, that it was found necessary for his own safety, again to place his person in security.

The Texan President, however, contrived with some difficulty to liberate him, and he then embarked in safety for the United States. He arrived at Washington on the 18th of December, and from thence was sent in a ship of war, by the American government, to Vera Cruz. No sooner had this unprincipled man again obtained power in his own country, than, forgetful of the noble sentiments and generosity which had guided the conduct of the Texan President, he again commenced his system of annoyance and petty warfare; thus proving that however much we may admire the magnanimity of Houston's behaviour, the policy which guided him was mistaken. His treacherous and vindictive enemy was left free to annoy and harass the man who so generously overlooked his cruelty and his crimes. The frontiers of the republic have been constantly disturbed by this implacable foe, and its progress towards settlement, population and prosperity, materially retarded.

The victory of San Jacinto terminated the struggle for independence in Texas. Since that event the Mexicans have resorted to every sort of intrigue, and pursued a course of policy, which has certainly answered the object for which it was adopted.

The Mexican policy evidently has been, by keeping the country in a constant state of agitation from "threatened invasion," to check the tide of emigration, which otherwise could have flowed into Texas. Since their defeat at Jacinto, however, the Mexicans have never undertaken another organized campaign against, or invasion of, Texas. It is true that marauding bands have attacked the frontier towns, and that constant apprehensions are entertained of their making still bolder inroads; yet notwithstanding these evident hindrances to emigration, the country is rapidly increasing in population, and there is little doubt that the Anglo-Saxon race, by whom this is chiefly effected, will ere long overrun the rich provinces of Northern Mexico.

Texas has now been recognised as an independent republic by most of the European powers, as well as by the United States of America. An industrious, agricultural population is rapidly pouring in from Kentucky and the Northern States of the Union, while England, France, and Germany, are contributing their share of emigrants to swell the increasing tide. The present population of this rising country may be estimated at eighty thousand freemen, and to these may be added twenty-two thousand slaves. In the province of Bexar there are a considerable number of Mexicans. The republic is divided into thirty-six counties:

Red River	Nacogdoches
Shelby	Harrison
Sabine	Robertson
San Augustine	Montgomery
Jasper	Harris
Jefferson	Galveston
Liberty	Brazoria
Houston	Fannin
Bowie	Jackson
Burnet	Victoria
Fort Bend	Gonzales
Austin	Bexar
Washington	Goliad
Milam	Refugio
Bastrop	San Patricio
Fayette	Travis
Colorado	Lamar
Matagorda	Panola

The constitution of Texas is modelled, with some little difference, after that of the United States; Texas being an integral, whilst the United States form a federal, republic.

The legislative power is exercised by a President and Vice-President, elected for three years, and a Senate, and House of Representatives. The members of the former at present consist of fifteen, and the latter of thirty-two members.

The common law of England, so far as it is not inconsistent with the constitution and the acts of Congress, has been adopted as the general law of the land. It must not, however, be supposed, that the colonists of Texas are at all behindhand in the art of making laws for themselves. On the contrary, they enact them with surprising facility. Austin, a town of inconsiderable size, on the Colorado River, is the nominal seat of government. It is, however, situated too near the Camanche Indians to be considered a safe place for the meeting of Congress. The Camanches are a hostile tribe, and very inveterate in their hatred of the whites. Washington, a town on the Brazos, is the actual seat of government. A meeting of the Indian tribes is to take place in a few months at the Waccoo village, some hundreds of miles from Washington, up the country. This meeting may be productive of peaceful and conciliatory measures.

Chapter XI

Island of Galveston ⚓ Curious Construction ⚓ Enterprising Course of the Texans ⚓

I have already remarked, that at a distance, the city of Galveston—in America every village is called a city—gives one, on a first view, no very high idea of its importance. The houses in general are small, though here and there, an overgrown rickety-looking building speaks of the larger means and higher pretensions of its occupant. The streets are disposed with not much regard to regularity; and the houses are built of wood, most frequently of planks nailed together, clinker-fashion. The whole affair has, I must say, rather a fragile appearance, and it will readily be conjectured, that when viewed from the water, any grandeur of effect must be quite out of the question.

The island of Galveston is about fifteen miles in length, and seldom exceeds two in breadth. I have before remarked, that on its surface it boasts but three trees, and those are not remarkable for size or beauty. The soil is rich, and is covered with the long, thick, and rather rank grass of the prairie. The island is intersected with several inlets of the sea, or bayous, as they are called. At present Galveston is the only town in existence on the island, but it is fast rising into size and importance. It is strange, that here, where bricks could so easily be made, the inhabitants should still continue on with their wooden tenements. The only bricks I saw in Galveston were those forming one solitary chimney. It is calculated that, on an average, these wooden houses last ten years, and in the meantime they are very liable to be blown down. It must not be supposed, however, that such an occurrence,which, by the way, is by no means a rare one—materially injures the building capsized.

The houses, in fact, and religious edifices at Galveston are formed to endure shocks of this description. They are all raised a foot or two from the ground, by means of small, but solid blocks of wood, one of which is placed at either of the four corners. This is ingenious. It raises the house out of the road, and in the summer keeps out the snakes, etc, to say nothing of the pigs. Were brick edifices to be recommended to the Galveston citizens I have no doubt that their reply would be, that, in the first place, the wooden houses occupy infinitely less time in their erection. To this I agree, but would it not eventually answer, in the necessity of rebuilding being less frequently required? Another excuse would be, that the foundation of the soil being light, the brick buildings would be more likely to weigh it down than the wooden ones. This may be the case, but cannot good foundations be made, and wet and light soil improved, and rendered capable of supporting the weight of an ordinary house? Another advantage of a wooden tenement—which, however, I am inclined to think is a questionable one—consists in its faculty of locomotion. It is no uncommon thing, to see a house of considerable size drawn by means of a movable windlass to a considerable distance.

The English church is at present in rather a dilapidated condition. During a recent hurricane, it was, in common with half the town and the Roman Catholic Chapel among the rest, thrown on its beam-ends, where it remained till it was raised up. The city of Galveston fell, as might a pack of cards built into temporary houses by a child at play! The Catholic priest, poor man, whose abode was in the vestry of his little chapel, took refuge during the hurricane in the Protestant church, which was the last to fall. He was afterwards gravely and severely rebuked by the righteous among his congregation, for his want of faith, and his taking refuge among the heretics. It might naturally be supposed that Galveston would remain, after this visitation, a heap of ruins. But no—in an incredibly short period of time, both houses and churches were raised from their recumbent position. No one was hurt, either in their persons or their pockets, and business went on the same as before. It is true, that the church windows were all broken, and are not yet repaired, but we were told that the clergyman had gone to Halifax, to obtain funds from the Bishop for that purpose.

I was quite surprised at the celerity with which houses are erected here. A very good six-roomed house is raised, from floor to ceiling, and rendered fit for habitation in a week. I do not mean to say that they are remarkably air-tight, or particularly well-arranged, but to build any house in so short a time is worthy of remark. I have heard, to pursue the subject of houses, of a description of building, which I am sure would serve well here, where mud is at a discount. It is, as nearly as I can recollect, to make a double wall of planks, each wall being at a distance of some eight or ten inches from the other. The space between the two should be filled up with mud, well pressed down. After a short time, this becomes as solid as brick. Houses built in this way, would, I am sure, be much more comfortable.

The external air would be much more effectually excluded; the inmates would have less to suffer, both from cold and heat. And there is no doubt, that the houses themselves would last for a considerably longer period than they do at present. I cannot assert that the process of building would be effected as speedily as it now is. Much more time would doubtless be expended and time, to these people is money. Perhaps, however, when the population is greater, and labour consequently cheaper, some improvements in these respects may be effected. The Texans are an impatient people. They drive to, and at, their ends, with greater velocity than any individuals I ever saw or heard of. Nothing stops them in their go-ahead career. The present, and how to make the most of it, is their *idée fixe*, and they are too much occupied by their daily business to have leisure to think calmly of results.

To "go-ahead," is essentially the motto of the Texan people; and let them once get well on their legs, and no people are better calculated to do it faster. I am not going to enter into their politics, but I thought from the first, and I have heard sensible Texans say the same thing, that they ought to lean upon some established power—say the United States—at least for the present.

But to return to Galveston. The city contains about three hundred covered buildings, which a bold person would, or might, call houses. There are also four churches; rather a considerable proportion, I should say to the number of inhabitants, which amount only to about two thousand. Then, there are temples, squares, theatres, botanical and zoological gardens; but they are only at present on the ground-plan.

Altogether, Galveston is a rising city and no doubt will rise in time to be of considerable importance.

CHAPTER XII

COURTEOUS TEXANS ⚓ LOFTY STATUS OF PIGS
CHEWING & SPITTING ⚓ FRENCH EMIGRANTS
CROSSING A BAYOU ⚓ IDIOT GIRL

There are many large and valuable stores in Galveston.
Under this denomination come all sorts of warehouses
and magazines, and what in England we should call shops.
There are three newspapers printed and circulated at
Galveston. These have a considerable sale, and as entire
liberty of the press is, of course, allowed, their contents are
often amusing enough.

The advertisements, likewise, are by no means deficient
in entertainment. The most numerous are, I think, those
of medical men, of whom Galveston boasts a large supply. It is quite a treat to a stranger, at least it was so to
me, to drive through this very original city, and note the
different amusements, callings, and trades. There are
plenty of attorneys' offices. Law is decidedly popular, even
in this new country; and I noticed no small sprinkling of
grog-shops. Some of the most frequented stores are those
containing drugs and chemicals, and every ship that comes
in is announced as containing leeches by thousands, qui-
nine by hogsheads and calomel by lots, to say nothing of
demijohns of castor-oil. Doctoring must answer here, if
anything does.

In this colony there exists a spirit of good-will, and mutual helpfulness, very pleasant to see. I believe this to be
the case in most new settlements, before refinement begets
selfishness, and the indulgence of luxuries hardens the
heart. If a settler happens to require the aid of his neighbour's hands, or working tools, in the performance of any
manual labour, the assistance is rendered as readily as it is
asked. This is saying a great deal, for no one seems to hesi-
tate a moment about considering his neighbour's property
as his own; and should the latter not happen to be in the
way, his goods are removed, *pro tempore*, without scruple.

I have reason to speak gratefully of the courtesy and civility of the Texans. During our stay among them, I experienced repeated instances of good-will. One in particular, which prepared me for the rest, I will mention here. The pier near which the yacht was anchored, extended a considerable distance into the sea. The landing was at all times difficult, more especially so at low water. To a lady, the clambering ascent, for there were no steps previous to my arrival, was almost impracticable. The morning after our arrival I prepared to go on shore in the gig, really dreading the difficulties which, I was told, I had to encounter. What was my surprise and satisfaction, to find, when the boat touched the piles of the wharf, that a most convenient flight of steps and a balustrade had been erected during the night. This had been done without any regard to expense and solely for my accommodation. The person to whom I was indebted for this really useful service, neither expected, nor would receive any remuneration. He was an alehouse keeper on the wharf, and a very well educated man, for any station of life.

Such occurrences as these may be called trifling, but they at least serve, in some measure, to illustrate the character of the people, and to justify my remarks on their willingness to befriend, and render assistance to one another.

The designation of "dry store," is that which is appended to by far the largest number of the houses of Galveston. Till I made inquiries, I could not imagine what these stores contained. The very name, too, was an anomaly; for the said dry store stands most frequently in water, or at least in mud and mire which, to English feet, would be scarcely fordable. Trifles such as these are totally disregarded by these hardy settlers, and their wives and families seem equally disposed with themselves to make light of difficulties. There is something very praiseworthy in this undaunted spirit of enterprise, and one feels that it both deserves, and will be rewarded by, eventual success.

Now I am on the subject of mud and mire, I may as well suggest that a very little trouble and expense would raise both houses and causeways above the inconvenience of wet. But, as I before remarked, these people prefer enduring evils to losing time in remedying them. At present, the numerous pigs are the only living creatures who benefit by the oozy prairie, which surrounds nearly every house in Galveston. The pigs here are as much considered, and I believe occupy as important a position in society, as those of Ireland. They are not, however clean feeders, those Galveston swine. Nothing seemed to come amiss to them, and they disputed the carrion food with the disgusting turkey-buzzards. Having observed this, I carefully eschewed pork during my stay. The pigs themselves are frightful. Their long tails are destitute of curl, even when suffered to retain their original number of joints. This, however, is seldom the case. The dogs, both wild and tame, are inveterate pig-hunters. The dogs being often hungry withal, the pigs frequently suffer, and it was a rare sight to meet one of these unclean beasts with either ears or tail.

Thus, all creatures here make up their minds to bear the ills which flesh is heir to. It is a truth, which at every moment is forced upon you, that those difficulties and discomforts, which would appear most formidable to us, are unfelt and unnoticed by them. Where an Englishman would sink, past redemption, in the mire of despondency, they, to their praise and credit be it spoken contrive to struggle through.

There is one large and flourishing hotel at Galveston besides several smaller ones. In the Tremont House, as it is called, assemble the fashionable portions of the society. The *table d'hote* dinner-hour is two and, after the quarter of an hour, which is the time an American generally allows himself to devote to this meal, has elapsed, they are to be seen reading the newspaper under the wide verandah of the hotel, in every variety of bodily contortion. I believe it is not in the nature of an American to sit still, or to sit straight. They are perpetually either rocking or balancing themselves in their chairs or, with legs hanging over the railing of the verandah, performing that frightful act of uncleanliness on which Mr. Dickens has heaped such deserved reprobation.

I wonder what the American ladies are about that they do not put a stop to this latter proceeding which, and I do not exaggerate, is mentioned with disgust in all civilized societies, whenever the manners and habits of our transatlantic brethren chance to come under discussion. I have reason to believe that the fair "ladies of the land" are as delicate and refined in their habits as they are well educated and beautiful. That they have unbounded influence over and are treated with marked respect and consideration by the hardy "sons of the soil" admits not of a doubt. Then why do they not, one and all, rise up and say to their husbands, their brothers, and their lovers, "Cast away that lump of tobacco, which disfigures your appearance, and renders your voice and manner of speaking ridiculous. I will have no chewing I will have no spitting. If you must smoke, do it in moderation, and with propriety, but let our floors, our hearths, be secure from pollution." American ladies, do this, and you may not only as now be proud of your countrymen as men, but vain of them as gentlemen.

But to give up being personal, and return to more general subjects. From all I could learn, and judging from the opinion of a skillful medical man, who had been a long time in the country, I should say, that the climate of Galveston Island is by no means unhealthy. Of course, in these latitudes the heat, during two or three months in the year must be very great. July, August, and September are the most trying months. Then the mosquito rages, and men doubtless long for trees, and cooling streams, and shelter from the sun. Of the climate, during the remaining nine months of the year, I heard no complaint, even among our dissatisfied countrymen. The scenery, if such it can be called, is totally without variety. A long monotonous prairie, with occasional tussocks of high grass, little plots of reeds and frequent bogs, cover the whole extent of the island. The soil is rich and well adapted to grazing purposes. There are a good many deer, which are sold in the market at about two dollars each. Fowls and turkeys, alias gobblers, are brought from the mainland, distant about four miles. The usual price of the former is tenpence, and of the latter one dollar each.

The only "drive" is on the sea-beach, and a most beautiful beach it is—so hard and smooth, with its fine sand, that you scarcely hear your horse's foot fall as he trots, or rather runs along—a light carriage behind him, and the broad prairie spreading far before. Occasionally you are—I was going to say—stopped, but I should have been wrong. No one is stopped in this country by anything short of a bowie-knife, or a rifle-ball. But your progress is delayed by an interesting bayou, through which you have to wade, or swim, as the case may be. There is neither time nor spare cash to erect bridges. Indeed, were the expense to be incurred, the probability is they would be washed away by the first rain or by a more than usually high tide. Bridges then being out of the question, nothing is left you but to make the best of such means of transport as are within your reach. If you fortunately chance to meet with any person who has lately crossed, you ask, "Well, Sir, is it swimming?" Should the answer be in the affirmative, and you happen to be on horseback, equipped for a journey, with your plunder (luggage) about you, you "up saddle-bags!" and boldly plunge into the stream. Should your route lie along the shore, the safest way is to go a good way out to sea—on—on—till you find yourself well out among the breakers. I confess that, at first, this struck me as rather an alarming proceeding but, in fact, it is much the safest plan. There is always a bar of sand formed across the mouth of these bayous, and if you can hit that, the depth of water is much lessened.

At the crossing of one of these bayous, we once witnessed a most comical scene. We were returning from a shooting excursion in a light carriage, and were accompanied by an English gentleman on horseback. We had crossed our last bayou in safety, when we found a traveller going in the contrary direction on foot, waiting patiently for a lift over the water. He was a Frenchman and his figure was rather an anomaly in these wild regions. He was accoutred in the foil costume of *la jeune France*: long hair, *pantalons à sous pied*, coat (guiltless of collar) and painted boots. Sure "such a man was never formed" to tread the pathless prairies, and how he got there, and who he was, I could not guess, and never have to this day. But there he stood, bowing and shrugging with a most cat-like horror of wetting his feet. He was evidently most anxiously looking out for an opportunity of crossing the awful-looking breakers dry-shod.

No sooner did our English companion perceive his situation, than he kindly offered to recross the water, provided the Frenchman would mount behind him. This, however, was sooner said than done; it being no easy matter for a gentleman, evidently not too well-skilled in equestrian exercises, to effect a location on the back of a fiery steed, quite unused to carrying any extra burden. The cavalier attempted to spring up, in spite of his narrow trousers but it was all in vain. After each successive effort he found himself stretched on *terra firma*. After many fruitless attempts, he changed his ground, and eventually succeeded in fixing himself in front, with his arms clinging closely around our friend's throat. In vain, however, the unfortunate rider, suffering for his philanthropy, implored to be released.

"Mais Monsieur," vociferated the Frenchman, in the true spirit of Sindbad's Old Man of the Sea. "Je suis très bien comme ça," he said, indicating that he was comfortable as he was and wished to continue on.

"If you are, I'm not," was the reply and, in a moment, the arms were transferred to the neck of the horse and thus, with legs dangling, and himself hanging on as if for the bare life, the poor foreigner was safely conveyed across the breakers. We laughed heartily, and would, I fear, willingly have increased our merriment, by seeing the foreigner struggling in the shallow water. Poor man! His troubles were not yet at an end. A small bundle which he had held in his hand had fallen from his grasp, and during his equestrian exploits had drifted well out to sea! What this precious bundle contained we had yet to learn. No sooner was its owner in safety, than hat in hand, and hair streaming in the breeze, he made his thanks to his deliverer. "Mille re-mercimens."

"Ce n'est rien, une complaisance de prairie, dans ce pays sauvage il faut s'aider un et l'autre," replied our English companion. In this wild country, we must certainly help one another.

"C'est vrai, et voyez vous, Monsieur, j'etais fort embar-rasse, c'est que je portais le bonnet de Madame ma femme." Here he discovered his loss, which in the agitation of the moment had passed unnoticed. He had lost his wife's bon-net in the commotion.

He asked desperately if we had seen where it had been deposited. The Englishman pointed silently to the sea, and we left our friend on the beach, shrugging his shoulders in impotent despair.

Now that I am on the subject of emigrant Frenchmen I must say a word on the extreme fitness of these people to cope with the inconveniences of a new country, such as Texas. They are more light of heart, and less easily depressed than the English settler; added to which, their wants are fewer and more easily supplied. If a Frenchman, in the distant and scarcely inhabited prairie, finds himself in want of a dinner, he takes his rifle, cries, "à la chasse," and is as proud and happy if he returns with a small lark, to regale himself after his toil, as an Englishman would be had he brought home a fat buck.

One evening, as I stood on the wharf, waiting for the gig to come off from the *Dolphin*, I witnessed the disembarka-tion of one hundred and fifteen emigrants, shipped by the authorities from France. They were a motley group; most of them well-clothed, and one and all looking cheerful and happy. Among them, I remarked a poor old man, erect and strong. He was dressed like a farmer, but from his car-riage, I thought must have been a soldier in his youth. He had on a blouse, with a fur casquette on his head. His wife carried his gun, and he was surrounded by his children. He told me he had left his farm, near Verdun, to settle in Texas. In his own country he was a poor man. Here, his children (he had eleven of them) at any rate would not starve. "Madame," he said, "we are not lazy. We are here to work." There was a promise of success in the old man's energetic tone, as he uttered these words. It was, he said, very pleasant to be greeted by kindly words in a foreign land, on his first landing. He was one of Napoleon's old soldiers. "Je ne suis pas aristocrate, moi." (What egotism there is in a Frenchman.) *Moi!*

The tears stood in the old man's eyes, as he offered me a pinch of snuff. It was all he had to give and I received the offering in the spirit in which it was made. His old *tabatière* was modelled after the *petit Caporal's* cocked hat. It was of tin, polished and shining from long use.

Among the group stood an idiot girl. I was much struck by her appearance. Though her deficiency in intellect was evident from a certain wandering gaze in her dark eyes, which it was impossible to mistake, her countenance betrayed but little of that vacuity which is so generally indicative of her class. Such pitiable objects as decided idiots frequently have something revolting in their manner and appearance. With this poor emigrant, however, there was nothing of this, and I looked at her with unmixed feelings of interest and compassion. She was not exactly pretty, but her features were small and interesting, and of all the party, her person appeared the cleanest and her attire the least untidy and neglected.

I was sufficiently interested to inquire her history, and learnt that she was the daughter of poor parents in the neighbourhood of Verdun. An object of compassion from her birth, she had nevertheless not been quite a useless burden upon her parents. Her docility was remarkable, and she learnt to be useful in various little matters. Annette—for that was her name—was very deaf and she had an impediment in her speech, which rendered her utterance extremely painful. Still "through the gloomy vaults of the dull idiot's brain" meandered ideas peculiar to herself, and when the difference between right and wrong was put before her, the natural goodness of her disposition led her to refuse the evil and choose the good.

It happened that the child of a farmer in Annette's village—he was the very old Buonapartist with whom I found her on the wharf—strayed away one summer's day, and was not missed for several hours. He was a little boy of some three years old. Annette was present when the loss of the little plaything of the house was discovered. She witnessed the agony of the mother and the manly grief of the old farmer. That night Annette's little bed was unoccupied.

One day, then another passed away. The country was scoured in all directions in search of the missing ones, but without effect. On the third evening, when the mother had almost given up hope in the sickness of despair, Annette gently entered with the young boy in her arms. Noiselessly she stepped, and the mother saw and heard nothing till she felt her child's warm kisses on her cheek! Inquiries were showered upon both—where had they been? In what situation had the idiot girl discovered the lost child? They could not tell—the girl's poor head was weak and wandering, and her companion was but an infant. Something he told of a hollow tree, and of Annette's cloak being wrapt about him. She had fed him too with bread which she had brought—and this was all they knew. Soon after this poor Annette became an orphan, and the father, grateful to the feeble-minded girl who had saved the child of his old age, brought her with his family to this new country, and she was unto him as a daughter. When I saw Annette the hand of the rosy-faced boy was in hers. She was evidently a favourite and a playfellow. I have no fear, but that the poor girl will do well in the wilderness. There is here such an universal feeling of kindness towards childhood and helplessness. She looked happy and careless like the rest, and I am certain she will never want a friend, as long as Texan hearts remain, as they are now, in the right place.

How little did any of these poor people conceive of the difficulties that awaited them! "Is not this Bexar?" they asked immediately on their landing. When they were told that they had some hundreds of miles of difficult country to travel over before they could arrive at the promised land, though they looked disappointed for a moment, the spirit of hope was soon awake again, and like the pilgrims of old they went on their way rejoicing.

Notwithstanding the hopeful, and even joyous expression which I remembered on the countenances of these emigrants, the sight altogether left a sad and painful impression on my mind. I can fancy I see them now, those pale cold faces, and shivering forms interspersed among bales of cotton on the unsheltered wharf. A bitterly cold and fierce norther is blowing upon them, and their scanty garments are but ill-prepared to screen them from its violence. Heaven only knows whether they will ever realize the fortunes they have come so far to seek, but as I bade them adieu, I wished them success from the bottom of my heart.

After this interesting sight, we went on board the *Dolphin*, with two of our diplomatic friends, Captain Elliott, and Monsieur de Cramayel. As usual, the affairs of the republic, especially as regarded the important subject of emigrants, were discussed. We all agreed that it was incumbent on all governments sending out parties to this new and little known country, to obtain every information which could be useful to the settlers, previous to their departure. In case of failure, also, or of sickness, there should be means of relief at hand, and large families should not be permitted to leave their homes with even the possibility of starvation before them. From Captain Elliott I always gained much valuable information in regard to this young and interesting country.

Our acquaintances in this little settlement were necessarily few, and we were really obliged to those among them who were willing to share the monotony of our sealife. I beg to offer many thanks to the corps diplomatique of Texas for the agreeable variety of their society.

I regret extremely, that owing to our living on board the *Dolphin*, I did not extend my acquaintance among the pleasant society which I am aware the city of Galveston affords. I hope, at some future visit, to be able to make amends for the loss which was caused by those unavoidable impediments to visiting—stormy days and foaming seas. We were not in a situation to be hospitable at the time of our anchorage in Galveston Bay.

———

CHAPTER XIII

MEALS ⚓ CAPTAIN CARY ⚓ BOGS
⚓ A GALVESTON FORT
⚓ IMPROVIDENCE & IDLENESS OF TEXANS

There is not much variety of amusement at Galveston. Game, however, was plentiful in the neighbourhood and of this we took advantage, and never missed a day without going out to try our skill. Horses were to be hired in plenty, and not very bad. There is a certain Captain Cary, in Galveston, who keeps what is courteously termed a livery stable. He is a free negro, who with great labour and perseverance saved up money to the amount of a thousand dollars, and purchased his freedom. Horses are to be had from Captain Cary at half a dollar a day, with a sort of carriage included.

In this vehicle our little party daily packed up their guns, and sometimes their fishing-tackle, and sallied forth in quest of adventures. Their sport was very varied. When the wind was northerly, there were flocks of seabirds, in numbers almost incredible, ducks of every description— the delicious canvass-back, the mandarin, the pintail and our common wild duck—all good. But the most numerous kinds were scarcely eatable, being hard and fishy. The geese were the most difficult to shoot being very shy, and from the want of cover in the prairie, they generally saw us in sufficient time to get out of our way. Mr. Houstoun, however, contrived sometimes to bring one down, and at distances of one hundred and fifty yards. But they are not worth eating, for no keeping makes them tender, and they taste much more of fish than fowl.

No one must be surprised at our attempts to eat nearly everything we shot. Our dinners, with the exception of game, consisted always of beef. Mutton was not to be had—a sheep being quite a sight at Galveston. Pigs, to be sure, there were, but they fed so uncleanly, upon snakes and dead dogs, that resorting to them was not to be thought of. Turkeys and fowls were scarce, and we had had enough of them on the voyage. The venison is good, but destitute of fat. The price of a deer is about two dollars. Soon after our arrival, Mr. Houstoun went to the mainland, and came back with a magnificent deer, which he had brought down with small shot. It caused great jealousy among the Galvestonists. "I say, Captain, so you've been using up our deer, I see," said one of these gentlemen to him, when he returned triumphant with the spoil.

I remember, on the same day, that I took a drive on the sea-beach. The day was fine and I saw many beautiful, and some curious, birds. There was the pelican standing drowsily in the shallow water and, as we approached, wheeling away with his heavy lagging flight. There were beautiful herons of various kinds, and a flight of spoonbills of a brilliant rose-colour, like the flamingo. More inland, the bright-plumaged cardinal darted past us, while the yellow larks skimmed above us, in vast numbers. It was a pleasant day, and I well remember it. Mr. Houstoun was so pleased by his success with the deer, that the day following we tried our fortune again. We were not very systematic in our arrangements, and were easily beguiled out of our path by any game that chanced to come in our way.

Bogs are frequent, and not a little dangerous, as there are scarcely any visible signs of them, and if you are unlucky enough to get well into one, the chances are rather against your soon getting out again. In the neighbourhood of these bogs snipes are very plentiful, and Mr. Houstoun had left me in charge of the carriage and was fast filling his pockets with those birds, when I espied a fine deer bound out of the rushes, not ten yards behind him. Unluckily, he neither saw nor heard him, and I had the mortification to see the animal get away without a shot being fired at him. Soon after we saw, by the help of our glass, two deer feeding together at a distance. They were extremely shy, and our only plan was to surround them, making the circle smaller by degrees. I took up my position at one angle; Captain E., who accompanied us, at another; and Mr. Houstoun, with his rifle, at the third. The deer stood a moment at gaze, evidently doubting at which point to make his escape. Unluckily for himself, he chose the strongest position, and while in full career, he received his death wound from Mr. Houstoun's rifle.

I must confess, that anxious as I always was that the shot should not miss, I always felt a reaction of regret when I saw the prey stretched lifeless before me. On this occasion, though they assured me the deer was to all intents and purposes dead, but I could not see his quivering limbs, and leathern coat, stretched almost to bursting by convulsive sighs, without reproaching myself for having been a party to his assassination. I felt still more remorse when we discovered that his companion, the friend perhaps of years, would not leave the spot where he had fallen, but kept hovering about, just out of gun-shot, long after the remains of his companion had been removed.

I must here tell an American anecdote of deer-shooting. One of our acquaintances, as a proof of the great tenacity of life in these animals, informed me, that he had once shot a deer, had cut its throat, and half skinned it when, rather to his surprise, the animal suddenly rose, looked about him, and finally trotted off. "He required another ball in his heart to finish him—and that's a fact, Madam."

Wild swans are very numerous, but too shy for sport; the price of a swan's skin is a dollar. The best bird I tasted in Texas was the prairie hen. It is a delicious compound of pheasant, grouse and partridge. People that have been in India say that it resembles the jungle fowl of that country. It is as large as a pheasant, with spurs or tufts of feathers on its heels. We killed quantities of snipes, and plovers— sometimes twenty at a shot. The inhabitants do not waste their ammunition upon such small game, except the boys, who from the age of five years are entrusted with a rifle and dangerous enough are these inexperienced sportsmen to harmless passersby. The perseverance of these people when a deer is in question, is remarkable. They will creep in a horizontal position in the long grass for hours, sometimes, perhaps, not advancing more than a yard in a minute.

Our livery-stable keeper, Captain Cary, earned a great portion of his freedom-money in this way, owing to man's love of sport. A drunken rascal he was, with a head covered with black wool and shaped like a sugar-loaf. He let out a great many horses to our sailors at different times; and when we first arrived, they seemed to prefer a ride to the grog-shop rather than a hunting ground. There was every variety of apple-toddy, eggnog, gin-sling, hot tom-and-jerry, and juleps of every kind advertised at the numerous barrooms, in most tempting array. It was quite amusing to see them mounted on high-stepping horses, riding as only sailors do, as hard as they could go, without any definite object—their hats at the back of their heads, their loose trousers above their knees, and full three feet of daylight between themselves and their saddles. At the risk of their own lives and the horses, they would come galloping down the slight wooden pier, shouting and hallooing, for the admiration of their comrades on board. This love of equestrian exercises, however, did not last long. The charms of "Social Hall," "Ten Pin Alley" and the "Travellers' Friend" soon seduced them, and more than once their leave was broken, and they returned intoxicated to the vessel.

The mustang, or wild horse, I was not fortunate enough to see in any numbers. They are small, strong, and wiry, but, as I before remarked, difficult to tame, and apt to be vicious. I saw one just lassoed, with the Mexican who had caught him, on his back. The rider was using great, but I suppose necessary severity. I do not know which looked the wildest, the horse or his rider. On the day that I saw this animal, we had rather a disagreeable adventure, namely, being nearly swamped in a bog in the prairie. Our horse floundered in, but luckily the hind wheels of the carriage were on *terra firma*. By this means we were able, after a good hour's labour, to rescue the poor animal from his disagreeable situation.

It is really quite melancholy to see the innumerable bones of animals, which are scattered over the face of the country. During our drives and rides, we were constantly stumbling over these dismal-looking remains, bleaching in the sun. The bones are principally those of horned cattle, which have sunk too deeply in the bogs to be able to extricate themselves. No greater proof than this can be required to prove the immense quantity of cattle that exist in this country. Often I have perceived the head and shoulders of an unfortunate animal just appearing above the surface of the bog. Life being still in the creature, we have thought it advisable to send a merciful bullet through its devoted head. Mr. Houstoun, on one occasion, was on the verge of putting a period to the sufferings of a poor beast, thus doomed to a living grave. He was, however, deterred by the recollection of a piece of advice he had previously received. The Texans are particularly sensitive about the interference of strangers in any of their affairs, and it is more than probable, that the shooting of a cow, however well-intentioned the act, would give rise to disagreeable language and possibly to measures of retaliation.

There are many kinds of excellent fish at Galveston. The best of these is decidedly the red fish. It very much resembles the cod in flavour and grows to the length of fifteen feet. We found it excellent when salted. There are likewise immense quantities of gray mullet which, though certainly an inferior fish, are nevertheless very welcome when no other, nor better sorts are to be procured. At low water, they were taken from the pier by means of a casting net. Oysters are much in demand, oyster soup being a favourite delicacy among the Americans. They are large and coarse, and by no means highly flavoured. We often took gray mullet ourselves with a casting net and, occasionally, in the bayous, Mr. Houstoun hooked a red fish, which was a pleasant variety in our sports. The bait for them was a piece of crab or oyster. I was disappointed at finding so small a variety of shells along the coast. For the first few days after my arrival, I wearied my eyes with looking for treasures of

this description. I soon, however, discovered that I must
give up the search in despair. I never found, notwithstanding this deficiency, that the drives along the sea-beach were
either dull or monotonous. There were always ducks to
circumvent or surprise, and pelicans to watch as they stood
unconcernedly in the water, and generally, travellers to enter into conversation with. I regretted that the time was
drawing near when we were to leave the island. We are,
however, looking forward to returning when the weather
is finer and the prairie not so wet.

The sea-fogs were just now very disagreeable, and
it must have been extremely unsafe for ships to venture
near the land. On the 9th of January a large vessel was
seen. This was an event of importance, and it was quite
delightful to perceive the masts and sails of what we plainly
perceived was an English man-of-war, breaking the line
of the horizon. By degrees, and as the vessel approached
nearer the land, she was pronounced to be the *Electra*, an
English corvette. Her arrival on the Texan coast had been
expected, and the pilot went out to her immediately in his
little schooner. The sea-mist, which had partially cleared
away, came on again so thickly, shortly after his departure,
that he found it impossible to find the ship. In consequence
of this, the *Electra* stood off to sea again. This sort of
weather continued for about a fortnight. It is true, we had
occasional glimpses of sun, but they shone through such
a curtain of misty haze, as to be as unlike the bright king
of day as possible. It is very curious, the suddenness with
which these mists roll away. During this time there was
no rain, and our sporting amusements went on as usual.
The day before that on which we intended bidding adieu,
for the present, to the young Republic, we had some rifle
practice with the seven barrel. A deserted house was the
object, and the owner's old boots the particular aim. Mr.
Houstoun gained credit from the lookers-on for the cor-
rectness of his aim at this singular and original target.

Not far from the scene of this exploit is the fort of Galveston! Not willingly would I speak in disparaging terms of

any of the warlike defences of the city, but I cannot really advise the good citizens to trust too much, or too implicitly to them. Their safety in case of an attack by sea, lies in the difficulty of access to their coast. The bar at the mouth of the harbour, and the shallowness of the water, form a natural barrier to invasion, by means of that element. For the same cause, a navy is almost a useless possession to themselves. I believe the President always strongly objected to having the Republic burdened by the purchasing, fitting up and maintaining the expense of ships of war. In the present financial condition of the country, a navy is a worse than useless incumbrance.

The extreme apathy and indolence of these people, when there is no present and personal good to arise from their exerting themselves, is really wonderful. Love of country, though I believe it to be strong within them, is as nothing compared with self-interest and aggrandizement. I believe the same observations would apply to most individuals throughout the world, but I could not help being struck with its peculiar applicability to these Republicans. As a proof of this, I may mention that, lying in the harbour of Galveston, were a brig and a steamer, both vessels of war. They were both aground, and were literally falling to pieces for want of repair, a prey to marine insects and vermin of all kinds. A little money and a very slight degree of exertion, expended in time, would have saved two valuable vessels to the Republic, and also their harbour from exhibiting a most unsightly monument of their improvidence and idleness.

[EDITOR'S NOTE: *The vessels mentioned here are the steamship-of-war* Zavala *and the schooner* San Bernard, *both of which were left to rot at Galveston for want of the funds to do even the most essential repairs to keep the vessels afloat. The* Telegraph and Texas Register *for December 14, 1842 comments on the* San Bernard, *suggesting, "she might be set afloat again for a sum not exceeding three hundred dollars."*]

The revenue of the country is not at present sufficient to play ducks and drakes with. What it may be hereafter time will show, as well as the disposition of the people as to its expenditure. In the meantime, the money arising from the sale of these vessels would have been a start. Not long ago a large steamer went on shore on the island about ten miles from Galveston city. She belonged to a Galveston merchant, and contained a large cargo of cotton. She very soon broke up, as a heavy norther was blowing at the time, and very little of her besides her engine was saved. A good many bales of cotton were floated on shore, and we used to meet portions of the iron-work being hauled (Anglice: carted) along the beach to Galveston. Altogether the loss must have been a heavy one to the proprietor. Cotton, harmless as it looks, sometimes turns out a most dangerous cargo. If, at the time it is packed, it happens to contain the least degree of moisture, it is apt to ignite in the same manner as hay when pressed into a heap, in a similar state.

Our kind friend, Monsieur de Cramayel, the Charge d'Affaires for France, had sent me a most beautiful little live hawk, of a species quite new to me, which he had shot, but it was only "seriously" not "dangerously" wounded. The sailors—who certainly are the most tenderhearted people in the world, as far as dumb animals are concerned—nursed it through its illness, and soon made it quite tame and sociable. We had by this time accumulated quite a menagerie on board. My favourite dog, I have related before, died of a sunstroke at Jamaica: long may the graceful boughs of the coconut tree wave over his tomb! We had still, however, old Rake the setter, who is I regret to say, far gone in decrepitude, and second childishness. Like many other better dogs than himself, he has had his day. Still "sans eyes—sans teeth—sans everything" the old dog always finds a warm berth, a kind word, and the best of dogs' food that can be had for asking. Besides this worthy animal we had two mockingbirds, an eagle and a goat. The latter we found a most useful animal, though not equal in beauty to her predecessor. She was bought at New Orleans with her kid and the kid soon found its way into a pie. Those on board with harder hearts than I could boast of, ate of it with great satisfaction. I heard the poor goat wandering about the decks over our heads, in search of her child, and uttering dismal bleatings, while the flavour of her progeny was under discussion. Had I had the heart to partake of it, I am sure I never again could have looked poor Nan in the face with any degree of assurance.

We had serious thoughts of continuing our course southward, to visit Vera Cruz, and thence to proceed to Mexico. Several circumstances however deterred us from following this plan. In the first place we were by no means sure that, coming from the port of a hostile country, we would be well received by the Mexicans. Another reason was, the want of a tolerable road between Vera Cruz and the capital. Three hundred miles over rocks and stones amongst brigands and thieves was enough to turn back the boldest of us. To New Orleans, therefore, it was decided that we should again betake ourselves.

The *Electra*, after a fortnight's absence, or rather after standing on and off the shore, had at length succeeded in coming to an anchor outside the bar. She has brought despatches for Captain Elliott, and we are to take him out to the corvette in the yacht.

January 26—We took our pilot on board, he having assured us that there was sufficient depth of water on the bar for us to go out of the harbour. I was really quite sorry to say adieu to this island, where we had lingered so long. We had on board our friends of the diplomatic corps, who were bound, as the Yankees say, to pay a visit to Captain Darley, on board the *Electra*. We passed the formidable obstacle of the bar without any difficulty, and soon after, put both pilot and passengers into the boat of the former, with many farewells and good wishes. We passed close to the bows of the *Electra*, and remarkably well she looked to us, accustomed to Yankee and Texan craft as we'd become. The wind was favourable, and we steered a direct course to the southwest pass of the Mississippi.

If we escape the dangers of plague, pestilence, famine and shipwreck, and live to return to Texas, I shall, I have no doubt have something more to say about the young Republic. "It's a fine country and that's a fact."

CHAPTER XIV

WINTER ON THE MISSISSIPPI ⚓ SNAKES ⚓ ⚓ AMUSEMENTS IN NEW ORLEANS

January 29—The land was sighted ahead, and in the afternoon we received the pilot on board. The weather was fine and quiet, with occasional light airs. The pilot told us that the yacht would have to cut her way through several feet of mud, and every stitch of canvass was crowded on the vessel to enable her to dash bravely through, when she should arrive at the shallow part of the water. We were not long kept in anxiety for, though we perceived no change in her usual smooth and even course through the water, the schooner was slipping gently and safely through the soft mud. At one moment, however, (and that at the shallowest spot) she scarcely seemed to move and we began to fancy she was fixed, and might remain—as the Yankees say, "from January to eternity." A few seconds put us out of our suspense, for a puff of wind suddenly arose and carried us in safety into deep water.

I have forgotten to mention a lighthouse, which we left behind us at the southwest pass and I must revert to it here, as there is rather a singular story attached to it. The situation is I think a precarious one, at least it has the appearance of being so, the lighthouse having been erected on a sedgy bank formed by an accumulation of mud and snags. These insecure oozy-looking lands extend in all directions about the various entrances to the Mississippi, and give it the appearance—I have before remarked upon—of unhealthy desolation. The lighthouse in question was built by the government of the United States, at a considerable expense, as they were aware of the great necessity of such a beacon at the mouth of the river. Soon after the work was completed, an unexpected claim was set up to the land, or rather mud, on which the lighthouse had been built. The parties, who thus inopportunely appeared, founded their claim on a title, which was derived from some old

Spanish grant. This title they produced, but they offered to forego their claim for the moderate sum of, I think, thirty thousand dollars. The cause was tried and, to the great annoyance of the government, it was decided in favour of the new claimants. The government, rather than remove their lighthouse, consented to comply with this exorbitant demand. The whole affair is a fine specimen of Yankee cunning, and shrewd lying in wait for the unwary.

The two months that had elapsed since we last visited the Mississippi had worked a great change in the appearance of the woods. The trees, which were before clad in all the beauty of their autumnal verdure, were now bleak, gray and leafless. It is true that, here and there, an ilex or some other evergreen, relieved with its rich hues this dismal appearance, but they were but rare and I continually regretted the change that had taken place. The long hanging moss, so much like the gray and venerable beards of some aged patriarch, was pendant from the trees and showed more conspicuously than ever, from the want of leaves. One could not, as before, be cheated by the beauty of the decaying vegetation into a forgetfulness of the deadly insalubrity of the climate and country. The morasses were now displayed in all their horrors and one almost shuddered to pass such cradles of pestilence and disease.

The river was much higher than it was during our former visit. The breaking up of the frost, and the consequent melting of the snow in the northern country, had caused it to rise many feet. The tide was running three or four knots an hour, and it would have required a very strong wind in our favour, to enable us to make head against it. Unluckily for us not a breath of air was blowing, and on this, our second day in the river—after many attempts to progress, which ended in our making stern-way only—we let go the anchor and determined to go on shore.

The weather was intensely cold, and the water used for washing the decks immediately froze after being dashed over them. A bright sun was shining all the morning, and yet the water remained unthawed throughout the day.

We really could not keep ourselves warm in the yacht, as the state of the decks entirely prevented us from taking our usual exercise of pacing up and down the vessel and we did not at all relish being confined in the cabin, while such a brilliant sun was shining over head. An expedition on shore was, therefore, agreed upon, and the gig was manned. We landed with some little difficulty, as the banks are at that spot abrupt and rather steep—at least I thought them so, when I found myself obliged to attempt the ascent.

I soon perceived that I had gained nothing in warmth by the change from the yacht. Walking I found impossible, as the ground was so rough, and sitting still was freezing work. A happy idea at length struck us—that of making a fire on the ground under the trees. We set to work to collect sticks and dried leaves, and soon made a satisfactory heap. This done, we endeavoured to produce a light, by rubbing together two pieces of dried wood—Indian fashion. Do what we would, and strive as we might, we could not succeed, and yet we naturally felt that half the romance of the situation would be destroyed by obtaining a light in any more artificial manner. At length, however, we gave up the attempt in despair, and were thankful for a lucifer match which the doctor happily had in his pocket. The fire burnt bravely, rushing along the ground over the dead leaves, and warming the whole air to a distance of at least a hundred yards. I was constantly obliged to change my position, as the fierce flames approached, and seemed ready to lick my feet. The warmth was quite delightful, and I would at any time prefer such a woodfire to Newcastle coal in the best and most polished of fireplaces. Following my example, the crew of the gig, who had been wandering listlessly about the woods, made themselves a fire also, and sat round it to warm themselves.

While I was thus employed, Mr. Houstoun amused himself with shooting. There were plenty of rabbits, and they were easily shot. They were however not worth eating, when cooked. I do not know in what respect they differed from English rabbits, but they neither looked nor tasted the same. Numbers of beautiful birds were flying and sporting about; their bright plumage being seen to great advantage on the leafless boughs. I thought it grievous to shoot them, and when they brought me cardinals, blue-birds, and bright-coloured woodpeckers, I felt how much rather I would have seen them glancing about in the bright light, and sunning themselves in the warmth of heaven. They were now stretched lifeless and stiff upon the earth, these poor woodland forest minstrels! Never more to sing their joyous songs or flit about the dancing leaves!

But how still and sombre that primeval forest seemed! Not a sound broke upon the ear, except when the report of the gun reverberated through the woods, and startled the slumbering echoes from their long repose.

Here and there were blackened stumps, showing that the devastating hand of man had been busy there, and had lain low the stately trees which had grown in that vast forest for centuries. Around the prostrate forms of the dead giants clung the sad passion-flower, and the twining creeper, as though loath to part with the faithful pillar that had been their support in life. The whole surface of the ground was so thickly covered with dried leaves, that it was difficult to make any discovery of the descriptions of plants or herbs, which vegetate under the trees. The monotonous brown of the earth's covering was, however, varied by frequent tufts of the fan-plant, as it is here called. This graceful plant shoots up its broad fan-like leaves, of the most vivid green, and its peculiar shape and hue are calculated to give an appearance of tropical vegetation to the scenery.

We had been informed that wild boar and deer were to be found in the forests in considerable numbers. However we were not fortunate enough to see anything of them, and I confess myself rather incredulous as to the fact of their existence in these woods.

My fire had, after the lapse of a couple of hours, burnt low and we made preparations for going on board. On our return to the gig, we perceived the men very busily engaged; so much so, that we came upon them unseen.

They had found a small snake, which the warmth of their fire had probably aroused from its torpid state, and they were endeavouring to make sure of their prisoner. To effect this, they were trying to tie a piece of ropeyarn round the creature's body. The snake had, as one of the sailors expressed it, "hove off his tail," in the course of his capture. This circumstance considerably increased the difficulty of the attempt. Having with great care adjusted the yarn to his satisfaction, the man whose prize it was, deposited the reptile in the crown of his hat. Happily for the poor man, we returned in time to prevent the consequences of his imprudence. The snake was one of a most venomous species, and we immediately turned the tide of his sufferings by ordering him to be destroyed.

All night we lay at anchor, and the yacht ran no little risk of injury from the vast number of logs and trees which were floating down the river. Owing to the unusually high floods and tides, the stream was at times almost covered by these disagreeable hindrances to our progress. Trees of forest growth and stature, uprooted in their strength, came upon us with resistless force, and it required constant care to prevent collision when we were underway. A lookout man was always stationed "forward," to watch their coming and to direct the helmsman how to steer. These moving timbers were, however, not so dangerous as the snags— namely, trees, or parts of them—that have a strong hold on the bottom.

Thus sped our time, and a long and rather weary four days it was before we arrived at the city. The night before we reached it the yacht underwent a signal misfortune, which certainly occasioned some variety, though of not a particularly agreeable nature. It was the night of the 1st of February, dark and still and foggy. A small steamer coming up to the city, hailed us several times, to know if we wanted steam, her commander no doubt conjecturing that we were at anchor in despair of making further way. The lookout man on deck answered "No" several times, upon which the steamer, (as we suppose out of envy, malice and

hatred) ran on board of us, and did us all the mischief in
her power. Our fore-topmast was carried away, as well as
the larboard whisker, and part of the bulwarks on the larboard bow was stove in. The next morning all hands were
employed in clearing away the wreck, which having been
done, we made sail somewhat shorn of our fair proportions.

At one o'clock we arrived again at New Orleans, and lost
no time in sending on shore for our much wished for letters. One of Mr. Houstoun's first occupations was to find
out the name of the vessel, which had so signally insulted
us, and to demand satisfaction. The steamer proved to be
the *Swan*, a tug, and her owners found themselves obliged
to make good all the damage we had received. [*EDITOR'S
NOTE: Mrs. Houstoun makes mention, in her 1881 work
A Woman's Memories of World-Known Men, that Henry
Clay was lead counsel for them in a most important lawsuit
at New Orleans. This suit may have related to the settlement with the owners of the* Swan.]

The appearance of the city was now much more gay and
cheerful than it had been during our former visit. The car-
nival had begun and masks were visible in the windows of
the stores. The walls were covered with announcements
of forthcoming balls, both in the French and English lan-
guages. Plays were in great vogue and the Parisian taste for
horrors was also prevalent here. "La Mansarde de Crime,"
and such like mysterious tragedies, I saw announced for
constant repetition. The streets were much dryer, and the
shops—I beg their pardon, the stores—were more conspicuously and tastefully arranged than in the winter. The
spring fashions had already made their appearance. Ladies,
gaily dressed in every colour of the rainbow—beginning
with the parasol, and ending with the shoes—were prom-
enading the streets in all directions. Indeed, it seemed that
in proportion as business, owing to the season of the year,
had declined, pleasure had risen fifty per cent.

There are but two drives in the neighbourhood of New
Orleans—the old and new "Shell-Roads." These roads are

raised by artificial means several feet above the morass, which almost surrounds the city. They are formed upon piles, and are thickly covered, as their name implies, with small seashells. From this road, you look down on a swamp on one side and a canal on the other. Both roads, in the hot season, are described as literally swarming with alligators and mosquitoes. Happily for us, the time of the year for these creatures had not yet arrived. During our stay, I saw but one young alligator, and the mosquitoes were not yet brought into light and mischief.

Though still, in what we in England call the depth of winter, the vegetation was as forward as it often is in an English May. The tender green of the beech was everywhere visible, and the buds of the hawthorn were almost visibly bursting forth under the influence of the warm sunshine. Wildflowers, such as prefer moist and watery places, were beginning to show their blossoms, and among them I noticed several descriptions of briar, which were very pretty. Birds were welcoming the spring with their small twittering notes, but cheerful as their voices sounded in the still air, we missed the full chorus of our English woodland vocalists. No nightingale, no skylark. I missed almost all of my old favourites and was only consoled in their absence by the sound of the cuckoo.

One of the shell roads leads to the Lake of Pontchartrain. This lake is of salt water and its shores are low and flat. There is a sort of village on its banks, which is considered and used as a watering-place; and though not more than six miles distant, may be called the Brighton of New Orleans. Many of the opulent merchants have built villas at Pontchartrain, and during the summer months when business is at a standstill, they migrate to the shores of the lake, and refresh themselves by bathing in its salt waters. New Orleans is thus almost deserted by the rich inhabitants during the hot and unhealthy season.

It is on Sundays that the Shell Road ought to be visited. It is then crowded with pleasure-taking citizens. Not a carriage is left in the streets unhired, and by far the greatest

number are filled with negroes. It is quite delightful to see
how thoroughly they enjoy themselves. Their happy laughing faces are shining out at the open windows, and each
carriage is packed as full as it can hold. The slaves are seen
grinning and chattering incessantly, and with a vivacity and
excitement unknown to those of whom Sundays brings not
the happy variety of freedom. Another employment of the
slaves, on a Sunday, is the bringing in, on their own account, large supplies of the Spanish moss from the country.
They collect it from the tall trees in the neighbourhood, and
it well repays them for the trouble. It is principally used in
making beds, and enough for such a purpose may be collected in a few minutes. It requires but little preparation,
and the beds thus made are remarkably comfortable. I have
so often described this moss (*Tillandsia Usneodes*), that I
need not say much more about it. In the neighbourhood of
New Orleans it appeared to be particularly thick and long,
growing frequently to the length of three or four feet, and
almost hiding its parent tree. The effect of setting a dead
tree on fire, with its clothing of dried moss, is very curious.
We tried the experiment once, and the appearance of the
flames on the rapidly ignited moss was beautiful.

During one of these Sunday drives, I first saw and admired
the astonishing pace of the trotting horses in America. The
perfectly flat and smooth Shell Road is remarkably well
adapted for showing off their powers. The carriage used is
as light as possible, and looks as if much less weight than
that of a man would break it down. The horse I saw was
said to be "a considerable fair traveller, with most particular good bottom." I should, I am afraid, be suspected of
an Americanism, did I venture to assert how fast he went,
but the pace struck me with wonder. He passed at a trot,
like a flash of lightning, and it was a fair trot, not a run, or
anything like it. The best and fastest trotter was a Canadian
horse. These are generally of a small size, and I fear much
cruelty is used to break them into trotting in this astonishing manner.

CHAPTER XV

SOME FLORIDA INDIANS ⚓ CHIEF TIGER TAIL

I had expected to find every sort of Indian fancy-work in plenty at New Orleans, but I was disappointed. There was but little in the stores, and the prices asked were quite unconscionable. For a small hunting pouch, worked with beads, and not very curiously, the demand was fifty-two dollars; nearly fourteen pounds! We often met Indians, both men and women, wandering about the streets. They were scantily clothed, with an old blanket wrapped about them for their only covering. They were often in a state of intoxication (with their long shining black hair falling over their faces), and shivering with cold. The time at which they were most frequently to be seen was early in the morning, and they generally attended the markets.

During our stay at New Orleans a party of Florida Indians were brought in as prisoners, with their squaws and children. These Indians have for a long time occasioned great annoyance and trouble to the government of the United States. They are naturally fond of war and, although greatly reduced in numbers, are constantly engaged in hostile insurrections. Who can wonder at the efforts made by these poor and suffering people to regain possession of their country. Swampy and unwholesome as that country is, still it was their own, and the Indian tribes are never the first to forget their fatherland.

Some parts of Florida are productive and healthy, but by far the larger portion is wet and marshy, well suited certainly for the produce and increase of snakes, frogs, alligators, gnats and mosquitoes, but not an enviable residence for human beings. In common with the swamps in the neighbourhood of New Orleans, cedar and cypress grow in the Florida marshes to a prodigious size, as also the live oak. It is in these swampy forests that the slender remains of the once powerful tribes retreat for shelter from their enemies. That the whole race of Indians on this continent must hate the whites with a bitter hatred, no one can doubt. On every occasion they have broken faith with them, and have made themselves lords of the soil by stealing their birthright from the original inhabitants. Gradually, but surely, have the aboriginal Indians disappeared from the face of the world, driven out by the progress of civilization. It is not that by intermarriages, and other causes, the generation of red men becomes insensibly mingled with the whites, but that by some inevitable decree of Providence they dwindle away, and are lost to the world forever.

The Florida Indians are passionately addicted to hunting, and by this means they provide themselves and their families with food. Deer, bear, and wolf's skins, besides beeswax and venison, are articles they sell to strangers. They traffic also in squirrels' skins, which are beautiful and very valuable. In short, could the Florida Indians overcome their longing to be free, they might live in comfort enough. Those we saw at New Orleans, amounted in number to about two hundred, and they were constantly being augmented by fresh captures.

The poor creatures were kept in the barracks, which are situated about three miles from the city on the banks of the river. They were allowed the free range of the barrack-yard, but limited enough must such a liberty have appeared to them, accustomed to the free air of their native woods. We paid them several visits after their arrival and the sight interested me extremely. Most of them were fine athletic-looking men, muscular and well proportioned. I should say that they more resembled the Gypsies we are in the habit of seeing in Europe, than any other people. Their complexion is of the same dark hue, and their hair long, straight and shining. Some of the warriors were still in their paint—a hideous combination of colours which covered their bodies, red being the most prevailing tint.

The squaws were not remarkable for their personal charms. I saw but one who could be pronounced, in the least degree, pretty. She was very young, almost a child in appearance, and bore her infant on her back. She was nestling at the feet of a young and fine looking warrior who was the son, I was told, of a great chief. Occasionally she raised her dark expressive eyes to his face, not presuming to address him, but watching his movements, and anticipating his wishes, with the patience and submission peculiar to the Indian wife.

The rest of the women were employed in various ways. They were evidently considered as infinitely inferior to their lords in the scale of humanity, and all the menial offices were left to them to perform. Their mode of bruising the Indian corn, which forms their principal article of food, is by beating the grain in a large wooden trough, with heavy pieces of wood. It must have been very hard labour, yet the squaws performed it without receiving the slightest assistance from the men, who, I have no doubt, would have felt themselves degraded had they lent a hand to the work. Others of these hard-working females were boiling potatoes for the daily meal, and one and all bore upon their backs a little patient infant.

The poor little creatures were tightly swathed, like diminutive mummies, and had no power to move any part of their persons, excepting their large round eyes, which kept staring about in restless activity. There were a number of children of all ages and sizes playing about, and most of them were pretty and interesting.

I was very much struck by the extreme gravity and silence preserved by the whole party, men and women. Even in their amusements, the same dignified composure was visible. We often found the young men playing at a game, which greatly resembled the old English sport called "Hockey." They displayed much skill and activity at this exercise, the old men in the meantime looking gravely on. Some of the warriors were stretched on the ground wrapped in their blankets, while others were leaning, with folded arms, against the walls.

Among the prisoners was a great chief and warrior. His name was "Tiger Tail," and it was one that had often spread terror and dismay amongst his enemies. The chief was now old and his strength was on the decline. He was patiently awaiting the summons of the Great Spirit, to enjoy the reward of a brave warrior in the happy hunting-grounds of the blest. But once more, however, the war-whoop had sounded in his ears and, scenting the battle afar off, the aged chief prepared to tread his last warpath with the young warriors of his tribe. Gallantly they fought, but the Manitou had turned away his face from his children and, after a fierce struggle, they bent their heads beneath his displeasure and were led away captive. During this last engagement, Tiger Tail was severely wounded, and from the nature of the hurt, his sufferings must have been very great. Notwithstanding this, he refused every offer of surgical assistance and with true Indian stoicism, looked as composed and as mentally unsubdued as if he were seated at the council-fire of his tribe.

The skill and bravery of Tiger Tail had on former occasions caused considerable loss to the American troops, and his capture was a source of peculiar congratulation to them. During their march in the winter season through the vast forests of Florida, the Indians had been unavoidably subjected to much hardship. The children in particular must have greatly suffered. I was told (by means of an interpreter) that one poor little fellow, a boy not five years old, had been lost in the forest on their march. Three months elapsed before he was found. During all that time he had been alone, and had existed literally upon fruits and wild honey. He was a remarkably intelligent-looking child, as indeed they all were. When he was discovered in the forest, the boy was in very good preservation, and seemed likely to remain so. A plump, merry-looking little urchin he was, and there was that in his eye that would have made a warrior in the palmy days of Indian power.

The prisoners were remarkably well fed and cared for, and on the whole did not look unhappy. They were occasionally allowed the indulgence of performing their national war-dance, and this was done invariably at night. The scene was lighted up by torches, which they brandished in their hands. The stamping movement of their feet was accompanied at intervals by the most discordant whoops, and the whole ballet, though extremely curious, was anything but a graceful exhibition.

The first time we appeared amongst them, the Indians exhibited no marked signs of wonder. They looked at us askance and rather suspiciously, but once, only, did I see them roused to anything like animation. The object of their curiosity was my sable boa, and I shall not easily forget the silent wonder with which some of the grave old hunters regarded it. One of them, without any ceremony, took it away from me in order to examine it more closely. A little circle was then formed, and they deliberated upon its nature and origin. The prevalent opinion certainly was that it was the full-length tail of some animal, a creature to them unknown, on whom Nature had bestowed a "fly-disperser" of unusual length and beauty. After looking at it for a long time, one of them endeavoured to fasten it on the back of a brother hunter, who stood near. Having done this, he proceeded to curl it up in order to make it look as naturally like a tail as possible. The joke was hailed by the rest with a momentary laugh, but in another second their countenances were as still and as impassive as before. I had no idea that they could be half so facetious.

We generally distributed some small coins amongst them; money, however, they appeared to set but little value on. A much more acceptable present, I have no doubt, would have been some whiskey or rum. In common with all savage tribes, they were passionately fond of ardent spirits, not the least among the evils for which they have to thank their civilized successors.

I believe that it is the intention of the government to send the prisoners to St. Louis, with the object of settling them in the Western Prairies.

Chapter XVI

Negro Slaves ⚓ Lack of Religious Observance ⚓
Favourite Sports ⚓ Commerce of New Orleans

There is a railroad from New Orleans to Pontchartrain; rather an indifferent one, certainly, for the carriages are not even superior to our "second class" vehicles, and there is not even the satisfaction of going quickly over the ground.

The carriages which stand in the streets for hire are, as I before remarked, particularly good and comfortable. They are usually driven by slaves, and at a very good pace. We employed the same carriage and driver nearly every day during our stay. The former was a species of calèche, and the negro, who performed the office of charioteer, was the most communicative individual I ever saw. He was a very merry fellow, black as jet, and as shining as a plentiful supply of coconut oil could make him. His pockets were always full of nuts of various kinds, which he cracked and ate during the short pauses in his conversation. He often talked to us on the "Slavery question," told us how much money he had the opportunities of earning on his own account, and begged to assure us that it would by no means answer for him to be free.

The recollection of this man induces me to say a few words upon the apparently happy life led by this much-pitied race at New Orleans. Among the list of grievances, I have heard it asserted that they are kept strictly apart from their "white brethren," and are evidently considered, by this marked separation, as a degraded and inferior race. This, at New Orleans, is certainly not the case. I was constantly in the habit of seeing well-dressed American children, evidently the offspring of respectable parents, playing with little piccaninies, as black and as curly-headed as little niggers could well be. A perfect system of equality apparently existed among them, and in the course of their merry games the laugh of the black child was as clear and ringing as that of his white play fellow.

During our drives through the streets, especially on Sundays, the display of negro finery and taste was very remarkable. If we happened to overtake a particularly well-dressed person with a Parisian coat, a glossy hat and well-varnished boots, we were sure to be surprised by seeing a black face appended to these advantages. I saw such "persecuted" negro slaves frequently. They appeared to have no other occupation than that of flourishing about their gold-headed canes, and fixing a glass in their eye. Gloves (which are an unusual sight at New Orleans) they generally indulged in, and with one hand gracefully placed in the coat pocket, looked worthy—at least from behind—of figuring in the Tuileries, or St. James's Street.

No one pays higher for his outfit than the negro in the slave states. He gives his money too, so carelessly, and with such an independent air. I have heard of their giving eighty dollars for a suit of clothes. Their industry, and efforts to procure money, are highly praiseworthy. They are in the habit of giving their masters a certain sum of money, (generally, I believe, about two dollars a day) in lieu of their services. Their time, then, is their own, and they are at liberty to make as much more out of it as they can. From what I saw and heard, I am inclined to think that many of the domestic slaves would not accept their liberty, were it offered to them.

There is scarcely any spectacle more affecting in idea than that of a human being made to be an object of barter. I went to America strongly prejudiced against this unnatural traffic, and prepared to view every instance of it with horror, and every slave with compassion and sympathy. I became, however, after a short time, somewhat moderated in my opinions. Though still regarding the slave trade, generally, in the same light, I began to think that the slaves themselves were not quite so much to be pitied as I had imagined. The first time I saw a slave sold I was affected almost to tears, but after contemplating their cheerful, happy faces, and seeing how well and kindly they were generally treated, I learned to view the scene with different feelings.

A slave sale is in some respects a laughable sight enough. The American auctioneer is not to be outdone by that prince of auctioneers, George Robins himself, in the exercise of his vocation. I once saw a very small "lot" put up. It was a poor-looking creature about four feet high, and appeared certainly not much accustomed to stand in high places. He stood up, however, boldly enough, by the side of the auctioneer, dressed in the smart clothes kept for the especial purpose of making the poor fellows look their best.

The auctioneer began, "This fine young man, gentlemen, is warranted to be only twenty years of age, sound in wind and limb—he has an excellent character, and a good temper. Moreover, gentlemen, he was born in the state of Mississippi, and is warranted to be a first-rate field hand, and a terrible good cotton-picker. It 'ud be a privilege to have him, gentlemen." All this time the object of such eloquent praise stood on the elevated platform and, instead of (as one would imagine) looking distressed and unhappy, seemed only rather bewildered and grinned throughout the ceremony from ear to ear.

There certainly is a great absence of religious feeling and observance in this city. This may be attributed, in some measure, to the admixture of the Catholic and Protestant faith, professed by its various inhabitants. There is, however, I imagine, a deeper cause for the want of religion observable here. There is no religion having national authority, and thus in democratic countries and particularly among a hard-headed and unimaginative people like the Americans, devotional feeling becomes weakened and extinguished, when the outward observance of the rites and ceremonies of religion is in no degree a part of the government of the country. The subject altogether is too important, and involves too much learned disquisition for me to venture to touch upon it. I can only repeat the broad fact that religion is treated with no respect at New Orleans.

I have before remarked that Sunday is their great day of amusement. This, however, alone would not establish the fact of their negligence in religious matters. We do the same unfortunately in England, and in almost all parts of the European Continent, and should not be the first, therefore, to throw the stone. But the ceremonies of religion, church-going, etc, are not thought of here. They scarcely even think it necessary to profess a faith. This subject is one under frequent discussion between the wise men of the Northern and Southern States, and numerous arguments arise in consequence. The former asserts that in the north, it is absolutely necessary to the character of an individual, that he should be nominally a member of some religious persuasion or other. Be it Catholic or Protestant, Shaker or Quaker, follower of Johanna Southcote or an Anabaptist, it did not much matter, but one or other he must choose. He must, they say, be something; whereas at New Orleans "Nobody is anything."

The favourite sport on Sunday is that of rifle-shooting. Thousands flock to the ground where the performance takes place, and great is the emulation excited among the aspirants for fame. The mark is a turkey, which is fastened to the flattened stump of a tree, and the distance from it to the marksman is about seventy yards. The turkeys used for this purpose are brought down the Mississippi, by dozens, in flat-bottomed boats. The American sportsmen failed in impressing us with a high opinion of their skill as rifle shots. They talk a great deal about it but that, we all know, is no proof of superiority.

One of the New Orleans Society, who enjoyed the reputation of being one of the best shots in the United States, showed us a perforated target, of which he appeared extremely proud. He had laid a wager, that at a distance of seventy yards he would put half a dozen balls into a target. A wafer was placed in the centre, and none of the balls were to enter at a greater distance than five inches from the wafer. He had come off victorious in the match, and the target was laid up among his family relics, as a precious and honourable trophy of his skill. We remarked, previous to the wager being explained to us, that the balls were rather wide of the centre, but his *amour propre* was too great to receive a check easily—and he it was who boasted that he could "pick off" a man at the distance of a thousand yards across the Mississippi.

A fearful tragedy was acted shortly before our departure from New Orleans. A large bank stopped payment, and the announcement was attended by an excitement among the inhabitants almost unequalled. Men were seen rushing about through the streets, some with bags of dollars on their shoulders, and all with dismay plainly marked on their countenances. During the course of the day, the various banks in the city were emptied of their cash. But it was not till the following morning that we learnt the most painful part of the story, namely, that the president of the bank, a man much considered and respected in New Orleans, had committed suicide. He left his house the day that the bank broke, and twenty-four hours after was found dead in the Yellow Fever Burial Ground, having stabbed himself through the body. This sad instance of irreligion, and moral cowardice, was the more deplorable, as the unhappy man had the misfortune to possess a wife and a large family of children.

We were told that it was necessary to keep a constant watch over sailors, when in the harbour of New Orleans, as they are frequently in the habit of escaping. It was now becoming late in the business season; a great number of the ships had sailed. Many of those still remaining found great difficulty in procuring seamen for the voyage home. On hearing this, Mr. Houstoun took an early opportunity of informing the crew of the *Dolphin*, that he had no desire of retaining any man in the vessel against his will; and that if any of the "ship's company" felt disposed to go, they had better take their departure at once, and openly, instead of skulking off at the last moment, and leaving us without sufficient hands to work the ship.

Thus prepared, we "lay upon our oars," and awaited the result. There is a thoroughly organized system here for entrapping English sailors, who are highly valued, both as merchant and men-of-war's-men. The Americans are incessantly endeavouring to entice the men from the various ships to which they belong. The pay they offer is enormously high; thirty dollars (six pounds a month) have been frequently given, and it may be imagined that very few sailors are impervious to such high bribery as this.

Merchant ships at New Orleans generally have their cargo stowed by contractors, who are experienced in the business, and who employ blacks and Irishmen for the purpose. The affair being arranged in this manner, it becomes almost a desideratum with the captains of merchant vessels to get rid of their hands as soon as possible. They are thus spared the trouble and expense of keeping them during the six weeks or two months that their ships remain in the harbour. When a vessel is ready to sail, the captain has recourse to what is called a "crimp," of which there are plenty, and this individual undertakes to man the ship. At two or three o'clock on the morning of departure, the captain goes into the forecastle, counts over the number of heads attached to so many drunken bodies and, finding the number stipulated for, he pays the agent the promised reward, and goes off as soon as he can.

The ship is, of course, immediately taken in tow by a steam-tug, and she is perhaps well out of the river before her heterogeneous crew are roused from their deep sleep of intoxication. One can fancy the absurdity of the waking scene. Each man having been, probably, in a state of perfect unconsciousness when taken on board, finds a difficulty in comprehending his situation. The man used to sailing in a little schooner, with perhaps but two hands on board, finds himself in a large ship, on the deep sea, with fifty strange faces around him. The freshwater sailor, who has been for years on board the Mississippi steamboats, and has become so used to the loud voices of their high-pressure engines, that he can hardly sleep without their lullaby, awakes—feels himself bounding on in silence, and cannot understand how he can be moving on without noise, smoke, or jerking. In like manner, the fisherman, who had never contemplated the possibility of his leaving his native river, awakes in a liner bound for Liverpool, and in bewildered astonishment gazes on the stupid countenances of his companions in misfortune. It is no uncommon thing for landsmen to pass themselves off as sailors, in order to gain the tempting wages offered to them. On one occasion, the doctor was witness to an amusing scene, in which these self-styled able-bodied seamen were actors. They were going through a regular course of practice, to enable them to pass muster, and to prevent the immediate discovery of their trickery.

No attempts were made to prevent our men from coming in contact with bribery and corruption. Here, as in every other port that we visited during our cruise, they had permission to go on shore whenever they asked for it—half of their number were always away from the yacht and it rarely happened that they broke their "leave." One day, however, to our great surprise, for we had seen no previous marks of disaffection or desire for change, we were greeted by the unwelcome intelligence that two of our men were missing. It was supposed they had gone over to the Americans. They had escaped during the night, in silence, and without any witness, as far as we could prove. The lookout man declared that he had not seen them take their departure, but we could not believe him; he felt, however, that he could not have betrayed his messmates, and we did not press for his confidence.

The two deserters were the only married men on board, and I suppose were anxious to return to their domestic comforts, as we afterwards learnt that they had taken service in a merchant brig bound for England. Subsequently to this period, we continually noticed well-dressed men, who were evidently "crimps," endeavouring to inveigle and entice away the men who formed the crew of the gig. Directly these men perceived us approaching, they hurried away with every mark of confusion.

Had Mr. Houstoun thought proper to follow the example set him, we might soon have found substitutes, by resorting to the same dishonourable means which were employed against us. As it was, however, we were not long delayed by a deficiency of hands. The service of an English yacht is sure to be a popular one, and the new men were pronounced active, and sharp. They were both Englishmen, and had lately served in a man-of-war.

I should say, speaking of the Americans in the daily habits of their lives, that they are a particularly methodical people. The same thing is almost invariably done at the same hour, let it be "liquoring" or eating soup. There are regular soup houses here. Their soups principally consist of oysters and gumbo, the latter a root peculiar to the country and collected by the Indians. With this same regularity, they enter the gambling-houses, of which, be it remembered, there are many. For a somewhat cold blooded people, it is marvellous to me how fond the Americans are of this species of excitement. It exists in all shapes, and their horse races are attended more regularly and more energetically even than our own. The betting, too, on these occasions, is most spirited.

Another of the remarkable points in the character of the New Orleans citizen is, as I was informed, his fondness for duelling. The nearness of their birthplace to the Equator may possibly account both for this and for their gambling propensities. The hot blood of the south has certainly a little to do with these peculiar vices. I have heard that duels take place most frequently in the hot season. At this period some are said to become irascible and to be easily excited, and it is just as well for peaceable men to keep out of their way. In the winter, they become quiet and phlegmatic. The cold air chills their blood, and they at once cease to be dangerous.

I will give one proof of the extremely methodical habits of the New Orleans citizens, and of the adroit manner in which certain matters are managed here. The post office is a large building, in the centre of which there is a bar or "liquoring hall." A clock of conspicuous appearance also decorates the entrance. The merchants, etc, are in the daily

habit of calling for their letters at the post office, there being no delivery in any other manner. The man who kept the
bar—and a cunning man he must have been—remarked
that at a certain hour all the merchants, after securing
their despatches, went off to another house to liquor. He
took great pains to ascertain the exact hour at which this
ceremony took place and, having done so, made his arrangements accordingly.

It appeared that before going "on 'Change," the merchants, as though actuated by one simultaneous motive,
took their morning "liquor" at half past ten. The hands of
the post office clock pointed at a quarter past ten when the
letters were delivered, and the men of business immediately
hurried off to take their invigorating draught. Our friend
at the post office, craftily and in secret, contrived daily to
move back the hands of the clock some ten minutes. The
merchants looked up. "What!? As I'm alive, it's half past
ten a'most; it's infarnal late. I actilly must take my liquor
here today, sir." And so they all did. And after a time, it
became a confirmed habit to take their early dram at the
bar of the post office. He was a very smart man, that gin
sling and sherry cobbler seller. I believe that the "liquoring" hour often tells the New Orleans citizen what o'clock
it is, so regular is the habit and so indispensable is it to his
comfort.

It is impossible not to reflect with admiration, when one
walks through the streets of New Orleans, on the immense
distance to which goods are conveyed by the people who
purchase them. Every fifth store is a hatter's and, to judge
from the flourishing state of this branch of trade, "awful
good" hats must be in great demand. Numbers are sent
to the Yankees in the Far West, and as the dress in those
distant settlements is very savage and primitive, the vision
of a very large shining hat on the head of one of these skin-
clad settlers must be very charming.

Another remark I made at New Orleans, connected
with a much more important branch of trade, may not be
uninteresting. At New Orleans, I saw a gown of printed

cotton, which had been purchased at one of the stores. The pattern was pretty, the price very moderate and the colours indelible. The cheapness of the cotton I thought so remarkable that I was induced to ask "whence it came?" The reply was, that it was of American manufacture. And so it was. Even I, unskilled as I am in commercial matters, was struck by the possible consequences of the perfection to which the Americans have brought their manufactures.

I had never thought much on the subject, but had always supposed that all kinds of cotton and woollen goods were imported into America from England. To my great surprise, however, I found that nearly everything of this kind that we saw was of native manufacture, and that the prices of them were no higher than in England. It is a positive fact, and certainly an important one, that in the year 1826, one hundred and fifty million yards of calico were imported into the United States. Last year the quantity was reduced to fifteen million! It appears to me that America has, thus far, derived benefit from her almost restrictive tariff, for she is now, as far as regards the manufacture of cotton, woollen and iron goods, independent of other countries. The manufacturing of these articles is so profitable a business, that several English companies are establishing factories in various parts of America. When the Yankee spirit of enterprise and go-aheadism is taken into consideration, it may fairly be conjectured that, at no distant period, they will become formidable rivals to Great Britain, and will greatly interfere with her exclusive privilege of supplying the world with the articles above mentioned.

I have laid in a stock of new books for the voyage, for at no place can a temporary library be procured at a less outlay than in the United States. Bulwer's novel of the *Last of the Barons*, was sold at two bits—about eleven pence— and every other work in proportion! A work published in England comes out almost simultaneously in the United States, and English works of standard authors are eagerly bought, and read—I suspect—mostly by the ladies.

CHAPTER XVII

HENRY CLAY ⚓ AMERICAN SOCIETY & MANNERS
⚓ 2ND DEPARTURE FOR TEXAS

Mr. Henry Clay was at New Orleans. He is their great orator and a Whig, and it is supposed by many that he will be
their president at some future time. There was much public
dancing, driving, eating and speechifying in his honour,
for among the characteristics of their English origin, that
of exercising their eating and drinking powers in behalf of
a popular character, still remains in all its glory. Mr. Clay
is deservedly popular. He was making a sort of progress
through the States, but I am told does not pay his travelling
expenses out of his own purse. This makes a vast difference, and is the strongest possible proof of the orator's
popularity. The affections of the multitude seldom endure,
after an appeal is made to their pockets.

The last tribute paid before his departure, to the orator's
high and well-deserved reputation, appeared in the shape
of a public ball. Invitations were sent on board the yacht,
but unluckily they arrived the day after the fete. By this
means we were prevented from witnessing what was, no
doubt, an interesting national display. I heard, however,
the events of the evening described, and Mr. Clay's polite speech to the New Orleans ladies was much admired.
[*EDITOR'S NOTE: Mrs. Houstoun notes in her 1881 book,*
A Woman's Memories of World-Known Men, *that she visited with Mr. Clay and Captain Elliott in the Houstoun's
sitting room of the St. Louis Hotel. She mentions only a bit
about Henry Clay's physical appearance and the fact that
they discussed the possible reasons why certain famous intellectual men married ignorant and foolish women. This
meeting is not mentioned in* Texas and the Gulf of Mexico.
*Shortly after this meeting, she says, Clay acted as counsel
for them in a New Orleans lawsuit.*]

One of my greatest sources of amusement, was in observ-
ing how different are the sayings and doings of a people

speaking the same language, and descended from the same parent stock as ourselves. In the stores, you will see people who, should you happen to meet them the next day, will be prepared at once to claim your notice by shaking hands with you. This custom, strange as it at first appears to the inhabitant of aristocratic countries, is very easily accounted for. Let it be remembered that, in this country, no "honest calling" precludes a man from the right of being called a "gentleman." Whilst you are possibly stigmatizing him as "forward" or "impertinent," he is not in the least degree conscious that because your fortune may consist of lands, place or funded property, and his in dry goods, you are, therefore, in any way privileged to consider yourself a greater man than himself.

It struck me, however, that the manners of the Americans were deficient in that real dignity which lies in finding one's right place in society and keeping it. In such a society as exists in America, all stations are ill-defined. Nor can there ever be a standard of good breeding, where so many causes concur to render the grades of society forever fluctuating. Much, therefore, is left to the intuitive tact and natural good sense of each individual, but the peculiar sensitiveness of the Americans renders them perhaps ill-qualified to manage these delicate matters well. This is particularly noted when they are brought in contact with foreigners. The American who, in his own country and towards his own people is courteous and polite—neither vainglorious, nor apt to take offence—becomes in Europe, or amongst Europeans (from this very want of knowing his station) abrupt, rude and offensively boastful. He lives in constant fear of transgressing those rules of etiquette of which he greatly overrates the importance, and, fearful of not being enough considered and aiming at achieving a trivial and unworthy importance, he ceases to be the manly, independent character for which nature and education intended him.

But to return to the impression produced upon us by the apparent familiarity of an American's first approach.

The Englishman, wrapped up in his armour of aristocratic absurdity, need not be alarmed at the advances of the well-meaning Yankee. The latter has his share of pride and that not a trifling one, and he is the last man in the world to force his acquaintance where there is the slightest chance of its being unwelcome. I allow that some things here are startling enough at first, and I confess that I did not quite like hearing my maid called, "the lady that waits upon you." One is also certainly apt to imagine undue familiarities and disrespect, where nothing of the kind is intended. But wait a little. Divest yourself of a few of the prejudices engendered and fostered by our conventional state of society, and we shall soon be less shocked and more willing to give our friends across the water credit for good feeling and good sense, though perhaps not for good taste.

The English are too apt to assert as an undeniable fact that "the Americans are ungentlemanlike," thus arrogating to themselves the right of deciding upon the manners of a whole nation. But let us ask, on what grounds they claim this exclusive censorship? We have, I admit, set up for ourselves a standard of refinement and *savoir faire*, very different from anything we are likely to meet with in the United States. But does it, therefore, follow that we must be right, or that, allowing that our habits are more refined, there are not advantages in their democratic state of society, which more than counterbalance those of which we are so proud?

In aristocratic societies, where all is polished, there is more, much more that is false. The soft, and pleasant veil of refinement, in rendering vice less revolting, greatly increases its growth. And in a society such as ours, where the display of natural feelings is repressed by the cold rules of ceremony and what is called good breeding, great risk is run of their being extinguished altogether. The genuine kindheartedness of the Yankee is not checked by these cold and unnatural laws, and vice with them, being seen in all its naked deformity, unadorned and hideous, is never mistaken for what it is not but is reprobated as it deserves to be.

Originality and absence of affectation are the essential characteristics of American manners. (I speak of the gentleman of the United States, when in his own country.) Whatever is original and natural, carries with it a certain respectability. But directly this is lost, indifferent imitations take its place and the imitative American, like everyone else in similar circumstances, becomes ridiculous. The manners of the Americans in general, however, are not bad, and it can only be alleged against them that they have no artificial manners at all. This, in our estimation, is a grievous fault; and it must be admitted that infinite pleasure is taken by our countrymen in turning into ridicule the peculiarities of a people, of whose real excellencies they are too prejudiced to judge impartially. That the ridicule is returned by the Americans, and with interest, and often with as much legitimate food for its exercise, there is no doubt. The manners and habits of the English, differing so essentially from their own, are not likely to escape with impunity. Whilst the members of our aristocratic community are laughing contemptuously at the want of courtly breeding displayed by the Americans, the latter are still less lenient to our devotion to trivial etiquette, and what they consider our servile adulation of rank and station.

After all, what can be the motives which induce two great nations to be constantly attacking each other in this puerile way? They are on different sides of the wide Atlantic; surely there is room enough in the world for both. The hostile feeling, existing between the countries, is kept alive by the constant attacks of authors, many of whom are ignorant of the nature of really good society. These people cross the Atlantic from the east and west. A clever, but possibly an underbred English writer, makes a tour of the States, sees absolutely nothing of good American society and publishes a book, criticising that of which he or she is totally unqualified to give an opinion. This work is then sent across the Atlantic, as a faithful picture of the habits and national characteristics of a great nation. Upon this, there follows squib after squib from either side. The great features of national character are disregarded, and the points of attack are small personal defects, faults of language and coarseness of behaviour. Animosity is excited in both nations, for who can deny that ridicule is harder to bear than abuse. Neither the English, nor the Americans, find it easy to forgive an affront. The feeling of jealousy and suspicion, once thoroughly aroused, will not be easily allayed. Owing to this inveterate feeling, the English traveller in the States finds the greatest difficulty in arriving at truth; whilst the American in England sees everything through a mental vision distorted by prejudice, jealousy and vindictiveness.

One of the principal charges brought against our friends across the Atlantic is that they are in the habit of boasting, both of themselves and their country, in an indiscriminate and offensive manner. If we were not endowed with a considerable share of pride ourselves, we should not complain so much when we meet with it in others; for what renders the vanity of others so insupportable is that it wounds our own.

The Americans are proud, and justly so, of their self-earned freedom, of the liberal constitution of their country, and of the place in the scale of nations in which their own exertions have placed them. It is unfortunate, however, that they cannot bear their honours meekly, but do injury to their own and their country's cause, by their habits of exaggeration and self-praise. There is a want of quiet and genuine dignity about the American's sense of freedom and equality. If he feels that the advantages he thus enjoys are great, let him value them in silence and let their fruits be seen. The American, however, would not be half so boastful, did they feel that they were correctly judged and rightly appreciated by us. That they will be so in time, I have little doubt, but time must elapse before either party will be softened. It is a good genuine brotherly hatred, the strongest of any when it once takes root because, in fraternal feuds, jealousy has always more or less a share.

But it is not only in their personal habits that the Americans find themselves exposed to attack and criticism. A strong feeling against their good faith and trustworthiness certainly exists, both as regards their public and private relations. In this respect, I can make but few remarks, and those certainly cannot be in their justification. Amongst themselves, it is well known that there hardly exists a man who, for the sake of realizing a profit, however small, will scruple to employ any means in his power to overreach his neighbour. This being known and acknowledged, it excites among them neither fear nor indignation. The struggle between these acute calculators becomes neither more nor less than a keen encounter of their wits, in which honour and high feeling have no share.

It is true that both parties, (where the means employed are no secret) start upon equal terms. But such freedom of action (to speak of it in the mildest terms) must, to a certain degree, blunt the susceptibilities, and cause an absence of gentlemanly and honourable feeling in their money concerns, both public and private. Notwithstanding all this, I believe that such better feelings do exist. I am convinced that in proportion as an American will exert all his energies to shave his adversary on change, so he will be true as steel to the friend whom he has once admitted to his confidence.

The only apparent aristocracy in the United States is that of wealth, and heaven knows the idol is in no want of worshippers. It has, however, been impossible for even this democratic and money-making people to root out of their English natures their respect for rank and their zeal for personal aggrandizement. They have a way of talking about titles and hereditary distinctions, from royalty to the last made peer, which is meant to mark their contempt for such aristocratic follies. It is done, too, with a bravado, which is often intended to shock the prejudices of their English auditors. The very frequency with which they visit these topics, however, sufficiently marks the degree of importance which they attach to them. I saw instances of this without end and even heard of an American gentleman who, being confined to his bed during a long illness, seriously amused himself with reading the Peerage from

beginning to end! In short, I should say that no people
bend the knee lower at the shrine of hereditary rank than
the Americans. I verily believe, that if Queen Victoria were
to take an excursion across the Atlantic (a circumstance
which, in these days of locomotive Sovereigns, seems not
quite impossible) her Majesty might travel from New York
to "Virginny," with true-hearted Yankees harnessed to her
travelling carriage. I do not know, however, if I could venture to affirm as much, if royalty were to pay them a visit
under any other form than that of youth and beauty.

I think it is De Tocqueville who remarks on the fondness
of the Americans generally for tracing back their origin to
the first colonists of the country. Certainly, with all their
jealousy of the Mother Country, they are exceedingly
proud of their Anglo-Saxon origin. I have also noticed,
that notwithstanding the very equality of which the Yankee
so frequently boasts, as marking the superiority of his own
nation over that of every other people, he is most anxious
to disclaim the existence of the same in his own person. By
some means or other, he is always attempting to prove that
he is a splendid exception to the general rule, and that he
is a great man on his own account—a very triton among
the minnows.

Another petty cause of still more trivial quarrels is a habit
to which the Americans are remarkably addicted, namely,
that of drawing incessant comparisons between the two
countries. If the institutions, the habits or even the public
characters of Great Britain are under discussion, an American immediately sets to work to find some parallel in his
own country, the merits of which he hopes will throw those
of the opposite party into the shade. Violent and provoking
language is often the result of this injudicious conduct; and
unfortunately, even in private society and in the presence
of ladies, Americans are too apt to lead the conversation
to these unsafe and disagreeable subjects. As an instance
of this, an American gentleman one evening said to me,
speaking of the apartment in which we were sitting. "I expect now, you've not such lofty rooms as these, Ma'am, in

the Old Country?" And then again, "Why now, don't you diet in public at the hotel? You mightn't do it in England, but here we never do insult our females."

It is difficult, in offering an opinion on the American people, to avoid giving offence to one side or the other. Few travellers in the United States will venture to be sincere in their remarks. The English are not satisfied if the dish of American abuse served up to them is insufficient to satisfy the cravings of their appetite, whilst the Yankees are equally indignant if they are spoken of in any other terms than as the "greatest nation on the face of God's airth." Of their public debts I have said enough, and will only add that they cannot expect to be popular in England, so long as thousands are losers by their dishonesty. On the other hand both parties should remember that they are descended from the same parent stock, and this ought to be a motive, as soon as possible, for burying their grievances in oblivion.

The national character of the Americans is the same as our own, but modified by a widely different form of government and habits exclusively commercial. That these habits are among those that "tame great nations," there is no question. I fear it is equally true, that when "men change swords for ledgers," "ennobling thoughts depart." In some respects, they may be better than those who live in the land of their fathers, and in others worse. Let us therefore, hope for peace between them.

For my own part, I confess that after a short residence, I entertained towards the inhabitants of this fine specimen of an American city very different feelings from those with which I entered it. It is true, indeed, that my experience of their character and my time for observation were both limited. Still, during the season of our residence, thousands met at New Orleans from all parts of the American Union. This is always the case during the winter and business months. I was informed, that perhaps nowhere could so good an opportunity be found for strangers to see a considerable variety of character and incident. The Americans are, I should say, hospitable, warm-hearted and generous, and inclined to be so most particularly to the English who visit their city.

As for the middle and lower classes (for, notwithstanding their boasted equality, such distinctions do and must exist), I should pronounce them to be far superior, in education, conduct and address, to the corresponding class in our own country. The knowledge which each man possesses that he may, by good conduct and superior attainments, raise himself to the highest consideration enjoyed among his countrymen, must, in almost all cases, have the effect of stimulating the mind to good and useful endeavours, and preventing the increase of disorderly, idle, and useless members of the community.

Our intention, in returning to New Orleans, had been to ascend the Mississippi to a considerable distance and thus to see as much as we could in a short time of this wonderful river, and the great and rising cities on its banks. Our purpose was defeated by unsatisfactory accounts of the state of the country. The snows and ice had not sufficiently melted to render travelling agreeable. I was extremely disappointed at finding that my plan for making a northern tour could not be carried into execution. It is, however, only postponed, and I hope at some future time to extend my knowledge of America beyond its present narrow limits. I have said that in Louisiana the nature of the people is kind and liberal—what it may be in the Northern States, where the climate and other causes may contribute to chill the feelings and deaden the quick impulses, I have yet to learn.

I can hardly imagine a more pleasurable excursion than that of ascending or descending the Mississippi in one of the great river steamers. I went on board one of the largest, the *Missouri*, before we left and was really astonished at the comfort of the interior. There is so much room for everyone and such space for walking exercise, that confinement in her would, I think, be no punishment, even for a considerable time. And then there would be the constant variety of scenery, the change of place—all delightful. But the time has come when we must take our leave. I see the little fleet that forms the Texan navy busy in making preparations for a warlike cruise, and I hear our men singing and joking, in their delight at the prospect of a change. The order is given to weigh anchor and we float down the stream once more. As we approached the mouth of the southwest pass, we perceived two large cotton vessels bound for Liverpool and drawing about sixteen feet of water, sticking fast in the mud. We were told that they had been in the same situation three weeks, and that it was not unusual for vessels to remain there double that time. They looked very forlorn and uncomfortable.

Chapter XVIII

SECOND ARRIVAL AT GALVESTON ⚓ TEXAN NEWS
⚓ THE TRINITY RIVER ⚓ GALVESTON HARBOUR
⚓ FALSE ACCOUNTS OF CRIME IN TEXAS

After a short and prosperous voyage, we were again at anchor in Galveston harbour. Immediately after our arrival, we received the cordial greetings of our kind friends, and were congratulated on having a third time braved the dangers of the bar in safety. Our first inquiry was, of course, for news, and we were in hope of hearing the reply so commonly made in Europe, "Nothing at all going on—all as flat as possible."

Just at present, in this struggling country, every hour brings with it its event, and not a day passes without being marked by some endeavour (often a successful one) of these energetic settlers to raise their country into strength and prosperity. The most important among the events which were in progress was the advance of a body of Mexicans. They were said to be approaching the town of Bexar, but not in any considerable force. The Texans did not seem in the least afraid of them; indeed, I rather thought our friends would not object to having another brush with the enemy. [*EDITOR'S NOTE: The January 25, 1843 number of the* Telegraph and Texas Register *noted that a springtime attack by the Mexicans was almost certain, according to some members of Congress. The editor of that publication opined that it most likely would not happen owing to Santa Anna's want of troops. But Mrs. Houstoun's opinion that the Texians might like another swipe at the Mexicans was likely the popular opinion of the time, on the heels of the Santa Fe, Somervell and Mier Expeditions and the 1842 invasions of San Antonio. Folks back home were hopping mad and wanted to spring the Texian prisoners held at Perote.*]

The President was still up the country at Washington, and it had been announced that the lady of the General (the "Presidentess," or whatever her title may be), had given birth to a son. May he one day fill the office and enjoy the honours now so worthily borne by his sire. [*EDITOR'S NOTE: Sam Houston's first son, Sam Jr., was not born until the month the author returned to England—May 1843.*]

Another circumstance which had lately occurred had caused great satisfaction. A steamer, by name the *Ellen Frankland,* had returned in safety to the harbour after having made a successful voyage up the Trinity River, to a distance of between four and five hundred miles from its mouth. This was the first occasion of such an undertaking having succeeded, and it forms almost an era in the commercial history of the country. The voyage must have been a peculiarly interesting one, and Mr. Houstoun had decided to take a passage on board, when the *Ellen Frankland* went her next trip. Our stay, however, was not long enough for us to take advantage of such an excellent opportunity for seeing the country. When this interesting and adventurous little vessel tried her fate again, we were daring the dangers of the deep on our way back to Old England.

Captain Frankland, the owner of the steamer, assured us that the navigation was perfectly practicable, even to a point within a distance of sixty or seventy miles of the Red River. This part of the country had been lately granted to a joint company of English and American speculators, who had already introduced a great number of settlers. I have heard, also, that an English company have lately undertaken a speculation, which appears likely to prove not only a source of considerable profit to themselves, but also to be in its results extremely advantageous to the interests of the country generally. The intention is to run iron steamers, with a very light draught, up and down the Trinity; the steamers having flat-bottomed rafts attached to them. The successful result of Captain Frankland's expedition has proved that there do not exist in the Trinity River any great or insurmountable impediments to navigation. This cannot be said of the generality of the rivers in Texas, which are shallow and full of snags and hindrances of all kinds. As regards its position with reference to the United States, the navigable capabilities of the Trinity must prove of immense and incalculable benefit to the city of Galveston, in a commercial point of view, and the citizens are already anticipating the numerous advantages they are likely to derive from the discovery of this invaluable water-privilege. It is now ascertained that a canal, connecting the Trinity with the Red River, would not be by any means an expensive undertaking, the distance being about sixty miles and the country perfectly level. There can be no doubt that all the vast quantity of cotton, and other produce grown on the Red lands, would then be transmitted direct, by means of the canal and the Trinity River, to the town of Galveston, instead of being put on board steamers in the Red River, and being sent by a long, dangerous and most circuitous route to New Orleans.

The Americans attach such importance to this Red River trade that the United States Congress has repeatedly voted immense sums to clear away the wood drifts which are constantly accumulating. These drifts put a stop to navigation for months at a time. I fancy that the citizens of the republic enjoy not a little the idea of overreaching and circumventing the Americans. They are perfectly aware that, should this mode of transit be established, a grand field will be opened to them for all sorts of smuggling transactions. Unlawful goods will no doubt be introduced into the United States in sufficient quantities to supply the whole western country, and American produce will doubtless be exported from Galveston by the Texans, greatly to the dissatisfaction of their *ci-devant* countrymen at New Orleans.

In considering the state of commerce here, there is one truth plainly evident: that the Texans will soon monopolize the whole of the Mexican trade. This has hitherto been conducted by trading parties from the United States who, after traversing the entire extent of the Great Western Prairies as far as the Rocky Mountains, meet, and transact their negotiations with the Mexican traders at Santa Fe. When it is considered that Santa Fe is only distant from

Galveston five hundred miles, one may form some idea
of the commercial advantages the Texans would possess
over the Americans. The latter have, for years, found it
worth their while to pay the enormous duties charged for
the admission of English cotton goods into America. The
merchandise has then been transported from Philadelphia
or New York, upwards of four thousand miles to Santa Fe,
and a great part of this distance on the backs of beasts of
burden. What a price the poor Mexicans must have paid
for their purchases, to allow these enterprising traders a
profit, and one good enough to satisfy a Yankee calculator.

It might naturally have been expected that these signs of
the present, and visions of the future, would have aroused
the government to take some measures in order to render the entrance of the harbour less dangerous. Nothing,
however, has been done. As long as the men in office and
authority perceive no actual good resulting to themselves
individually from the furtherance of any public work, they
will not endeavour to forward it. They are not sufficiently
disinterested to expend the public money upon the public
alone.

The harbour of Galveston, if properly buoyed, would be
by no means a bad one. The entrance is perfectly safe for
vessels drawing ten feet of water, and there are times when
ships drawing twelve and even fourteen feet, may venture
in. It is, without any question, the best harbour in the Gulf
of Mexico, and there is no doubt that no other port than
that of Galveston will ever be of any commercial importance
in Texas. In the present state however, of this neglected
harbour, no company either in England or America, will
insure vessels bound for the port of Galveston.

We had determined not to put implicit faith in the numerous surveys and charts of the different harbours lower
down the Gulf, and had resolved, if possible, to see and
judge for ourselves. The intention was to send the government pilot, a clever navigator, in his little schooner down
to Matagorda and Aransas. After ascertaining the depth of
water on the several bars, we should then know where we

might venture to take the yacht, and Mr. Houstoun would possibly have an opportunity of enjoying some buffalo-hunting, which he was very anxious to do.

The *chasse* in Western Texas is far superior to any that can be hoped for here. Considerable herds of buffalo and wild horses still exist there, and deer in great numbers. The country also, near the sea in Western Texas, is described as being elevated. Instead of being, like other parts of the country, low and almost under water, the undulating hills approach in the vicinity of Aransas almost to the sea-beach.

A great deal has been said about the vast extent of crime in the Republic of Texas. If we are to believe many of the writers of the day, murderers are to be met at every town, life is not safe for a moment, and private property is never respected. The whole of the population are described as dishonest and bloodthirsty, the very refuse of the vile. There is said to be no law, and that public justice is unknown. That these accusations are almost entirely false I have no hesitation in asserting. Indeed, even by a mere glance at the general character of the people, one must feel that they are undeserved.

Let us ask, is an irresistible longing for freedom the characteristic of a mind degraded by crime? Do felons, thieves, and assassins fight for their country as the Texans have done? I should say, certainly not. The refutation of the charge becomes still more clear and positive when we recollect that it was not for pay that they fought, but that they were actuated by one spontaneous impulse of patriotism, and the love of honest independence. "Sound, healthy children of the God of Heaven," they could not submit to the degrading yoke of the Mexican.

But there is another circumstance which tends to give the lie to these accusations, and to establish the fact that the Texans are at least not worse than their neighbours: the fact of the almost non-existence of courts of law in this country. This is nearly the only one in the long list of accusations brought against the colonists in Texas in which there is truth. The rarity of the criminal acts (which

I maintain there is in this country) is rendered still more remarkable by this circumstance. Lynch law is the only description of retributive justice to be looked for here. And if we compare the annals of crime in other countries (where men are restrained by the strong arm of the law) with the list of offences committed here, we could easily prove that the primitive proceedings of the Texans are not productive of murders, thefts, and immoralities. In a country where there is no police and no executive authority, it is something to say—and it may be said with truth—that theft is almost unknown. Should such a misdemeanour be committed, summary justice would be administered by the unanimous voice of the people.

As to the charge so often brought against them of shooting and stabbing, I aver, that were any other people possessed of the same power of killing their adversaries with impunity, they would much more frequently avail themselves of the privilege. The Texans, almost without exception, carry their national weapon, the Bowie knife, about them and this alone, one would imagine, would lead to a frequency of assassinations. It is proved, even among our own people, that the use of the knife, when found conveniently at hand, can hardly be resisted in moments of passionate anger, and this in a country where punishment is sure to follow. The Texan, to a certain degree, is allowed to take the law into his own hands. But should it afterwards be pronounced by the unprejudiced voices of the people that either the punishment of his enemy was undeserved, or not warranted by the first duty of self-preservation, he becomes himself amenable to punishment by means of lynch law. That this state of things cannot continue long, I am well aware, nor can it be doubted that the increase of population, the introduction of luxuries, and innumerable other causes, will soon alter entirely the face of society. At present, however, the Texan people go on remarkably well, with their primitive system of administering justice.

During the months we remained in Galveston harbour, there was no single instance of malicious crime—no street fights—no apparent drunkenness or tumult. It is true that on New Year's day, one man was shot, and doubtless this fact would, to those ignorant of the details, furnish a strong argument in favour of the popular opinion of the prevalence of crime in Texas. The circumstances were as follows: Some children were quarrelling in the street. From words they came to blows, when their respective parents, who had been drinking together, thought proper to interfere. "I say, sir, you call your children away, sir." This gentle remonstrance not being duly attended to, the speaker went forthwith for his rifle, and was in the act of presenting it at the head of his foe (probably only as a means of intimidation) when he received his deathwound from the other's pistol. No notice whatever was taken of this misdemeanour.

Two well-known German noblemen, sent out by their government to report on the condition of Texas and its supposed advantages as a field for emigration, were travelling through the country at the same time as ourselves. They have given it as their opinion that, considering the state of the laws, no country was ever so free from crime as this. The case of manslaughter I have related was perpetrated on a day of public rejoicing and misrule. The parties had been drinking at one of the numerous bars, their passions were excited, and the whole affair was the work of a moment. It is due the survivor to add that the children of the deceased were received and provided for by him in the most liberal manner he could afford.

I have asserted that the Texans are willing (beyond most other people) to assist each other. At the same time I wish not to affirm that the person who confers the benefit will not expect a *quid pro quo* in some shape or other. In a society such as this, where "taking your neighbour in" is called smartness, and inveigling him out of some portion of his lawful property goes by the gentle name of "shaving" him, one must not expect to meet with much delicacy in the arrangement of accounts between man and man. As a proof, however, of the rarity of theft, even houses containing valuable property are left untenanted and unsecured, and this without any fear of their being entered by a marauder.

As Galveston increases in size and importance, there will doubtless be more law, more justice, and more crime. At present, in this small community, the eyes of each man are on his neighbour. They unite for their common security, and the rowdy fellow is held in check by the consciousness that, should he offend and shock the prejudices of society, tarring and feathering would be his reward.

I never heard of Texan heads being submitted to the examination of a professor of phrenology, but I should imagine that the bump of invention would be found largely developed. A man will inform you, with the gravest face in the world, that he has seen in the prairie a buffalo weighing two thousand stone! And another, that he has met a Camanchee coming home from market to his wife, with the legs and arms of human beings slung over his shoulders, to dress for supper!

When two Texan gentlemen are engaged in a dispute, however violent may be the discussion, the courtesy of the "sir" is never omitted. On the contrary it is repeated at every third word, and mixed up as it is with the oaths and denunciations with which they always interlard their discourse, the effect is curious enough. They always end their anecdotes with "and that's a fact, sir, by God," pronounced with great energy. The manner it would be in vain to describe, but the more unfathomable the falsehood, the greater is the energy they employ in the utterance of these expressive words. "Seeing the giraffe ahead" is one of their singular but every day expressions. An acute Kentucky man giving an account one day to Mr. Houstoun of a speculation in which he had been engaged, and speaking (of course with the universal nasal twang) of a smart Yankee who was plotting against him, and whose designs he had detected, wound up with "I stopt there sir—I went no further. I saw the giraffe ahead." The origin of this quaint expression I was not able to discover, but they understand one another so perfectly, their crooked ways and their turnings and windings, that it is really amusing to watch the progress of a game played between two able combatants. I have often thought, however, that they are apt to overreach themselves by too much cunning.

Every thought and every idea here resolves itself into money. In their getting up and lying down, in their eating, drinking and sleeping moments, in the home of their wives and children, and in the barroom of the drinking houses— dollars, and how to obtain them, seems their one sole and engrossing thought. Whether or not they are attached to their kindred, I cannot say, but certainly, to judge from the very little time they seem to spend "in the bosom of their families," domestic life can have but slight charms for them. The Texan ladies generally, I fancy, lead rather secluded and quiet lives, and are reserved and silent.

The society of Galveston invited us to a ball at the Tremont House, and I greatly regretted not being able to accept the civility, but the weather was extremely cold, and the return to the yacht at night neither safe nor pleasant for a lady. Were I asked what is the national religion of the Texan people, I should answer none. It is true the places of public worship are more than sufficient, and that everyone attends the service on Sunday, and that the religious observance of the Sabbath is not more neglected than it is in Catholic countries in Europe. On the other hand, the feeling of devotion and the respectful upholding of religion is apparently absent. I may wrong them, and I trust I do, but I judge from their conversation, from the education of their children and not a little from their constant habit of profane swearing. This renders the society of Americans, generally, extremely painful to those who are accustomed to treat the sacred name of the Deity with awe and respect. It is very distressing to hear little children practising their first powers of utterance in mocking their Creator, and older boys, of almost every class, vying with each other in taking his name in vain.

CHAPTER XIX

SUFFERINGS OF EMIGRANTS ⚓ CLIMATE ⚓ PRODUCTS OF TEXAS

I was sorry to hear from Monsieur de Cramayel that the French emigrants who arrived at Galveston during our former visit, were not, as we had supposed, sent out by the French government, but by one of their speculating countrymen, and that they had already suffered considerably, from various unanticipated causes. In transporting so large a body of emigrants through the country, arrangements ought to have been made for their support, and to defray the necessary expenses of the journey. [*EDITOR'S NOTE: The French arriving at Galveston were among the first to arrive in Texas under empresario Henri Castro's, bound for Castroville. Monsieur de Cramayel and Castro were anything but friendly with one another. The Monsieur frequently attempted to "blow the whistle" on what he believed to be Castro's fraudulent endeavors and wished to prevent further French colonization in Texas.*]

I confess I cannot but regret that some thousands of our starving population cannot be conveyed to this country. The colonization of New South Wales and New Zealand is doubtless advantageous to Great Britain, and certain speculative companies may derive benefit from it; but it may be questioned if the same good fortune generally attends the poor colonists. In the latter colony (New Zealand,) we have lately had sad proof that the hardships and sufferings of the settlers are not of a trivial nature. The difficulties with which these people have to contend are not merely confined to the severe labour of hewing down the giant trees of the forest, and to the slow and wearying process of clearing land, which is obtained from the New Zealand Company at thirty shillings per acre. The circumstance to which I allude, is the melancholy fate of Captain Wakefield and his companions, who were not long ago destroyed by the aborigines of the country.

It cannot be denied, that as a field for settlers, Texas has considerable advantages over almost every other country. Its climate, except the lowlands, is excellent, and the settler has to encounter neither the extreme cold of the winter season, nor the scorching summer heat of the more Northern States of America and Canada. In the latter countries, also, the settler labours under the immense disadvantage of having to clear his land of the primeval woods before he can hope to establish anything like a farm. This is labour which he is spared in Texas, where the vast and productive prairies need but little improvement at the hands of the agriculturist. As compared with New South Wales and New Zealand, Texas has neither the poor soil and drowths of the former, nor the high-priced and thickly-wooded lands of the latter. Lastly, Texas is within a month's or, at the outside, six weeks' journey of England. By passing through the United States, it may even be accomplished in twenty-four days, without difficulty. This of itself is by no means a despicable advantage.

I believe that the accounts generally given of the productiveness of the soil in Texas are not exaggerated. The climate in the rolling country, at a distance of seventy or eighty miles from the sea, is no doubt extremely healthy, perhaps as much so as any in the world. It is also comparatively free from mosquitoes and reptiles. The lowlands, however, between the rolling country and the sea, are, from all we could learn, scarcely habitable for Europeans. We saw a few Germans, who had been settled on the banks of the Brazos in the low country for five years, but they had repeatedly suffered from fevers, though they were now to a certain extent acclimatized. A more miserable looking set of objects I never beheld.

Another evil, and one scarcely less to be dreaded than the fever, consists in the myriads of mosquitoes, which are so venomous and troublesome as to render existence hardly endurable. We were only in Texas in the winter season and had, therefore, happily no opportunity of judging with our own persons the extent of the nuisance. There can be no doubt that this low country, whose soil, however, is un-equalled in richness, can only be inhabited by people from the Southern States of America—Louisiana, Mississippi, etc. The inhabitants of those provinces are accustomed to even more unhealthy situations than the Texan lowlands, and without the benefit of the constant fresh sea breeze, or trade wind (as it may almost be called) which blows over the latter. It has, I believe, been asserted, that the productions of this part of Texas can be brought forth by slave or black labour alone. This, however, may be disputed.

I shall now endeavour to give some account of the products of the country, which are, I should say, acquired by less labour than is perhaps necessary in any other part of the globe. This arises from the circumstance of the prairie being already half cultivated by nature. It is, generally speaking, perfectly level, and no trees or shrubs interfere with the course of the plough or the spade of the agriculturist. The soil is of great depth, and not a stone or even pebble can be discovered on turning up the earth. In the low country, cotton, sugar and tobacco will be the great staples and, it is said, their quality is equal to the best that can be produced in any other climate. In the rolling district, cotton, indigo, rice, wheat, rye, barley, oats, and all the common vegetables of our own country, grow with wonderful luxuriance.

Wheat, it is supposed, will come to greater perfection in the more hilly and less fertile district further to the north. Here, also, the apple and pear trees would doubtless thrive and produce abundantly. The climate of the southern portion of Texas is said to be too warm to permit the inhabitants to enjoy these fruits in perfection. Indigo, and that of a very fine quality, is found growing wild in various parts of the country. Grapes, peaches and plums seem indigenous, and are found growing wild in the woods. There can be no doubt, indeed, that the soil and climate are calculated to produce most of our English fruits in the greatest abundance and, in addition to them, many of those found in more southern climes.

The prairie lands everywhere afford the very finest pasture, and cannot be surpassed for grazing purposes. So
luxuriant is the growth of every kind of herbage that,
throughout the year, cattle grazing in the open country,
are generally found in excellent condition. All the care that
is required in rearing stock, is easily obtained by employing
a Mexican or two as herdsmen, an occupation for which
they are admirably fitted, and which they are said to fulfill
with fidelity.

Whilst we were in Texas, the price of an ox, or of a cow
and calf, was five dollars, about a pound sterling—the
dollar being valued at from forty-eight to fifty-two pence.
Horses and mules could be bought at from thirty to fifty
dollars. Whilst we were at Houston, a hundred pigs were
sold at a halfpenny per pound weight. The mildness of the
climate, and the fact of its not being subject to the extremes
of heat and cold, is very favourable to the increase of stock,
poultry, etc. One of the most experienced and sagacious
men in the country was of the opinion that no speculation
would do so well in Texas as the breeding of sheep; not
only on account of the increasing demand for wool in the
United States, but also to supply the wants of the settlers.

And now having detailed many of the temptations offered
to European emigrants, I feel bound to mention what seem
to be the disadvantages attending the settling in Texas. The
first and most apparent of them is the difficulty of purchasing land with a good title. It was the opinion of some of the
cleverest lawyers in Texas that the titles to three-fourths of
the "located" lands in Texas were of a doubtful character—
not perhaps absolutely invalid, but admitting of a lawsuit.
I dare say the attorneys themselves are generally too glad
to undertake any case for a chance of a share in the spoil
which, here, as in more civilized countries, is by no means
inconsiderable.

Wood, in many parts of the country, is very abundant but
I suspect that as population increases, there will be found
very frequently a want of this essential. Supposing the settler has acquired his land in a healthy and desirable location

and has made all his arrangements necessary for farming, etc., he will constantly be required, in his intercourse with his neighbours, (if, as is most probable, they happen to be Yankees) to practise a degree of ingenuity and cunning in trading transactions, of which, few of our countrymen can boast. I heard, that owing to this deficiency in the art of "shaving," nine times out of ten when an English settler had done business with a Yankee, the substance of the confiding John Bull had gradually diminished, until his whole means had found their way into the possession of his more experienced, but less scrupulous, neighbour.

Many tempted by the extremely low price of land have been induced too choose "locations" far removed from the protection of civilized beings. And not a few, in all probability, have built their houses as near the river as possible. Here, after a time, if the settler escapes the fever and ague, he most likely finds himself unable to endure the utter loneliness and solitude of his position, together with the hardships and deprivations necessarily attendant upon such a residence in the wilderness. His house is abandoned, and either falls into decay, or is destroyed by the bands of roving Indians, who are not very scrupulous in regard to any flocks or herds they may chance to find unprotected.

But it may be asked, how are these evils to be provided against? I should say, easily enough. In the first place, settlers should be gregarious. Companionship lightens toil, and promotes a spirit of emulation. And it is the more necessary for our countrymen in particular, that they should settle in herds, because they generally have a defect in their character which stands in the way of their success as settlers. This defect is peculiar to our middle and lower classes, and is not found among the Americans. The fault of which I speak is the difficulty they find in adapting themselves to occupations to which they have been unaccustomed. The ploughman is a ploughman only; he cannot use the axe, make a fence, or perform the commonest carpenter's work. The carpenter, on the other hand, would be sadly puzzled to use the plough or spade. And so, in like manner, with all. The American settler can generally turn his hand to anything, and no kind of work comes amiss to him. I believe this may also be said of him, that although he is always on the lookout for a good thing and would do his utmost to overreach his neighbour in what he considers fair trade, he will generally be found kindhearted, good-natured, and willing both to assist and lend, if required. This I fancy is generally the case among early settlers, in a young country like this. I could find many more arguments to prove that English emigrants should only go to Texas in bodies, and then not without someone capable of directing them; but that I think the fact must be self-evident.

Chapter XX

Patience & Perseverance of Settlers
⚓ Story of a Young Emigrant

No settler in a new country should enter upon his vocation without having on hand an immense stock of perseverance. Patience, under sickness and distress, is also another invaluable quality, the exercise of which will be often called for in the life of an emigrant. Let no one expect that his bed in the wilderness will be one of roses. The charms of this wild life will, on the contrary, often be varied by disruptions and hardships of every description. I was much interested by an account I heard of a young emigrant, whose story afforded proof of the truth of my remarks.

This settler was a young Scotchman, who, having saved a few hundred pounds, and seeing no "opening" in his own country, decided upon trying his fortune in the plains and prairies of Texas. His knowledge consisted of some practical information on agricultural subjects and on the price of livestock, in England—in short, of farming details which apply exclusively to practice in the "Old Country."

Jamie McLeod, for so I will call him, had married a pretty Irish girl, Nora, of tolerable connections and good education. She possessed, withal, a light heart and a happy temper—no trifling characteristics for domestic life in the wilderness. Land, as I have elsewhere observed, is temptingly cheap far up the country, so the Scotchman easily made a purchase of a considerable tract. He and his young wife, with a little helpless child, travelled by slow degrees, but cheerfully and full of hope, towards the rolling country above Washington.

They had not been long in their new abode when they discovered that the location was ill-chosen. They had built their log house in a hollow instead of on rising ground, which is everywhere at something less than a mile distant from the river. It was therefore damp and unwholesome. In short, the McLeods, like many other settlers, had rashly followed their own ideas and neglected to ask the advice of experienced dwellers in the country.

The consequences of this imprudence soon made themselves apparent, and in a short time McLeod was stretched upon his bed in a low and lingering fever. Nora's helpfulness was now of essential service. Strong in body, with hardy peasant nerves and a genuine Irish spirit of good humour and trustingness, she nursed her sick husband, milked the cows, minded the house and took care of the baby. Fortunately, in this rich soil and land of prolific produce, the means of existence were easily procured, at least for a season. Nora's stock of poultry was not easily exhausted, for the domestic fowls breed and rear their young much more frequently than in most other countries. Of the pigs and other animals, the same may be safely averred. Thus Nora and her little family continued to live on.

But McLeod's was not a temporary malady. Week after week sped by, and still he lay there, a useless, powerless man. The nature of his complaint affected his spirits and he seemed fast sinking into a state of helpless despondency. In vain did Nora, with her bright face and cheerful voice, slightly indicative of her Hibernian origin, endeavour to console him. When the sick man indulged in sad prophecies of the poverty which he insisted would ere long come upon them, Nora would gaily repeat to him the Irish proverb, "Cheer up, my darling, there's a silver lining to every cloud." But they could not live upon smiles and cheering words; and proverbs, however true, are as unprofitable as they are stale.

By degrees their livestock diminished. Some strayed, others were shot by some wandering riflemen, a few fell sick, and a tribe of Indians, who were encamped near, did not scruple to lay their hands upon such as came within their reach. Happily for Nora, these Indians belonged to a friendly tribe, otherwise her fear of them would have been still greater than it was. She could not accustom herself to their wild and savage appearance, and the dread seemed mutual, for the Indians seldom approached the abode of the white man.

McLeod had sunk a considerable portion of his little fortune in the purchase of land, stock, etc, trusting to his own industry and exertions for the future support of his family. After a time, then, the destitution which the sick imagination of the poor Scotchman had so long anticipated stared them in the face. The wife, notwithstanding her hopeful spirit, began to despond, and her husband's health grew daily worse. The feeling of sadness and gloom was a new and unaccustomed one to Nora. So new was it, that at first the unwelcome tenant could find no abiding place in her heart. She was determined, however, to hope, though she saw her husband's face grow paler and thinner day by day. She would obstinately look forward to better times, though their supply even of daily food was fast dwindling away, and though she saw no present means of relief from their distresses. Nora ceased not to exert herself for the support of those she loved. Night and day she toiled; the garden was dug, and, in anticipation of future wants, was sown and planted by her hand.

Neighbours she had none; she was alone in her troubles— not a friend to assist or to advise. Notwithstanding all this, Nora still talked hopefully, still boasted of the "silver lining" which was to shine out of the dark cloud that hovered over their destinies. But her heart was heavy within her, and her bright eyes were often dimmed with tears.

It was winter and heavy rains had deluged the country. The log house of the McLeods was surrounded by mud and wet grass. One cold bleak morning, Nora opened her door and gazed for a moment abroad. The gloomy prospect struck a chill into her heart. A keen northerly wind was blowing fierce and strong. It came howling through the trees, and scattering the fallen leaves into her face. Nora had not been in bed during the previous night. Alarm for her husband, and the care which his illness momentarily required, had afforded ample employment both for mind and body. Suddenly she heard his voice calling her name.

It appeared to her that he spoke in a stronger tone, and she hastened to his bedside full of hope. Alas, her hope was in vain. She saw his eye lighted up by delirious fever and, to her terror, perceived that reason had deserted its throne!

With the strength lent by the fierce fever that raged within his veins, he raised himself from his bed, and was with difficulty restrained from rushing towards the door. His actions were violent and he heaped bitter imprecations upon her, and upon his child. At this moment a horrifying sound struck upon the mother's ear. There was a sudden shriek, and then the fearful shouts of fifty savage voices burst loudly and suddenly forth, startling the echoes for miles around. And well did Nora recognise the feeble cry she heard. It was the voice of her little boy who had been playing in the garden, in unconscious glee. Quicker than thought, she sprang to the door, and gazed distractedly on the scene before her. Her darling was in the hands of the Indians, of Indians, too, who were totally unfamiliar to her.

In a moment she guessed the truth—that the dreaded Camanchees were upon them! In vain she struggled to free him; in vain did the child hold up his little hands, and implore help from her, who never yet had been deaf to his prayers. Amidst the stunning sounds of the terrible war-whoop, the petted child was held up before his mother's eyes, and while she was forcibly held back, the scalping-knife did its revolting work! The bright sunny curls were hung at the belt of the savage who performed the deed, while the boy was flung palpitating, and barely possessed of life at the feet of his parent.

It was now Nora's turn to suffer, and another of these relentless savages speedily seized hold of his now unresisting victim. Another moment would have decided her fate, when the arm of her enemy was arrested by the appearance of a new actor on the scene—a gaunt form, who, (without any previous warning) approached the group, and attracted the attention of all. It was McLeod, whose wild ravings could not be restrained. Deliriously unconsciousness of his danger, he stalked in amongst them. His wild actions and strange gestures sufficiently attested to the wandering of his mind, and the Indians stood appalled. Tall warriors in their fierce war-paint bent their heads reverently before him. Impressed with the notion of his being inspired, and acting under the especial protection of the Great Spirit, these untamed and revengeful children of the forest shrank awestruck from his presence.

Slowly and in silence they retreated, and ere another minute had elapsed, Nora was left alone with the husband who had so unconsciously saved her. On the ground, on the very spot where he had so lately played in childish glee, lay the bleeding body of the dying child. Who can describe the feelings of the mother, as lifting him in her arms, she tried to hope that the outrage he had undergone would not prove a mortal injury. Cases *have* been known of recovery after scalping. I myself saw a young man at Galveston who did not appear at all worse for the operation.

Gently and tenderly Nora laid her child on his little bed, and then, only then did she return to her painful task of soothing and quieting the invalid. With gentle words she persuaded him to return to his bed, but even then she could not leave him for a moment. At intervals she heard the faint and feeble moan of her suffering child, but though the mother's heart was torn within her, she could not desert her post. Towards the evening the sick man became more composed, his ravings suddenly ceased, his eyes closed, and a deathlike calm spread over his features. Nora listened, but in vain for his breathing; she felt that he was dead, and that she was alone. She did not weep, however, but sat in a state of stupid insensibility. She was roused from this trance of despair by a sound, small and low, but a sound which once heard, can never be forgotten—the last sound of parting breath! It was small and low, for it was the breath of a little child—the signal that its pure and innocent spirit was about to meet its God! In a moment Nora was by its side, on her knees, imploring with wild eagerness for its young life, and covering its little hands and face with kisses. The struggle was brief, and when the mother saw that it was dead she fell senseless.

She recovered, she knew not how, and it seemed as though a fearful dream had passed over her. Oh that sad and terrible awakening after affliction! The doubt—the fear of the reality—and then the gradual, and overwhelming belief in the worst! Poor Nora felt all this, as gradually she roused herself into sense and life. It was all true—her child, her first, her only one was taken from her. She could not weep, hers was a hard tearless grief. Suddenly, however, the thought of her husband crossed her mind, and a dim recollection of his last sad moments caused her to shudder as though body and soul were parting asunder.

Mechanically she rose, and approaching his bed, leant over what she imagined was but the senseless clay of him she loved. Her head rested on his breast, when she thought—could it be fancy?—that it throbbed slightly and feebly. Breathlessly she listened. It was no delusion—he was alive! Death had not claimed his prey, and he might yet recover.

Poor Nora! The eyes, which were dry when heavy affliction struck her, overflowed in salutary drops under the sudden influence of joy. Her first impulse was one of deep and overpowering gratitude, but her thankfulness was, like her grief, silent and subdued. She sat down beside the bed and patiently awaited till he should awake. For several hours did she watch, by her husband's side, and morning was again stealing over the sky when he awoke, and in feeble accents whispered her name. His reason was restored, and Nora felt that all present danger was over. Hours sped by—hours spent by the grateful wife in ministering to his recovery. He was weak as an infant and she dared not tell him of their loss—that their child lay near them, a lifeless corpse.

The next day, after Nora had as usual been addressing words of encouragement to her patient, and carefully concealing from him her own deep distresses, she was startled by hearing horses' footsteps approaching their abode. In a few minutes, a man on horseback stopped at the door, and without ceremony entered the house. Nora did not rise, for the hand of her sleeping husband was clasped in hers, while silent tears chased each other down her pale cheeks. Her baby lay unburied nearby, and for her feeble husband, where was she to find the means of recruiting his exhausted strength? She had had but little food for many days, and how could she seek for more?

She hardly raised her head when the stranger entered, so absorbed was she with these melancholy reflections. The traveller, unconscious of her sorrows, addressed her with a cheerful, hearty voice, "Good morning, marm. How's your man? Ill, I don't doubt—these here diggins ar'nt wholesome anyhow, I reckon." Saying this, the stranger, who was a portly man of respectable appearance, seated himself without ceremony in the chimney corner.

Shelter is never refused in the prairie, and to that he was welcome. Gladly also would Nora have set food in plenty before her guest, had she any. She gave him, however, of that which she had, and the stranger soon learned the almost destitute condition of his young hostess. The traveller possessed a kind and friendly heart, and a well-filled purse withal. Liking the appearance of the young settlers, and admiring the order and cleanliness of their cottage, he pitied their misfortunes, and hastened to procure necessaries and comforts for the desolate inhabitants of the watery prairie.

Having then cheered the sufferers with words of hope, and seen the remains of the dead infant decently interred, he left them, promising to return. Two more weeks sped by. McLeod had left his bed, and sat weak and trembling by the fire, while Nora, though her thoughts often wandered to the grave of her child, looked at him with eyes full of gratitude and happiness. Their talk was of the kind stranger, and of their hopes that he would soon return. And when, soon after this, they again saw his benevolent countenance, and heard his loud hearty greeting, what joy was theirs! The stranger was a rich landholder and cotton-grower, and being in want of an overseer on whom he could depend, he fixed upon McLeod to fill the office. He gave his protegés a pretty house, located in a healthy clearing, not many miles distant from their own property. McLeod was to be a man with authority, and they soon had where-withal to live in comfort and contentment. When Nora entered her new habitation, leaning on her husband's arm, she looked up in his face. "Ah, now Jamie," she said, "and didn't I tell you there was a silver lining to every cloud?"

CHAPTER XXI

ABUNDANCE OF GAME ⚓ SEVERE NORTHERS
CLASSES OF LAND TITLES ⚓ LIVESTOCK
⚓ GALVESTON ENCROACHES ON THE GULF

A few weeks had made a considerable difference in the aspect of the country. The prairie was already beginning to put on its summer mantle of flowers, and immense flocks of migratory birds were darkening the air. Wild-fowl also, and all kinds of game, were in much greater abundance than when we were here last. Mr. Houstoun was delighted with the snipe-shooting, and he was tolerably successful, frequently killing twenty in an hour. He was also fortunate enough to kill a very rare bird in the country, called by the inhabitants the Sand-Hill Crane, which resembles the bustard very much, both in appearance and in flavour, but is considerably larger. The Sand-Hill Cranes are very difficult to approach, and only appear after two or three days of severe northers.

These northers being peculiar to the Gulf of Mexico, I must endeavour to describe them. They most frequently occur after a few days of damp dull weather, and generally about once a fortnight. Their approach is known by a dark bank rising on the horizon, and gradually overspreading the heavens. The storm bursts forth with wonderful suddenness and tremendous violence, and generally lasts forty-eight hours. The wind after that period veers round to the east and southward, and the storm gradually abates. During the continuance of a norther, the cold is intense, and the wind so penetrating, it is almost impossible to keep oneself warm. The weather is generally clear, and frequently the northers are almost unaccompanied by rain.

The description of the tremendous hurricane that occurred last September, as it was told to us, is intended to give one the impression that on some future day the flourishing city of Galveston may be swept away by the overwhelming incursions of the sea. I endeavour to think such an occurrence is not likely. On the occasion I have alluded to, such was the force of the winds and waves, that many houses were turned topsy turvy, and some were floated many hundred yards from their original position. The greater part of the island was also under water for many days, and boats were in request to go from one house to another. Such a storm as this, however, had never occurred before in the memory of the oldest inhabitant, and some fishermen who had been resident there more than twenty years, asserted that their previous experience presented no parallel for such a destructive hurricane. [*EDITOR'S NOTE: The storm referenced here is the September 18, 1842 hurricane. The strong Category 2 storm drove the Gulf over the island and caused an estimated $10,000 (1842 figure) in damages. A smaller storm followed on October 5, 1842.*]

An stronger argument in favour of the city never being entirely submerged is the fact that the accumulation of sand, which forms the island, continues increasing. It is proved beyond a doubt that the land is everywhere encroaching on the Gulf of Mexico. We saw an excellent old Spanish chart of the coast, which was made sixty or seventy years ago, and on comparing it with our own we found it on all important points remarkably accurate. The island of Galveston, however, is there represented as much smaller than it is at present, and Pelican Island (a large sand bank in the middle of the bay) is entirely omitted.

There can be little doubt, from the omission of Pelican Island in the chart I have referred to, and also from the manner in which it is known to increase in size, that half a century ago it was not in existence. This would lead to the supposition that the harbour is gradually filling up. But it is conjectured by many that as its limits decrease, the channel, probably formed by the Trinity River, will become deeper. The bar at its entrance is said to remain exactly the same, though the depth of water on it varies considerably according to the wind. After several days of very strong southerly winds, there is frequently as much as fifteen feet of water, and the depth throughout the bay, and even up the river, is increased several feet.

Vessels, however, cannot take advantage of this circumstance during the continuance of the southerly winds owing to the extremely heavy swell on the bar, which, notwithstanding the greater depth of the water, materially increases the chance of a vessel's "bumping" (a term the Americans use for touching on the sand-banks, and they seem to think nothing of the phenomenon.) It is no uncommon practice to make the crew and passengers keep constantly moving in line, from one side of the deck to the other, when there is not sufficient water to pass a bar without "rolling over," as this proceeding is called. We ourselves on one occasion assisted at a ceremony of this kind in a steamer.

The best period for entering the harbour at Galveston is after a southerly wind has been blowing pretty fresh for some days, and is then succeeded by a norther. Advantage should be taken, at the very commencement of the gale, to pass the bar (as vessels may lay over the bar with a northerly wind) or otherwise, the whole of the available water is blown out of the bay, and thus the depth on the bar is perhaps reduced to less than nine feet.

One of the evils, arising from the hitherto unsettled state of the country, seems to be that the people, instead of attending to their domestic affairs and agricultural pursuits, have occupied themselves (for want of better employment) in making a superabundance of laws, and acts of Congress. There are I do not know how many of these volumes already published, and many of them are so contradictory, and admit of so many interpretations, that it is to be presumed the Texan lawyers will never want business. A great proportion of these acts of Congress relate to the land laws.

As I have before mentioned the difficulty in getting good titles to land in Texas, I shall endeavour to give some account of the different descriptions of titles. There are of course various opinions on the subject, and I can only give my own, grounded upon information received from those whom we considered the best authorities.

The first titles I shall mention are those emanating from the Mexican government. Many of these are unconditional and indisputable, and are undoubtedly the best that can be found. There are, however, others, originating from the same source, but which are generally considered totally invalid, certain conditions having been attached to the grant, which were never fulfilled by the grantee. This has not, however, prevented many from setting up claims on the strength of these impresario or contract grants.

The second class of titles are those emanating from the government of the Republic of Texas. Of these there are various kinds, and they seem to have been granted so incautiously, and to have offered so many opportunities for fraud and deception that at present it is almost impossible to pronounce a particular title to be good or bad; that is to say if it has not been also patented by government. I shall divide the titles emanating from the Republic of Texas into four classes.

First—Those titles granted to all who arrived in the country previous to the Declaration of Independence.

Second—Titles granted to those who were actually present in Texas at the Declaration of Independence, or who took part in the campaign of 1836.

Third—Titles, the headrights of colonists who have arrived in the country and have become citizens at various periods, since the Declaration of Independence.

Fourth—Titles created by Government Scrip.

Of these four classes of Texas titles, the first is probably the best, as it is the earliest in date. With regard to the second class, it is only necessary to say that, within a very short period, fifteen thousand individuals had each claimed and taken possession of his league of land, which, by the Act of Congress, every person who participated in the struggle for independence was entitled to. Now it is well known that, at the period alluded to, there were certainly not five thousand fighting men in the whole country. The fact was, that thousands of adventurers had, immediately after the act was passed, flocked in from the United States, secured titles to land under false pleas, and forthwith returned to America. This was easily effected by representing themselves as having been long in the country, and in the confusion which prevailed at the moment, the imposition could not be detected. A commission was subsequently appointed by government for the purpose of inquiring into the validity of these titles, and their number was soon reduced from fifteen thousand to five thousand. Those whose claims were approved received patents for their land, but the remaining ten thousand titles were pronounced utterly fraudulent. It is notorious that many of these forged titles to land in Texas still continue to be sold in the United States.

The third and fourth classes of titles may both be considered good, if the original possessor was undoubtedly the first to "locate on," and register the lands selected. There is a land office for this purpose in each district, but the registers have sometimes been kept in a careless and informal manner, and there have been frequent changes of surveyors. As a result, I am informed that it has often happened, notwithstanding all possible precautions, that the same land has been surveyed, and what is called "located" by two or three claimants, one after another. If the titles however, be patented by the government, these accidents are not likely to occur.

To account also, in some measure, for the numerous disputes concerning titles to land in Texas, I must observe, that in a country so ill-surveyed and frequently so deficient in landmarks (particularly if the seller be dishonest,) it is not always easy to discover the exact position of the estate which is indicated by the title you have purchased. And it is by no means improbable that you may "squat" on some other person's domain, your own being perhaps some miles distant. The rightful owner of the land you have thus unwittingly appropriated is perhaps resident at New York, and may not think fit to acquaint you with your mistake till you have built a house, or perhaps laid out the plan of a city. Such proceedings are already as common in Texas as it is in the United States.

I have now endeavoured to explain the difficulties which exist in regard to procuring land titles in this country. Many such as I have described may be purchased all over the United States, and even in London but from what I could learn, all such should be avoided. It must not, however, be supposed that good and safe titles to land are unattainable. On the contrary, with proper care and caution, they may be obtained in the country with a good government patent, and with indisputable right. I believe, too, that the money paid will be trifling compared with that which would be expended for the same purpose anywhere else in the world.

It should be remembered, among its other advantages, that Texas comprises an extent of country as large as France, and that half its lands are still unappropriated. One of the evils attendant on settling in Texas, is that "aliens" cannot hold land in Texas. In regard to some land titles, this is certainly true, but the difficulty may be entirely obviated by a foreigner spending six months in the country. This trifling expenditure of time, which may be very usefully employed, confers citizenship and enables a stranger to hold land on the same footing as the Texan. It should also be added, that in the case of an alien holding land, the only party proceeding against him would be the government, and such an opponent has so rarely started up in any country, that not much fear need be entertained on that score.

Apparently no country can be better adapted for breeding purposes, in the case of mules and horses. It is supposed that it would be an extremely good speculation to export horses from Texas, where they may be bought for thirty dollars, to Havanna, where their price is from two hundred and fifty to five hundred dollars. The passage thither occupies about four or five days. If the Spanish government were so far to overcome its feelings against Mexico and acknowledge the independence of Texas, Cuba would become a great market for Texan produce of every kind.

Chapter XXII

GENERAL HOUSTON, PRESIDENT OF TEXAS ⚓
WHITTLING ⚓ UNCOMFORTABLE TRAVEL IN TEXAS

As we soon intend on making an excursion up the country and, if possible, paying our respects to the celebrated President, General Houston, I think that a short account of the history and character of the latter may not be unacceptable. Of the talents of this remarkable man, there can, and does, exist but one opinion. But there is, nevertheless, a strong party against him. From the want of other objects to occupy their time and attention, a large proportion of the people amuse themselves by abusing him, both in his public and private capacity.

The impossibility of a governor of a country pleasing and satisfying all parties is everywhere acknowledged. And the want of national funds under which the republic at present labours, greatly increases the difficulty. Every instance of adversity, and every deficiency of dollars, is attributed at once to the President's mismanagement or cupidity. The latter charge is so strange, and so utterly unfounded, that it finds but few believers.

There are several other causes of complaint against him. The principal one is his avowed dislike to going to war, which, in common with all people who have but little to lose, is a favourite pastime with the Texans. The advice of the President to his countrymen—"stay at home, gentlemen, look after your flocks and herds, and sow corn"—meets with but little sympathy from his fellow citizens. Another cause of his unpopularity with the fighting party, is his opposition to the existence of a navy in Texas. The President contends that they have no use for ships, and that the support of a navy is a useless incumbrance to the republic.

American sympathizers and "loafers" are objects of his especial enmity, and with reason, for no persons are so much to be feared. They are people who go about in search of promiscuous plunder, and it matters nothing to them whether friend or enemy falls a victim to their rapacity. If nothing is to be made of the Mexicans, they turn upon the Texans in search of prey.

It is well known that the Mexicans, in general, are not well-disposed towards Santa Anna, whose military despotism is ill-calculated to conciliate their regard. It is not difficult to believe that were they left to themselves, they would be friendly towards the Texans. As a proof of this, in the recent campaign on the frontier, most energetic proceedings, conducted with beautiful military skill were made by the Texans for the attack of Mier. Fire-eating parties of war-like citizens, armed and caparisoned, advanced simultaneously at three different points of attack, resolved to conquer or to die. What was their surprise to find that they had wasted all this valuable energy and courage without necessity. No opposition was made by the Mexicans to their entrance, but on the contrary, they were received in the most friendly manner and invited to eat, drink, and refresh themselves. The return made by the invaders for the kindness with which they were treated, was ungrateful indeed. In the dead of the night, they commenced plundering, and appropriating to themselves everything they could lay their hands on.

The men who proceeded with the Mier expedition were "loafers"—the dangerous and unprincipled set of people of whom General Houston is so anxious to free the country. One of the few respectable individuals who took part in the expedition told us that they were heartily ashamed of being there, and, for his own part, he felt "dreadful small" on the occasion. But to return to the character of the President. Old Sam, as he is universally called, is, I believe, a native of Kentucky and was educated for the law. He distinguished himself highly at the United States bar, and married an American lady possessed of great personal attractions. Differences subsequently arose between himself and his wife, the causes of which are not known. As divorces are easily obtained in this country, where mutual irritability is alone sufficient to establish grounds for entire separation, Gen-

eral Houston took advantage of this facility. To judge from
his subsequent conduct, he must have felt his domestic bereavement severely, and it seems to have been long before
he recovered from its effects.

In the year 1828, in a fit of disgust and despair, as it is
supposed, he took up his abode among a distant tribe of
Indians, I believe the Cherokees. He spent several years
among them, conforming himself to their habits, and even
outdoing them in some of their acts of daring and adventure. He is said to have taken to himself a squaw, but let
it be remembered that this is only hearsay evidence, and I
do not vouch for its veracity. It is commonly related that,
at this period of his life and in the society of these primitive *bon vivans*, General Houston grew so attached to the
dram-bottle that the Indians bestowed on him the sobri-
quet of "Drunken Sam."

Having now said all the evil, if such it can be called, of
his character we must turn to the bright side. General
Houston's bravery is worthy of the boldest days of chiv-
alry. His patriotism is sincere and unquestioned, and his
integrity without a stain. His talents as a legislator are of a
high order, and should those that are against him succeed
in electing a President who is opposed to him in politics,
they will find him most formidable in opposition. When we
consider how instrumental the President has been in securing their independence, we are the more surprised that
he should have enemies among his own people. In the enu-
meration of his qualities, we should, however, notice, that
he is caustic and severe. His superior talents render him,
perhaps, not sufficiently lenient to the faults and weakness
of others. These circumstances may, in some measure, account for his unpopularity.

General Houston has married again in recent years, and
his wife is said to be an accomplished and exemplary person. She possesses a great influence over the President,
and uses it with judgment and moderation. Owing to her
admirable advice, General Houston has broken through
those habits of drinking and swearing, which were former-

ly blots on his character, and the former of which injured his health. He is a man of education, and, besides being well read in polite literature, appreciates the elegant and standard authors of our country.

Whenever the President travels through the country, it is at the expense of the persons at whose houses he puts up, and whenever he makes use of a steamer he has the privilege of a free passage. I believe that during his public career, General Houston has neither saved nor made a dollar. On the contrary, he is said to be often in pecuniary difficulties. As a proof how convinced the people are of his integrity, in regard to not having amassed a fortune from the public funds, it may be mentioned, that not long ago, being in want of a little tobacco, and not having wherewith to purchase it, he could not obtain credit.

Parties are much divided, and the opinions of the people are showing themselves in various ways on the subject of the election of the next President. It is the prevailing topic of conversation. Indeed, it seems to me that both in the United States and Texas this sort of excitement is so popular, that no sooner is a President elected than there commences all the excitement of canvassing for and choosing his successor. At the present moment there are several persons who are about to "run," as they call it, for the Presidency. General Houston has bitter enemies, but he has likewise warm friends and partisans, who are among the best and most influential of the people. It is, therefore, not probable that the choice of a successor in the government will fall upon anyone inimical to him, or decidedly adverse to his line of policy.

Without using any undue means to make himself popular, the President is courteous and polite to persons of all ranks. Though I believe he is a Tory at heart, it makes no difference in his civility of manner to any parties or factions. The House of Assembly at Washington is open to the street. It has no windows, and anyone may look in who pleases. General Houston's greeting to the free citizens—carters or blacksmiths, as the case may be—is always equally kind and polite. It is, "How d'ye do, Colonel? How's Madam? Bad weather for the ladies!"

During this time, and while public business was under discussion, the honourable members of Congress were to be seen seated on candle boxes and sugar casks—in short, on anything they could find—and each man was whittling away without intermission. A piece of wood is placed before each senator, who, were it not for this necessary precaution, would very soon, in common with his honourable friends, cut the table to pieces. No sooner is a member seated than he takes out his knife, and never leaves off cutting away whether speaking or silent.

A great deal, certainly, is done with wood besides the national amusement of whittling. It is invariably used for building and the celerity with which they erect both churches and houses, is, as I have before remarked, wonderful. A troop of Franconi's horses (at least their owners called them such) on their way from Mexico to the United States, were at present amusing the good citizens of Galveston by their performances. In a day, there was built for them quite a large temporary theatre for the exercise of their manoeuvres.

Though some of the houses have a certain air of exterior neatness and decoration, comfort, at least domestic household comfort, is quite unknown in this country. The north winds blow through and through their paper houses, and they heed it not. Carpets, well-made beds and all such necessaries of life are unknown or despised. The traveller in Texas must set out prepared for every species of discomfort. His bed, if he should happen to procure one, will be disputed, or, if he should happen to prefer a compromise, perhaps shared, by some other traveller.

Monsieur de Saligny, late Charge d'Affaires of his French Majesty, chanced to be travelling up the country in this primitive republic. He was fresh from the luxuries and ornaments of a Paris life, not among the least of which are the comfortable beds which are everywhere to be enjoyed. To this agreeable mode of existence, Texas and its numerous inconveniences, must have formed a striking contrast. On arriving at one of the halting places at night, he retired to what he doubtless imagined would be a solitary couch. Though the winds of heaven were whistling through his log-built chamber and the bright stars peeping through the roof, the fatigue of the journey soon closed his eyes in slumber. He had not, however, slept many minutes, when he was awakened by the entrance of a most formidable looking individual. It was a stout Kentuckian, duly armed with bowie knife and pistols. While in the act of disencumbering himself of his upper garments, the man said, in a coarse, but not unfriendly voice, "Well, stranger, I guess I'll take the inside of the bed, if it's the same to you?" I believe the Parisian preferred passing the night on the floor to the misfortune of having a Yankee between the wall and his nobility.

No innkeeper in this country would ever dream of sending away a traveller on the plea of want of room, as long as one bed remained in his house half-unoccupied. It was with a perfect knowledge of the difficulties and inconveniences that awaited us, that we made up our minds to undertake an excursion up the country, and we were therefore prepared for all contingencies.

I may here remark that, on a previous occasion, when I accompanied Mr. Houstoun on a fishing and shooting excursion to the mainland, I could not help thinking how extremely eligible is this country for railroads. As far as I could see, and I was told it was the same for miles, the horizon was only bounded by the flat and pathless prairie. Oh, that such advantages of locomotion were now at hand! But then, though unquestionably we should have been spared many of the small and tedious troubles of the route, we should also have been deprived of the pleasure of seeing a remarkable country in its primeval state, and we should also have lost in interest what we should have gained in luxury and comfort. The weather was extremely cold and sharp northers were chilling us with their ungenial breath, but we were too anxious to see something more of the country to be easily dissuaded from our purpose.

The *corps diplomatique* were engaged to join our party, and the arrangements required for the undertaking being few and simple, we fixed an early day and forthwith took our places in the steamer bound up the Buffalo Bayou to Houston.

The first published view of the city of Houston, known as the "Alpine" view, was included in the 1844 British edition of this work. The fanciful image of the town girded by evergreen-covered slopes was copied in subsequent European works of the mid-19th century.

Chapter XXIII

The Steamer "Dayton" ⚓
The Town of Houston ⚓ Start for the Prairie

It was about two o'clock in the afternoon on a bright frosty day, that we put ourselves on board the Houston steamer, *Dayton*, Captain Kelsey. She was a small vessel, and drew but little water, a circumstance very necessary in these small rivers. The American river steamers differ very much in appearance from those to which an European eye is accustomed. They have the appearance of wooden houses built upon a large raft. There is a balcony or verandah, and on the roof is what is called the hurricane-deck, where gentlemen passengers walk and smoke.

On the occasion of our taking our passage both the ladies' and gentlemen's cabin were quite full, and I therefore preferred spending the evening on the balcony in spite of the cold. I had many kind offers of civility, but I could not help being amused at the terms in which some of them were couched. The question addressed to me of "Do you liquor, ma'am?" was speedily followed by the production of a tumbler of eggnog, which seemed in great request and I cannot deny its excellence. I believe the British Navy claims the merit of its invention, but this is matter of dispute.

We dined soon after our arrival on board and found everybody very orderly and civil. Certainly there was a strange mixture of ranks, but this made it more amusing to a stranger. The ladies, during dinner, were very silent, though the noise I had heard them making in their own cabin, five minutes before, was deafening. The supper consisted of alternate dishes of boiled oysters and beefsteaks, of which there was plenty, and the latter disappeared in marvelously quick time between the strong jaws of the Texan gentlemen. I confess to preferring meat which has been kept somewhat more than an hour, especially in frosty weather. On one occasion our dinner was delayed for some time, while the cook went on shore and "shot a beef."

There was fortunately water enough for us to cross Red Fish Bar, and we were fast steaming up Buffalo River. For a considerable distance from the mouth, the shores are low, flat and swampy, but as the stream narrowed there were high banks, and the trees were quite beautiful in spite of the season, which was extremely unfavourable to foliage and woody scenery. Such magnolias—eighty feet in height and with a girth like huge forest trees—what must they be when in full blossom! There were also a great number and variety of evergreens, laurel, bay and firs, rhododendrons, cistus and arbutus. It seemed one vast shrubbery. The trees and shrubs grew to a prodigious height, and often met over the steamer, as she wound through the short reaches of this most lovely stream.

It was late when I retired to my cabin, as the scene, lighted by a clear frosty moon, was so beautiful and to me so novel, that I could not make up my mind to leave it. I had expected to be much annoyed by the noise of the high pressure engine. To that, however, I soon be came accustomed. Of all sounds I ever heard, that of the negro slaves carolling out their nightly songs on this evening was the most dismal and unearthly. They were seated, some on the hurricane deck, and others at their work, but all joining in the same loud, weary, monotonous chaunt. The young girls have generally beautiful figures, and are as straight and upright as young pines. In the ladies' cabin especially there was one very pretty bright-eyed black girl, who seemed full of fun and good humour.

My berth opened out of the state cabin and, as the only partition was a Venetian door, I could not avoid hearing all the conversation that was carried on by my neighbours. Cards and drinking constituted no inconsiderable part of the pleasures of the evening, but with all the excitement of talk, tobacco-chewing and brandy, I never heard people more orderly and reasonable. Their talk as usual was of dollars. Politics, indeed, occasionally took their turn, but the subject ceased to become interesting when the pockets of the company could no longer be affected by the turn of affairs. There was no private scandal, no wit, no literature, no small-talk—all was hard, dry, calculating business. I heard many shrewd and hard-headed remarks. The fate of their country was talked over as a matter of business, and one rather important-looking gentleman made a stump speech on the expediency of Texas becoming a colony of Great Britain! I do not know the orator's name, but General or Colonel he must have been. Military titles are taken and given here with as little ceremony as the title of Count on the Continent. Upon our arrival in Texas, Mr. Houstoun sprang into a General at once.

There was a Baptist preacher on board. He was a thin, weary-looking man, with a cast in his eye, which was very comical. He had fought for his country and, though now a man of peace, delighted in displaying his knowledge of military matters. He was going to Houston to establish a school for young gentlemen, while his wife was to superintend the education of their sisters. This he said he was induced to do, so that his boys might not mix with their inferiors. He could not bear, he added, that his sons should be acquainted with vulgar boys, which they were obliged to do at Galveston. But the preacher didn't like it and now, at his school, he could choose the boys! Exclusiveness here!

Where shall we look for a country where true charitable feelings of equality exist? I may remark that my maid was obliged to wait till all these people had done their meals because, I was told, they did not like her to eat at the same table. Strange inconsistency but one that sufficiently shows the futility of any attempt to introduce a perfect system of equality anywhere. It exists in America but in name alone.

I shall not easily forget the night I passed on the Buffalo River. There was card-playing going on in both cabins, and occasionally I heard a card put down with a smart slap, and then "I guess now, that's the way to do business," and from another "Now sir, I've made an operation I expect." In the ladies' cabin, where a few favoured individuals of the other sex had the good fortune to be admitted, it was "Ah Miss Delia, I see the giraffe ahead, I do." And then a young gentleman played "Auld Lang Syne" with variations on the violin, followed by "The Boatie Rows," sung with tremendous applause by a young Scotchman with a fine bass voice, which would have been too much for Westminster Abbey.

At seven o'clock in the morning we arrived at the pretty town of Houston. It is built on high land, and the banks, which are covered with evergreens, rise abruptly from the river. There are plenty of inns at Houston, such as they are, and we took up our quarters at the Houston House, a large shambling wooden building kept by a Captain or Colonel Baldwin, one of the most civil, obliging people I ever saw. We had a sitting room which was weatherproof, though to keep out the intense cold was impossible. It was said that our landlord was anxious to add to the comforts of his house, but he had a great many bad debts. It was, he told us, a losing concern altogether. More went out than came in, and only that morning, Baldwin had asked a gentleman to pay his lodging bill and the reply was "If you come to insult me again sir, by God, I'll shoot you sir."

We went down to breakfast in the public room. The food consisted of tough beefsteaks, each as large as a good-sized dish, eggs hardly warmed through and emptied over the meat, and squirrels. Each guest did not remain more than five minutes, and on his retiring, his place was immediately filled by another hungry traveller. I looked on in silent wonder at their extraordinary powers of mastication. One old man in particular, in a green baize coat, outdid all the rest. I could not have believed any human being could have contrived to stow away such a cargo of "dry goods" in so short a time.

The weather had by this time changed, and a cold sleety rain was falling. It was not promising weather for sport, but Mr. Houstoun was determined to try his luck, and the whole *société* of the place kindly offered to accompany him on his expedition. Off they all set, on raw-boned high trotting horses, guns on their shoulders and exhibiting every variety of strange costume. As to any sport they had, they might as well have remained at home—the only event of the day being the breaking of our doctor's bridle, upon which his horse ran away. He was thrown but, happily, without receiving any injury. Houston, proud as the Texans are of it as a city, does not bear a close inspection. There is but one brick house in it, and I could not quite make out what its inhabitants meant when they talked of it as a great city: "The poetry of the country, sir, is Houston;" a very incomprehensible panegyric certainly.

Our dinner we had in private. The hotel was, as the landlord said, "in a fix," but our fare was not bad of its kind, there being "pork dodgers" and "dough doings" (corn bread,) chicken fixings and sausages. Rossetta, a negress with rings on every finger, waited upon us, and a hideous creature she was. Jerry, the black porter and a great thief, assisted. The tea was made in a huge kettle. We retired to rest fatigued enough. A piercing norther was blowing and whirling wildly round the fragile house, and forcing its way through the cracks and crannies, and putting out both fire and candle. The cold was more intense than anything I ever before experienced.

The whole town was in a state of excitement, for the Mexicans, who had recently entered Bexar and had marched off all its inhabitants as prisoners, were hourly expected. During the night there was a cry that they were at hand, but it proved only a false alarm. We were disturbed too, in the course of the night, by the importunities of an unfortunate man, who could not find a bed and who kept knocking at all our doors, saying he was very cold and must come in. He was what the landlord called a "rowdy loafer"—not a pleasant companion, as it is by these people and by these alone (who are not Texans) that gouging and bowie-knifing are practised.

Our ceiling was of canvass, and in the night we were obliged to "fix" an umbrella over the bed. I watched the feet of a restless cat as she wandered over our heads, her paws finding their way through the holes, which time had worn in our sail-cloth covering.

The prairie, as I have said, was in a very bad state for travelling. Roads, it is well known, there were none, and "plumbing the track," or, tracing the path of former travellers, is at all times difficult. However, we were resolved to see something of the country, and therefore hired a wagon for the purpose, drawn by two stout horses, and set off, in spite of wind and weather.

On leaving Houston, we ascended a hill so steep, as to seem almost impossible for a carriage, however light, to be drawn up it. Stumps of trees were left in the middle of the path, which lies through a thick forest. The trees are mostly evergreens, magnolias, bay, laurel, and cypress, and the forest itself has the appearance of an ornamental shrubbery on a gigantic scale. Notwithstanding the severe cold, the ground was beginning to be enamelled with flowers. There were violets, and a small flower like a jessamine but growing close to the ground in both blue and white. I saw also various salvias, and many other plants and flowers of which, not being a botanist, I can give no account. It was quite gladdening, after having been debarred so long a time from the sight of trees, to find oneself journeying through such woods as these. I began to think that the name of "Happy hunting grounds" was not misapplied. Texas signifies, in the Indian tongue, these endearing and happy-sounding words. I believe that those parts of the republic where the Indians still abide are the most worthy of the appellation.

Chapter XXIV

Scenery of the Prairie ⚓ Lipan Tribe
⚓ Death of the Lipan Chief

The birds here are many and various. Cardinals, blackbirds with bright red wings, mockingbirds and woodpeckers of every hue are the most common. As you advance into the interior, the woods become less thick and the country is more open. It is, in fact, a prairie, slightly rolling, and diversified with frequent clumps of trees. They are so tastefully arranged by the hand of nature, that you could imagine yourself in a finely-kept English park, where landscape-gardeners and studiers of the picturesque had expended their utmost skill in beautifying the scenery. Where the clumps of trees are at a considerable distance from each other, I was strongly reminded of some parts of Windsor Forest.

We saw great quantities of cattle grazing, and some sheep. The latter, I was told, are considered very profitable stock and sell at from three to four dollars each. The following manner of preventing them from straying, struck me as ingenious. In the month of March, the long prairie grass is set on fire. Where sheep are to graze, the fire is confined to small patches and, as they do not roam into the high grass, they keep eating down that which has been burned, till the owner thinks it expedient to prepare another spot for them in a similar manner.

One night, at our inn, the master's son, after setting our dinner on the table, coolly advanced his chair to the fire, remarking on the weather, and added, "Well, Gen'ral now, where did you go to? Tell us now. I guess you found it too cold. You haven't fixed any game anyhow." How surprised we should be in England at such familiarity as this! But here, you see at once the absurdity of either showing or feeling annoyance, as it is evident they are so very far from intending incivility. They are, moreover, so genuinely kind that I, for one, felt inclined to take everything as it was meant—in good part. An Englishman certainly feels, when he pays for his room at an inn, that even the landlord has no right to enter it, but he must divest himself of these peculiarities here. In other respects, the resting places for the night are as comfortable as goodwill and hospitality can make them. It is often difficult to persuade the worthy host to accept any remuneration. We were told by an Englishman, who had been in every part of the country, that he had often seen, when a traveller was not possessed of much ready cash, that a good song or a budget of news, invented or remembered, would be taken in payment for a night's lodging and an ample meal. Read this, rich men, who live in refined and populous cities—eat the dinner which has cost you as much as would have nourished a score of hungry wanderers. And when you are done, reflect on the humble lodging in the desert where, out of little, at least something is given.

About this time I made acquaintance with an Indian of the Lipan tribe, who came with a rabbit to sell to me. Some of his tribe were in a camp at no great distance. I was alone when he entered and he eyed me, evidently with fear and suspicion. The poor people. They have no reason either to like or respect the whites, and I did not wonder at his suspicion, though I did at his alarm. He was about eighteen years old, very gipsy-looking, with an eye singularly wild and piercing. He was dressed like a hunter, with a leather pouch, cow's horn for powder, a knife and a whistle. His clothing was scanty enough. It was a long time before he would approach me, and he seemed to have a great dislike to allowing me to touch his accoutrements. He had his rabbit in his arms and contrived to make me understand, by putting up his fingers, that he wanted two bits, about tenpence, for it. Having paid him the money, I poured out a glass of sherry, which I offered him, but he refused it with a look of disgust, and again retreated to his corner.

Knowing the fondness of an Indian for spirits, I concluded he was afraid it was poisoned. I was right in my supposition, for immediately afterwards, on seeing me put my lips to the glass, he rushed to me, seized it from my hand, and drank it off. He was a good specimen of his kind, and I was very glad to have had this interview with him.

The tribe of Indians to which my acquaintance belonged is not one of any importance, and their numbers have been much weakened by their wars with the Camanchees, of whom they are the hereditary enemies. It is much to be hoped that these wars with the Indians will be soon put to a stop to in Texas. The "happy hunting grounds," indeed, can never be what they once were to these poor people. But peace and freedom from oppression, they have a right to hope for, and General Houston, who interests himself much in their civilization and well-being, has on every occasion proved himself their friend and protector. A meeting of the tribes was to be held shortly, at the Wacco village on the Brazos, situated about two hundred miles above Washington, for the purpose of making treaties of alliance both between the whites and among themselves. The President is to meet them there and much was expected, both from his intimate knowledge of Indian habits and character, and from the respect in which he is held by the tribes. Some of his addresses to them are curious enough. I shall transcribe one of the latest, being a letter of condolence to the Lipans, on the death of their chief.

To the Chief of the Lipans
Executive Department, Washington,
March, 26, 1843.

My Brother,

My heart is sad! A dark cloud rests upon your nation. Grief has sounded in your camp. The voice of Flaco is silent. His words are not heard in council. The chief is no more; his eyes are closed. His heart no longer leaps at the sight of the buffalo! The voices of your camp are no longer heard to cry [that] Flaco has returned from the chase! Your chiefs look down on the earth, and groan in trouble.

The warriors weep—the loud voice of grief is heard from your women and children. The song of birds is silent. The ear of your people hears no pleasant sound. Sorrow whispers in the winds. The noise of the tempest passes. It is not heard. Your hearts are heavy.

The name of Flaco brought joy to all hearts. Joy was on every face! Your people were happy. Flaco is no longer seen in the fight, his voice is no longer heard in battle. The enemy no longer makes a path for his glory. His valour is no longer a guard for your people. The right arm of your nation is broken. Flaco was a friend to his white brothers. They will not forget him. They will remember the red warrior; his father will not be forgotten. We will be kind to the Lipans. Grass shall not grow in the path between us. Let your wise men give counsel of peace. Let your young men walk in the white path. The gray-headed men of your nation will teach wisdom. I will hold my red brothers by the hand.

> Thy brother,
> SAM HOUSTON

The landlord of the inn came in soon after the departure of the Indian and "fixed the rabbit" for me, as he called it. This was merely putting it into a box, with holes in it. I kept the poor little animal some time, in memory of my wild acquaintance, but soon after we returned to the *Dolphin,* he escaped and I heard no more of him. We had some excellent wild turkeys up the country, which were much better than the tame. On the whole, we enjoyed our inland visit, which we extended in various directions about Houston. In regard to the sport, or rather in the absence of it, the gentlemen of the party were disappointed. We began to think that the quantity of game up the country, and the ease with which it was said to be procured, were rather overrated. The want of success, however, might be fairly attributed to the badness of the weather.

CHAPTER XXV

DANGERS OF PRAIRIE TRAVEL ⚓ LEAVING HOUSTON
⚓ THE OPOSSUM ⚓ SLAVE TRADE

The city of Houston was our headquarters during our
stay up the country. Greatly did we regret that the state
of the prairie, owing to the constant and heavy rains, prevented our travelling as far as Washington, which city we
had intended to have visited. The scarcity and indifference
of the accommodations would not have deterred us from
such an undertaking, but, in a country where roads do not
exist, it is difficult not to lose one's way. The danger is
considerably increased when the trail of previous travellers
is obliterated by the rains. Plumbing the track (the Texan
term for tracing a road) is at all times a slow and tedious
operation. Between Houston and Washington there is a
certain space of two miles, which, when we were in the
country, was not traversed in less time than four hours, so
deep was the mire.

The Brazos and Trinity bottoms are overflowed for
weeks together in the winter season, and, in the absence
of causeways and bridges, are extremely difficult and
even dangerous to pass. In process of time, there is no
doubt that the banks will become raised, in a similar manner to those of the Mississippi, and the overflowings of
the rivers will be checked. At present, the aspect of the
prairie during the winter season, and the scenes which
are occasionally acted there, are more amusing to an on-
looker than agreeable to the parties concerned. Travellers
are seen knee-deep in mud, looking as though hopeless
of rescue. Dying and dead cattle are interspersed among
bales of cotton, which were in process of being hauled.
Altogether it requires a great spirit of enterprise to dare
the dangers of the route. We may fairly suppose that one
of the first public works which the Texans will undertake,
will be to establish a canal or railroad between the Brazos
River and Galveston Bay, in order to facilitate the transit

of the cotton, which is now hauled across the country, from the Brazos to Houston.

Our inn at Houston, though comfortable as Colonel Baldwin's extreme attention could make it, was cold and cheerless enough, and we were not sorry when the last evening arrived which we were to spend under its roof. We had our usual dinner of pork dodgers and a turkey fixed with sausages, varied with some dough doings in the shape of puddings, the likes of which I never saw before. Our surprise at their shape and consistency caused great delight to Rossetta, the negress in waiting, whose mouth distended to twice its usual dimensions with the violence of her merriment. Her laughter was contagious, and our last evening at the Houston House passed off in high glee.

We regretted very much that we were obliged to leave the country without being introduced to the President, but we hope, on a future occasion, to thank him in person for the gratifying messages we received from him.

[*EDITOR'S NOTE: Curiously enough, Mrs. Houstoun included in her 1881 book,* A Woman's Memories of World-Known Men, *a letter she had written to English poet, Rev. John Mitford, from Galveston in February of 1842. In this letter, she describes to Mitford a meeting with President Sam Houston while visiting the city of Houston with the French and English diplomatic corps. She describes Sam Houston as "wan and worn-looking" and states that he was quick to demonstrate his descent from the Old Country, and "claimed cousinship wish us at once." She further wrote that she'd never met a man who had done so much good service to State and humanity, "who was so simple and unobtrusive in manner, and who seemed to think so little of himself." Why a meeting with the leader of the Republic escaped publication in a travelogue pertaining to the Republic is very peculiar, indeed.*]

We were to leave Houston at eight o'clock in the morning. This arrangement gave me much satisfaction, as I should thus have an opportunity of seeing a considerable part of the country which we had previously passed in the dark. The frost was very severe, and the inhabitants asserted that the weather was unusually cold for the season of the year. They have an adage which tells them that no frost is ever known after the blossoming of the dogwood. This season, however, was certainly an exception, for the pretty shrub was in full blossom, but the thermometer was four degrees below the freezing point. The bayou is very narrow at Houston, and extremely winding. Some of the turns are so sharp that the steamer had great difficulty in getting round, and frequently touched the bank, both ahead and astern. Slow, however, as was our progress, I would have made it slower still. There was a bright sun shining above us and, notwithstanding the brisk cold air, I persisted in remaining on the hurricane-deck. I was at last, however, warned of the danger of my position, by receiving a pretty smart blow from the branch of one of the trees which nearly met over the stream. There were beautiful shrubs growing close to the water's edge, and down the steep acclivities had trickled rills of water, which were now frozen into icicles. The land was high, and interspersed with hill and valley on either bank. The nearer, however, we approached to the sea, the flatter and less pleasing the country appears. Gradually it becomes marshy, and has an unhealthy appearance.

There are quite as many passengers on board as when we ascended the river, and I certainly had reason to dread the night and the noisy talk which followed. The voices of Americans are in general disagreeable and pitched in a high tone. This is unpleasant enough in a man, but when such a voice proceeds from the mouth of a young and pretty woman, one really feels inclined to stop one's ears and refuse to hear the voice of the charmer. As to the habitual nasal twang (which before I visited the country I thought a fable, or at least an exaggeration of our fault-finding countrymen) it certainly exists in great perfection, and I have been at some pains to discover the cause. The fact is, their mouths are so full of their favourite weed that they cannot open them to speak without disagreeable consequences.

They are therefore obliged to employ their noses to perform the duty. But enough and too much has been said on
this disagreeable subject, and I only mention it *à propos* of
my sleepless nights on my narrow shelf in the steamer.

Breakfast on board was beef, and raw eggs after it, and
the infallible eggnog was drank by both ladies and gentlemen. Brandy is given freely. Nobody, however, appeared
to commit any excess, or seemed the least the worse for it.

There was a very pretty American on board who had
been a bride only a fortnight. She was not nineteen years
of age, and yet these were her second nuptials. Life is soon
begun in this country, especially among the female portion
of its inhabitants. While yet a child in years, the young
American turns into a "dreadful 'ansum girl'' at once, and
the consequence of this premature start is an early decay
of youth and beauty.

I was tempted, after breakfast, into the ladies' cabin, where
I remained because I was pleased and amused by what was
going on. The wife of the captain, who had more of the milk
of human kindness in her composition than would have
softened a dozen hearts in our conventional world, took
great pains to teach me the art of knitting, in which she
was wonderfully skilled. I, in return, answered her numerous questions about England. "Well I guess you've better
thread than this in the old country." "Do tell now, isn't this
pretty, sugar?" I told another lady (in return for some similar information) how many children I had left at home, and
then she marveled at how I could keep away from them.
She repeated the *bon mots* and accomplishments of her
own nursery brood till I began to repent of my temerity in
venturing among such a loquacious society. "I tell you now,
ma'am, my little boy always hides when he's told to go to
school, and I expect it's hard work to find him. He's a smart
boy is Washington Mirabeau, and that's a fact."

At dinner we had pig and parsnips, and the meal was,
as usual, despatched in an incredibly short space of time.
We were all much disappointed at an announcement which
was soon after made to us that, owing to the severe norther

which had been blowing for the last two days, the water was too low on one of the banks in the river to enable us to reach Galveston that evening. We were consequently obliged to run the vessel alongside of a sort of quay, and wait till the tide rose. A temporary bridge was constructed, and we all went on shore, some to shoot, others to visit a Colonel Morgan, close to whose house the vessel was lying, and some, like myself, to pass away time. It was extremely cold and we were obliged to walk briskly to keep ourselves tolerably warm.

Colonel Morgan's house was very pretty. Its owner was absent, so I went over it and took a walk in the grounds. The latter were well laid out, and the adjoining farm appeared, to my inexperienced eye, in good order. Some very fine sheep were grazing, and the wheat and barley looked very well. Mr. Houstoun had the good luck to kill an opossum, a strange-looking ugly animal, something like a badger, with its forepaws resembling human hands. When he brought the creature on board, the society were very anxious to have it cooked for supper, considering it, as they said, "first-rate eating."

The opossum is held in great respect by the Yankees, as a particularly "smart" animal. It is very difficult to take him, and he knows an ingenious trick or two for self-preservation. If he finds himself slightly wounded, and, after consideration, sees no other means of escape, he pretends to be dead and even allows himself to be carried home and his supposed corpse to be thrown aside. Directly he finds himself alone, he gets up and makes the best of his way to the woods again. This trick of the opossum is so well known, that when a slave is suspected by his employers of shamming sickness to avoid his work, he is compared to this cunning little beast: "Well I guess he's coming 'possum over us." It is difficult to deceive a Yankee, but the negroes often succeed when they pretend illness, for even as slave owners, these people have hearts, and kind ones too.

Some of the party who remained on board amused themselves with rifle-shooting, and I saw some good specimens of Yankee skill. A duck was discovered on the water, at the distance of fifty yards, and a sportsman assured us he would take off the top of its head, at that distance. He quite succeeded, and the poor little bird was brought to us literally scalped.

In the early part of the night I was, as usual, extremely amused with listening to the conversation of the acute calculators and cunning politicians that surrounded us. The future fate of the country, and its probable annexation to some other power was discussed, but what power was it to be? That was the question. France, they declared had been most anxious to obtain possession of them, but her propositions had not exactly suited them, and the affair had ended. England, they seemed to think, would be the most eligible country on which to lean, but it was doubted very generally, whether that power would have anything to say to them. This was public talk, but we were privately informed by a person worthy of credit that a negotiation for the sale of Texas, to which he had been a party, had been on the point of being concluded, between America and Mexico. The latter were to make over Texas, for a stipulated sum, to the United States.

The transaction, as he assured us, was all but concluded. The papers required only the signatures of the respective presidents, when the person charged, on the part of the Americans, with the necessary documents thought he might just as well do a little business on his own account. Instead, therefore, of proceeding direct to Mexico, he betook himself to Texas to purchase land. With the knowledge of the impending sale of Texas to the States, he knew that the value of his lands would rise swiftly and, thus, confidently made his purchase. His detour was the cause of considerable delay, and, in the interim, events occurred which rendered the projected compact impossible, and altered entirely the aspect of affairs.

Mixed up with these political conferences was a good deal of conversation on the interesting subject of the slave trade. This is a very engrossing topic here, and on this occasion, it gave rise to some rather violent speechifying. There were many greatly in favour of the continuance of slavery, and a few as strongly against it.

There was one individual who spoke well in favour of abolition. His reasonings were very right-minded and ingenious, and I admired the straightforward moral courage which induced him to stand boldly forward in the midst of so many opposers, and to advocate openly the cause which he had espoused.

After listening to the various arguments, for and against the possession of slave property, I saw no reason to change the opinion I had previously formed on the subject. I am as much as ever convinced that the slave-owners are the greatest sufferers by its continuance.

The almost absolute dominion which a slave-owner, at least in the plantations, possesses over his human property must tend, in the abstract, to render a master tyrannical and unmerciful. It has the effect of making them despotic, because the human mind is so constituted that the possession of power is seldom used with moderation. It cannot be doubted that harshness, and want of sympathy with the sufferings of others, are engendered by the necessity, which the furtherance of their own interests often lays them under, of parting kindred and near friends.

I am far, very far, from thinking with coldness and apathy on the fact that there are human beings in a Christian land living in a state of slavery and dark ignorance. There are, however, objections often brought forward, which are of a most trivial nature. It is said that the name of "slave" must be bitterly galling to those who have the misfortune to be called by this degrading term. That this would be the case were the present nature and habits of the people such as to render them susceptible of much fine feeling, I cannot but agree. But before the negroes can claim pity and sympathy on such a plea as this, they must have lived for years, and almost for generations, a life of freedom and voluntary exertion.

Again—that the slave-owner does not always follow the golden rule of doing to others as he would be done by, is true. That it is wrong and contrary to every right principle, moral and religious, to keep fellow beings in this degraded state, is equally true. At the same time, it may be asked whether the evil, as regards the slaves themselves, is not more nominal than real. The owner of a slave, when he purchases him, enters into an agreement, understood though not expressed, that the slave's services will be re-paid by food, lodging, and decent clothing; that the slave will be allowed sufficient intervals of rest, and a certain portion of time in which he may work for himself. Also the slave may look forward to eventual independence if he is able to earn it, or if his own good conduct may render him deserving of the boon. The life of the slave is protected by the laws. His good treatment is to a certain degree secured by the powerful argument that it is contrary to his owner's interest to ill-use him. All this I believe to be true, as also the fact that young children are not separated from their parents.

At present, what is the conduct of the freed slave, and how does he prove that he is either a happier or a better man because he possesses the gift of freedom? If there is any truth in the supposed degrading, and enervating influence of slave-owning, there is still more reason for believing that the forced servitude in which he is kept, together with the strong prejudice which exists against his race and colour, render the freed slave, in his present state of mind and education incapable of valuing his free position properly.

Chapter XXVI

Character of the Negro Slave
⚓ Stop at Harrisburg ⚓ Return to the Yacht

In the character of the negro slave, as in every other, both good and bad qualities are mixed. Courage, good nature, and gratitude, they certainly possess, but they also are vain, revengeful, cunning and indolent. The opinion is entertained by many, that their mental capacities naturally, are of a very mean order. Prejudice has, I think, much to do with this opinion. But it is certain that, until circumstances shall have called forth and the conduct of the negroes themselves shall have demonstrated that they are capable of becoming statesmen, mathematicians, poets or philosophers, the fact of their being on an equality of intellect with their white brethren will find but few believers.

It is evidently the policy of the Texan slaveholders to keep the negroes in a state of entire ignorance and mental subjection, and to reduce them as nearly as possible to the level of brutes. By this means they hope to justify their own conduct towards them, and to prevent any possible intermingling of the black and white races. It has been proved that, in the south, population increases much faster among the blacks than among the whites. And as the surplus population from other countries settles but slowly where slavery exists, it follows that in a short time the negro race will greatly exceed in numbers that of the white men. When this takes place—if not before—the struggle for freedom will commence, and how it will end, no one can exactly foresee. The slave-owners of Texas would willingly make us believe that one of their main reasons for supporting slavery is because of the impossibility of employing white labour in many parts of their territories. But we may fairly conclude that the real motive for their conduct proceeds from alarm that the negroes should make an immediate, and disagreeable use of their freedom were it granted them.

That they will do so at some future time can hardly be doubted, and it is almost to be wondered at, that any government should encourage the existence of slaves, when they are known to be increasing in such formidable numbers. Unless some decisive measures are taken, the day of reckoning must come. In anticipation of this crisis, and feeling how little aid can be depended on from the North, the southern governments have taken pains to prevent as much as possible the granting of freedom in individual cases, and are likewise most careful in checking the entrance of free negroes into the country. As a proof of this fact, I may mention that when we were on the point of engaging at Jamaica a black man, as steward's mate, we were told that he would not be allowed to go on shore in a slave country, and that were he discovered on board the yacht, Mr. Houstoun would be obliged to become surety to a large amount that he should not put foot on land.

In regard to the excuse principally alleged for continuing slavery—that of the necessity of employing black labour in so hot a country as Texas—it is affirmed by many sensible judges that the necessity for so doing is founded upon an erroneous opinion. It is true that were slavery abolished, the culture of land in some parts of Texas would be more laborious, and perhaps less productive, than it is now. But no one can believe that white men cannot work, or raise the produce of the country. In most parts of the republic, the climate is not hotter than it is in the southern countries of Europe. It is obvious that, were white labour in request, white men would work, and the country would become settled in an incredibly short space of time. When this advantage, together with innumerable other benefits attendant on the abolition of slavery (not among the least of which may be mentioned the rise of Texas in the estimation of European nations) are considered, it must be concluded that the blacks will ere long receive their freedom at the hands of their white masters.

It appears to me (short-sighted as I am in these matters and unqualified to give even an humble opinion,) that many of the evils attendant on freeing the blacks might be modified, and civil war perhaps prevented, by conciliatory measures being adopted gradually towards the negroes. They are capable of strong attachments and, though the work of years cannot be undone in a day, much might be effected towards paving the way to a better understanding. The only effectual mode of conciliation, namely, that of admitting the negroes to the society of the whites and to equal social rights, never (I should imagine) will be adopted, so strong is the prejudice against them. Still for his own interest, as well as for that of his country, each man should perform his part in the good work, and should bear in mind the following passage from De Tocqueville admirable writer on this question:

"Whatever may be the effort of the Americans of the South to maintain slavery, they will not always succeed. Slavery, which is now confined to a single tract of the civilized earth, which is attacked by Christianity as unjust, and by political economy as prejudicial; and which is now contrasted with democratic liberties, and the information of our age, cannot survive. By the choice of the master, or the will of the slave, it will cease; and in either case, great calamities may be expected to ensue. If liberty be refused to the negroes of the South, they will in the end seize it for themselves by force; if it be given, they will abuse it ere long."

Whilst the important discussion of the slave question was going on at one end of the cabin, the price of provisions and the tariff were the topics of conversation at the other. Everything, as I have before said, resolves itself into "calculation," and I had proof of this on the present occasion. One of the speakers declared that things in general were dearer than they used to be. He detailed the different and indispensable articles of food and clothing, and summed up their cost. This he called the expense of living. Having done this, he proceeded to make a bill of the items required on leaving the world. There was the doctor's bill, the coffin, the hearse, the burial fees, lawyer's ditto for making the will and the supper after the funeral. He concluded with, "Well, sir, I calculate, if living's dear in this country, dying's dearer still."

The negroes, I may remark, had a grand fight this evening, and their yells and oaths were fearful to hear. They were not interrupted in their pastime, nor did anyone appear even to notice the affray.

The battlefield of San Jacinto was pointed out to me, and the evolutions performed during the engagement described by one who had borne part in the action. The Texans always speak of this victory with pride and exultation, and they have a good right to do so.

A fire had recently occurred in this neighbourhood, by which the residence of a General Baker had been destroyed, and he himself reduced to great misery. Fires are now very rare in this country, but a Yankee remarked "they will be more frequent when insurance offices are established." There are several beginnings of cities on this bayou. One, in particular, I ought to mention, because it is a good specimen of the rest. It was planned and begun years ago by a foreigner of the name of Pellegrini; I believe a native of Savoy. This enterprising individual is as mad a castle-builder as I ever saw, and enthusiastic and sanguine beyond belief. We remained a short time, to land passengers before the city. The plan embraces churches, clubhouses, squares, terraces, theatres and, in short, all the concomitants of a great city. But in the meantime there exist but eight wooden houses and a fine sounding name: Harrisburg.

There was a slight accident, which happened to one of the engines, that delayed our arrival about two hours, even after we came within sight of Galveston. It was late in the evening of the third day before the steamer touched the upper wharf of that port. The gig was waiting for us with her crew of fine-looking English sailors, in their yacht-costume, each of them so clean and neat. What admiration they excited as they stepped from the gig on board of the dirty little steamer—none on board had ever seen the smart crew of an English yacht before, and the sight evidently filled them with wonder. In five minutes we found ourselves enjoying the quiet and comfort of our ocean home. One certainly never appreciates comforts till one loses sight of them. How often, during our short absence, had I sighed for the every-day luxuries to which we were accustomed on board. The decks never looked so white as now, and the brightly-polished guns and spotless paint were, in themselves, a perfect luxury to the sight.

CHAPTER XXVII

SEVERE NORTHER ⚓ HUMMINGBIRDS
⚓ EJECTING ABOLITIONISTS FROM GALVESTON
⚓ NATIONAL GUARD ⚓ TEXAN DUEL ⚓ DIVORCE
⚓ GOOD WISHES TO THE REPUBLIC OF TEXAS

The cold wind seemed to have been still more severely felt here at Galveston than it had been up the country, and one poor man had actually died from its effects. This dismal death, however, was not so much to be ascribed to the intensity of the frost, as to the extreme keenness and strength of the wind. The crew were fortunately always prepared, by the sudden falling of the glass, for these national northers, but if it happened that I myself had neglected to consult this unerring guide, I have been quite astonished at their arrival. I have known a calm, as still as death; not a ripple on the water and not a murmur on the breeze; when suddenly a sailor has exclaimed "Here it comes!" And, in a moment, literally in the twinkling of an eye, the wind was roaring through the rigging and the sea rising to a tremendous height. The schooner was tossed about at her anchorage and the water fell on the bar to its lowest depth.

The last norther, before our return, was particularly severe, but fortunately it left us fine spring weather. As proof of the power of the sun, rattlesnakes, alligators and mosquitoes were beginning to make their appearance. Of the former, I confess, I have a great horror and I am sure if I were ever to become a "settler," I should not have courage to brave them, as I saw done by the Galveston people. In order, I suppose, to make one's mind easy, you are told that "the Indians" know a helpful herb, which they call the "snake's master." I have no doubt that this is very consolatory to the Indians, but I cannot see in what way others are benefited by their knowledge.

I saw a poor little Scotch terrier fall victim to one of these reptiles. With all the spirit and valour of his race, the tiny dog rushed at his foe and, careless of his master's call,

returned again to the charge, even after having been severely bitten. He lived only about three hours after he had
received the bite, although all kinds of remedies were tried,
the most efficacious of which, we were told, was a spoonful
of gun powder poured down the animal's throat.

In the long grass, among which the snake was found, the
children of one of the inhabitants were constantly in the
habit of playing. I asked their father if he was not afraid of
their sharing the fate of the poor terrier, and his reply was
"No, they never have been bit," and that he believed "suck-
ing the poison out of the wound always prevented any fatal
consequences." The rattlesnake certainly does not take
you unawares, for their angry vicious rattle is heard long
before they proceed to the attack. I would, however, much
prefer keeping out of even hearing distance.

The alligator's eggs were just beginning to be hatched,
and the young reptiles came out in sunny days in great
numbers. The alligator, however frightful as he looks, is
not a creature to be much afraid of, as he is rarely known
to attack man. He is, moreover, so large and unwieldy that,
whilst turning himself about, there is plenty of time to get
out of his way. We took a young one on board the yacht,
about four feet long and very savage. He did not live more
than a fortnight, perhaps from being too much exposed to
the cold. I had also a pretty little flying-squirrel, which I
rescued in the streets of New Orleans from a boy who was
tormenting it. These creatures are very common here as
pets, and mine, though very shy, used to come on deck to
sun himself in fine weather.

One of the most curious creatures I saw in the country is
the "horned frog," as he is familiarly called. In shape, he is
not very unlike the ordinary frog, but with the addition of
a tail, about an inch and a half long. He is found in marshy
spots in the prairie, and is of a brownish-green colour,
spotted with black. He has horns on his head, which are
pointed, and about half an inch in length. He has also similar excrescences, though not of so great a length, on his
back. He runs with great rapidity and is altogether a most

wonderful little reptile. We had two of these animals in our menagerie, and hoped to preserve them till we reached England.

A few days before we left Texas, we saw, to our great surprise, an immense flight of hummingbirds. They had alighted in a small garden in the middle of the town, which, in default of better and sweeter flowers, was well-stocked with the yellow blossoms of the turnip-plant. I could have stood for hours looking at them. They seemed to be of every colour—crimson, green, blue—and sprinkled with gold-dust. They darted and glanced about in the bright sunshine, shooting out their long slender tongues into the yellow flowers, and making their tiny music sound through the little *parterre.*

We found it very difficult to take them alive, and many were sacrificed in the attempt. I had, however, three brought to me in little cages, and preserved them alive for some days, feeding them on bread soaked in honey, which they ate greedily. They sat on little perches and appeared to be much tamer than larger birds, roosting at night and eating throughout the day, without regard to the presence of human beings. They all died the death of pets, accident or overstuffing. Poor little things, they should never have visited the settlements. They were too fragile and too delicate for the contact of human hands. No one seemed to know where this flight of *oiseaux mouches* came from. The day after their first appearance was cold and cloudy and they were no more to be seen, having disappeared as suddenly as they came. It is strange, at what a great distance from land, these little creatures are occasionally seen. When we were more than two hundred miles out at sea, between Texas and the Havanna, a hummingbird settled on the rigging of the *Dolphin.*

As on board the steamer, we found the slave question the principal topic of conversation among the good citizens of Galveston. Many maintained that individuals have no right to interfere with their lawful property, and were so indignant with the abolitionists, that they banished the principal philanthropist from the city. The person in question was conveyed in a boat to the mainland, and there turned adrift to preach to the inhabitants of the woods and prairies. Another, a black man and by trade I believe a barber, had likewise incurred the displeasure of the inhabitants of Galveston, by advocating the cause of his race in the marketplace. He declared his life was in danger, and pretending to be a British subject, claimed the protection of the British minister. One of their own most respected townsmen did not escape their wrath. This person, having declared himself opposed to the abolition of slavery but still inclined to hear the arguments pro and con, was ordered to be silent on the subject. He replied that his was a free country, where everyone had a right to express his opinions. This right apparently was not acknowledged, for he was put into a boat and sent to the mainland: strange occurrences in a country calling itself free.

The National Guard of Galveston were kept constantly in battle-array, and paraded through the town. The guns, too, were kept in readiness to protect the town against the fleet which was every day expected from Campeachy or Vera Cruz. I cannot say that the artillery at the forts presented a very formidable appearance. There were not more than a dozen eighteen-pounders, one or two of which had been lying harmlessly on the sand ever since we had been here. In the yacht we fancied ourselves quite secure, concluding that the British flag would be treated with due respect. I had little real expectation, however, of seeing anything of the Mexicans, and was inclined to think that the excitement would end as it had begun—in words.

Our drives into the prairie were now much more agreeable than before. The weather was warmer, and the land much drier. There were also more living inhabitants—bluebirds, cardinals, etc. We shot some pelicans, and afterwards reproached ourselves for our cruelty, for they were quite useless for stuffing or any other purpose. There were immense flocks of curlew and plover, who were evidently on their passage to some other clime. The prairie was becoming quite gay with flowers. In many places, however, the settlers were setting it on fire, and a very curious sight it was—a sheet of fire flying rapidly before the wind. The cactus, or prickly pear, was beginning to blossom, and I expected in a few weeks I should recognise some of the glowing descriptions which travellers have given of the country. Alas! I had no chance of realizing my anticipations, for we were soon to take our leave of the Gulf. The pilot had returned from down the coast. He found at Aransas only six feet of water on the bar, and at Matagorda seven. He gave it as his opinion, however, that there were times when vessels drawing eight feet might enter the latter port with safety.

The Galveston pilot fell in with the Mexicans at Copano. This was a fortunate circumstance for him, for they gave him fifteen dollars for some tobacco which had cost him but three. This was a good "operation," and they begged him to return as soon as possible to do some more business, promising to purchase, on the same terms, as many thousand bales of tobacco as he could manage to bring. This circumstance shows us what the trade with Mexico is likely to be when peace is established.

I shall not be surprised to hear, before any long period has elapsed, that the valuable mines (I believe of gold, silver and copper) which are to be found in this country, are worked; to say nothing of the coal mines, which perhaps I ought to have placed first in the scale, at least of usefulness. When population increases, and the demand for wood, steamers and building becomes proportionately great, this necessary article will no doubt become scarce, and the working of the coal mines will then be a work of absolute necessity.

Cedar is the commonest and cheapest wood here, besides being much the most useful for building purposes. It is very valuable in the erection of wooden piles which are exposed to the action of water, as no insects or marine animals will adhere to it. This wood is the one most in use, too, for firing. As you pass near the houses where there are fires burning, the perfume is delicious.

On my last day at Galveston, I passed near the burial ground, and a sad sight indeed it was! I should not have been aware of its proximity had I not perceived a human skull under my horse's feet! On looking round I saw many similar relics, and hurried from the spot with a feeling of dismay and horror, which would be difficult to describe. The reason for this desecration of the dead is as follows. The sandy soil has so little depth that, no sooner are the dead deposited in the ground than they are denuded of their light covering, and the sea which washes the limits of the burial-ground claims its share of these neglected remains. The consequence is that the adjoining land is actually strewed by human bones in every direction.

Our last act and deed before we left Galveston, was watering and victualling the *Dolphin.* A large supply of salted beef was taken in, which I should not have mentioned, but for an accident which occurred in consequence, and which gave us a good deal of uneasiness. During the process of stowing the meat, it was necessary to remove some of the iron ballast, and for this purpose, an instrument of the same metal is made use of. It is about a yard long, with a handle at one end and a hook at the other. One of the men was tugging away at the handle of the rod, and another was lying down in the act of assisting him, when the iron bent slightly, the iron ballast immediately slipped off, and the man who held it fell backwards. The consequence was, that the iron hook entered the eye of the unfortunate man on the ground. By ill luck, our doctor was on shore at the time and did not return to the yacht for some hours afterwards. He did not at all approve of the treatment practised by the Texan surgeon, who had been summoned when the accident happened. The agony the poor man suffered must have been very great. He fainted away almost immediately and soon became delirious. He was a long time on the sick list, and eventually lost the sight of his injured eye.

I confess, I should not much like to trust a serious case in the hands of the Texan doctors. Some of them may be clever and well educated, but the medicines in general I believe to be bad, in spite of their frequent announcement as cargo, and the words, "drugs" and "chemicals" appended to so many of the stores.

A death by violence had lately taken place in this country; and, as the circumstances under which it occurred caused a considerable excitement, I think them worthy of narration, and the more so as they throw some light on the reputed frequency of violent deaths in Texas.

A Colonel H., a mild and benevolent man, had a quarrel (as even the mildest men will sometimes have) with one of his neighbours. There was no means of adjusting their differences and, accordingly, Colonel H. was informed by his adversary, in the usual terms, that he should take an early opportunity of shooting him dead. Colonel H. was not a particularly nervous man, and for some time after this pleasant announcement had been made, he went about perfectly convinced, from the character of his foe, that he would not fail to keep it to the letter. After a while, however, the suspense and anxiety became too much for his spirits, and he resolved to put an end to the affair. Acting upon this resolution he watched for an opportunity, waylaid his adversary and—mild man as he was—put a period to his existence.

This affair, which would have been called a murder by prejudiced and ill-informed historians, is but the Texan mode of managing a duel. It certainly differs from our way of settling a quarrel, but when all is said, I do not know that it is a much worse form of manslaughter.

I have omitted to mention the extreme ease with which divorces are obtained in Texas. During our residence of only a few months in the country, no less than forty couples were disunited, and this merely by taking an oath on both sides of mutual incompatibility of temper. This circumstance ought to be generally known; as it may be of service to those similarly situated to learn that by a six months' residence in Texas, they may enjoy the benefit of this liberating system.

I received a present on this, my last day in the republic, which, though of little value, I prized as proof of kindness of heart and good feeling. Mrs. Kelsey, the wife of the captain of the little Houston steamer, the *Dayton*, sent me a cap of her own knitting. I had particularly admired it when on board, and it was worked with great labour and skill. She looked for no return, and the circumstance was the more gratifying because I had seen her but once, and did not expect to renew my acquaintance with her. Such things are not common in the "old country."

If we set off such instances of good will as these (and I could mention many others) against the trifling annoyance occasioned by the apparent familiarity and want of refinement on the part of these young settlers, we shall be more satisfied with the real good we find among them.

I one day heard a rough Texan, dressed like a ploughman, ask one of our English friends for the loan of his gun for a few days; and another, trusting (and not too much) to his good nature, said, on another occasion, "Well, now, Commodore, I want you to lend me your bedroom for a short time, if you please." It is the consciousness of their own extreme willingness to confer similar obligations which renders these people so little scrupulous in making somewhat exorbitant demands of others.

But I must draw my Texas annals to a conclusion. We were, as the Yankees say, "bound to go," and to leave this land of free hearts and untrammelled actions, for one which owns a despot's sway—and for a colony where the broad hand of authority presses down the energies of the people.

Let me, before I bid adieu to the shores where we had so long ridden at anchor, waft good wishes to the land and to its inhabitants. May the country "go ahead" and prosper. May wise men lead her counsels and brave men direct her arms. Above all, may her financial and commercial character be unsullied. Then will her word be good in the Great Exchange House of Nations, and she may hope to stand alone—an independent republic—a great people among the powers that are.

CHAPTER XXVIII

LEAVING GALVESTON FOR HAVANNA ⚓ SEVERE GALE
MORO CASTLE ⚓ LADIES' MANNERS
⚓ VISIT FROM SPANISH AUTHORITIES ⚓ HEAT

March 31st, 1844—We took our pilot, Simptom, again onboard and made sail. The men, as before, were busily employed in shifting ballast. A north wind had been blowing for some days, but the weather was calm and fine. After crossing the bar, the pilot was discharged, and I then really felt that I had bidden adieu to Texas.

Gradually the low shores of Galveston receded from our view. I stood on deck as long as I could catch a glimpse of the land, and continued my speculative reveries on her present and future fate, till other objects arrested my attention, and till the horizon was bounded only by the wide and quiet ocean. I entertained such disagreeable recollections of the September gales that I rather dreaded putting to sea in March, but our master assured me that the vernal equinox was not at all to be dreaded and I felt my courage strengthened. All this day, and the beginning of the next, I had reason to be satisfied with the weather and reposed in confident belief of a pleasant and quiet voyage to Havanna. Alas, for the short-sighted anticipations of a woman!

In the afternoon of the 1st of April, as I was quietly eating my luncheon in the cabin, I heard distinct preparations for a gale. Darkness crept over the sky and I heard the voice of the mate, "Take in a reef in the fore stay-sail." I never liked the sound of the reefing process. We always carried a great deal of sail, and I knew it was never reduced without absolute necessity. Soon after, it was "Take in another reef in the foresail! Look alive!" The lowering of the mainsail soon followed, and by this time it was blowing a violent gale of wind.

The sea, in an incredibly short space of time, had risen to a great height and, instead of enjoying the placid motion of the waves reposing on my couch on the deck, I had to hold on and devote all my energies to prevent myself rolling about in all directions. There is certainly something very laughable in the efforts made by landsmen and women to keep themselves steady on the deck during a gale of wind. Our present storm, indeed, was really no laughing matter. At a late hour I retired to rest, but continued putting up my head out of my cabin every five minutes to inquire how the wind was, and whether there was any chance of its abating.

On such occasions as these, the appearance of daylight was always hailed by me with unwonted satisfaction. I liked to see my situation with my own eyes, and to have the power, at any moment, of applying for information to one or other of the crew. Of course they always comforted me with assurances that it was nothing—it was only blowing fresh. This always reassured me, but more than all the rest, I rejoiced to see their cheerful faces, and to hear that they could joke.

On the morning of the 2nd of April I went on deck early. It was not seven o'clock, but I had had a sleepless night, so I wrapped a large cloak about me and staggered up to see the state of affairs. What a scene of blank desolation it was! The decks were wet and slippery with the spray; everything looked out of order and forlorn. The watch on deck had on their rough pilot-coats and southwesters well secured under their chins, and were crouching under the bulwark, to leeward, to avoid the constant showers of spray. The sea was of one dull heavy leaden hue, except where the summits of the huge tumbling waves were crested with a snow-white foam. It is one of the most fearful effects of the tremendous waves in a heavy head-sea, that your view is bounded only by high walls of inky-looking water. Around and ahead the prospect is circumscribed by these tremendous bulwarks of the raging element, which seem ever on the point of engulfing you in their descent. As I stood on the poop, and the bowsprit pitched into the hollow pit of waters, it seemed almost like a perpendicular descent, and I closed my eyes for a moment as though all was over.

Before eight o'clock, a second reef was taken in the fore-topsail. There was no break in the clouds till about noon, when the sun for a moment appeared through a thin veil of gray. In the afternoon the weather became much more moderate. Reefs were shaken out, and I began once more to feel happy and at ease. The swell, however, was still very heavy, and we were told was likely to continue so, the Gulf of Florida not being notorious for the quiet of its seas.

We saw a great deal of the gulf-weed, which floated past us in large quantities. This seaweed is very light and pretty when first taken out of the water, but it soon becomes shapeless and will not bear drying. I believe a vast number of shipwrecks have occurred in the Gulfstream. There are fearful currents and eddies, and ships are frequently driven out of their course. From the narrowness of the channel, the sea is always in a state of commotion and after the violence of the late gale, the waves were more fearful than ever. We were all, I mean the "idlers," more or less prostrated, either by internal or external malaise. Poor Monsieur de Cramayel was quite *hors de combat*, with the best intentions of making a good fight against the enemy. He didn't taste food for five days, and to this moment I am at a loss to understand how he contrived to exist through such a period of inanition.

As usual, we went through the ceremony of every meal, as regularly as if we were on land. The cook was never put out by weather, and let the ship roll about as she would, he never made any alteration and his entrees were as good and as numerous as ever. The table, which was a swinging one, sometimes caused a little delay in the consumption of the viands. Often, when on the point of securing a mouthful on our forks, the well-spread board would mount up towards the ceiling on one side, and we were forced to wait its pleasure before we resumed our meal. This was amusing enough to me and, as no one was very hungry at such a time, the delay did not so much matter, but the noise is not to be described.

I believe the *Dolphin* to be (without partiality) as quiet as
a ship can well be, but the masts and bulkheads began, after their long rest, like giants refreshed, to labour out their
peculiar noises with a spirit unknown before. I was told it
was nothing, and certainly, after the first night or two, I
slept soundly and heard it no more. How we were flung
about! My swinging cot rocked to and fro like an insane
thing, whilst I felt myself a passive victim to its sport. One
night I found myself, with a sudden shock, prostrated on
the deck. I had been sleeping soundly, and at first could
not make out in the least what had happened. I soon, however, ascertained that the lashings of my cot had given way
from the constant strain upon them. Luckily for me the
bump upon the deck was not felt by my head, as it was the
lashing at the feet that had given way. It was not pleasant,
however, to find oneself, in the dead of the night, in an
angle of forty-five degrees. The occurrence recalled to my
mind some descriptions of practical jokes, related by Captain Marryatt, and I thought how hard it was for unwary
midshipmen, to be cut down at the head, when they least
expected it. The escape from concussion of the brain must
be narrow. It is to be inferred, from its unfrequent occurrence, that the young gentlemen in the navy, half a century
ago, were not very susceptible in that organ.

April the 3rd was rather squally, but it was only single-reef
weather, and I did not mind it. On the 4th, light breezes,
"out all reefs," delightful sound! But it was not to last, and
during the three following days it blew hard enough. The
current was running very strong, and we were driven forty
miles out of our course. I believe that nothing but the violence of the gale would have induced our poor passenger
to come on deck. I had not seen him for four days, when
all of a sudden he made his appearance on the companion
ladder. Sickness and suffering had made sad havoc with
his outward man, as indeed they had with most of us.

The weather on the 8th was more moderate, and in the
morning several sails were in sight. It was delightful to
watch them—to speculate on what they might be, and to

feel that this stormy stage of our aquatic journey was so nearly at an end. At eleven o'clock a.m. the man at the masthead sung out "land ahead." The wind was S.E. half east, and the current was driving us to the eastward. We gradually neared the land, and at five o'clock p.m. I heard the welcome order to clear anchors. Soon after, we sighted Moro Castle. The highlands were beautiful! Once more we rejoiced in the sight of the waving tops of the coconut trees, and felt the hot sun of the tropics.

But we had no time for admiration, as the British ensign was hoisted and flowing gaily aft. The little schooner had passed the Moro Castle, and was sailing up between the closely-packed shipping in such a perfect manner! She certainly excited great admiration, if we could judge by the faces and marked attention of those on board the ships through which she passed. I was prepared by description for the striking appearance of the harbour, particularly of its entrance. The Moro Castle is on the left, a high imposing building. On the right is the fort of Punteo, and the prisons built by Tacon, when he was Captain-General of Cuba. The bay, in which more than one thousand ships may anchor with safety, opens out beyond this narrow entrance. Our master almost always made a point of taking a pilot, and this was one of the few occasions on which he deviated from his rule. The yacht, after threading the mazes of this difficult navigation, brought up at six o'clock p.m. in seven fathoms water. Decks were immediately cleared and sails furled, and we prepared once more for a quiet life.

There was so much to interest and to attract attention, that I stood on deck absolutely staring at all the interesting objects I saw. There were ships of every nation, and we were soon boarded by a number of dingy-looking men from a wretched-looking boat bearing the Spanish flag. The deck of the schooner was soon crowded by these officials, for such I supposed they were, while some rushed below, examining her in all directions. An order was given at last that no more should come on board. They could not all have a right to board us, and civility evidently was not the object of their visit.

I had been so long in democratic countries that I was quite rejoiced at the sight of some faint symbols of royalty. And (I confess my weakness) the dirty crown, on the still more discoloured flag, was quite refreshing to my feelings. To be sure, it was but the crown of degraded Spain, the lowest of the monarchies of the earth, but I respected it nevertheless. I began almost to despair of being ever left to ourselves. No sooner was the curiosity of one party satisfied than another boatload made its appearance. They dispersed themselves over every part of the vessel, and poked their black and tanned faces into every hole and corner, filling our eyes and noses with tobacco smoke, and defiling the white decks of the *Dolphin* with the odious consequences of their national habit.

The fact was that they could not be made to comprehend the nature of our craft. She was armed—that was suspicious—but then we were evidently not a belligerent set—were we traders? No—they concluded that there must be concealed cargo somewhere, and consequently hunted about in all possible and impossible places for our supposed merchandise. Monsieur de Cramayel, with the dismal recollections of his late sufferings fresh upon him, remarked "I think it very natural. Of course they find it impossible to comprehend how any rational beings can be seasick for pleasure!" The Spaniards evidently could not understand it. They shrugged their shoulders, looked puzzled, and with most dissatisfied faces returned to their boats.

Then came the sharks in the shape of bumboat-women, entreating and coaxing the sailors to buy of them. Jokes were cut as they leant over the ship's side, and every now and then, when some adventurous individual completed his purchase, it was handed up in triumph, and the fortunate possessor began to discuss its real value coolly and at leisure. My attention was diverted from this rather amusing scene by perceiving an English man-of-war's boat pulling towards us. She contained, besides the rowers, only a midshipman, a small boy, who if only as a clean countryman of our own we were delighted to see. He had been despatched from the *Thunder* surveying ship, Captain Barnett, which was lying near, to make inquiries, and to ask if we were the *Charlotte* yacht. Having replied in the negative, (and it seemed that our advent had caused much speculation among our countrymen) we thanked Captain Barnett through his envoy for some kind and civil offers he had made us, and our new acquaintance took his leave. Except the *Romney* receiving ship, the *Thunder* was the only English man-of-war then at Havanna.

After dinner, a very polite aide-de-camp, attended by a Yankee interpreter (very boastful and very loquacious) came to make inquiries after the health of the crew. The surgeon made out his statement that we were all tolerably well and that no immediate anxiety need be felt on our account. A clean bill of health was therefore given us, and we were graciously allowed the liberty of going on shore. Early the next morning Mr. Houstoun took advantage of the permission and called on Mr. Crawford, Her Britannic Majesty's Consul-General, to whom he had letters to deliver, and we had the pleasure of dining at his house the same afternoon.

This was called the cool season at Havanna. No one complained of heat, indeed some of the old inhabitants pronounced it quite temperate. I could not understand this, for to me it was most oppressive. We had again recourse to our awning, and as one proof among many that our sensations did not deceive us, the fish that was bought alive in the market at ten in the morning was in an uneatable state at four o'clock on the same day. How fearful must be the heat during the reign of the yellow fever! The healthy season is said to commence in November, and to last till February, so that I fear we had slightly encroached upon the limits of the yellow fever dominions. The dews here are remarkably heavy. The deck early in the evening was quite wet, as though heavy rain had fallen during the day, and drops fell heavily from the masts and rigging. These dews are supposed to be particularly injurious to Europeans, and the latter should be particularly careful not to expose themselves to their influence.

It is the custom at Havanna to dine early, and a very sensible custom it is. The ladies remain at home during the heat of the day, lounging over their chocolate and cigars, or taking their accustomed siesta. When the sun has nearly set, their life of movement (if such it can be called) begins. Then it is that they enjoy their drives, and pay their visits of ceremony or affection. After dining with the Consul, Mrs. Crawford's carriages conveyed the whole party to drive on the Passeo, the fashionable promenade of the city.

Almost the only carriage in use is the volante. It is a description of vehicle peculiar, I believe, to Cuba I must, therefore, attempt a description of it, for the benefit of those who have not had an opportunity of seeing it. It is in shape not unlike a cabriolet on extremely high wheels. It is six or seven feet in height, and the wheels are above the head of the occupant. The shafts are extremely long, and the effect is very light and graceful.

The volante is driven by a postilion, almost always a black, and his dress is the gayest that can be imagined. Gold and silver are spread with a lavish hand on his person, and red and blue, and every gay and gaudy colour is chosen for his adornment. The famed Postilion de Longjumeau would sink into obscurity and shabbiness by the side of these black performers.

Sometimes a second horse is attached as an outrigger, and has a pretty effect. This, however, is not allowed within the precincts of the city. Gentlemen are not often seen with ladies in the volante. Two ladies generally occupy the only seat, which is extremely wide. The rate at which the postilions drive, considering the narrowness of the streets, is surprising. The mules here are more esteemed than the horses. They are, many of them, beautiful animals and I saw some of a cream colour, which I admired extremely. I believe very high prices are given for them, as much as from sixty to two hundred pounds. I was delighted with the appearance both of the ladies and their showy equipages, as they assembled on the Passeo. The volante itself is much ornamented with silver, and the harness is always plated, wherever plating can, by any possibility, be applied.

The ladies wear the mantilla and their costume, in their volantes, consists (as it appeared to me almost *de rigueur*) of white muslin décolleté, with short sleeves, and neither gloves nor mittens. Their dark hair is always beautifully shining and well dressed. Their heads are well set on, and at the back hang the elegant folds of the lace mantilla. Everyone has something to say of the surpassing beauty of the Spanish women. Their eyes! Their figures! Their walk! These are all described as something so exquisite that no women, of more northern climes, can venture to compete with them.

I confess I was terribly disappointed by these far-famed beauties. One volante after another rolled by, and not one tolerable face, taken altogether, had I seen. I have no doubt that the extreme heat of the climate, to a certain degree, increases the natural duskiness of their complexions. Certainly, in daylight, they were, I thought, much too yellow to be pleasing. By daylight, however, they are rarely to be seen. It is at night that they are viewed to advantage. They all use rouge, I was told, from early childhood. But their black eyes, which are magnificent, do not require this foreign aid to make them sparkle. I saw some reputed beauties in the morning, and thought them plain; while at night, I could not believe them to be the same persons, and felt inclined almost to change the opinion I had formed in the morning.

The walk of the Spanish women, which is described as being so peculiarly graceful, I had little opportunity of seeing. No lady walks at Havanna, nor do they even descend from their volantes when on shopping expeditions. Naturally indolent, this relaxing climate seems to deprive them of the little degree of energy which nature bestows on them. Their accomplishments are as limited as their sphere of action. They whisk about their large fans with surprising dexterity, and this seems to be one of the principal employments of their lives. They speak a little bad French, do a little indifferent religion, get through a considerable amount of flirtation, and not a little scandal. The evening drive on the Passeo is the grand event of every day. Gossip then goes on at a great rate, as every passerby is scanned and scrutinized. Appointments are made, and reputations are sneered away. Great care is taken during the drive, that the long white drapery should hang out over the step of the volante, it not being etiquette for the flouncings and embroideries to be gathered within the carriage. I was warned of this by a young lady with whom I was driving, and who was shocked at seeing me endeavouring to save my gown from dust, and the contact of passing wheels.

The Passeo de Tacon was constructed by the governor of that name, and is really a most striking promenade. There are fountains and statues and everything requisite to make a delightful city drive. On Sundays it is crowded by volantes, both private and hired. Tacon made many improvements in Havanna and its neighbourhood. It is a pity that this fine colony should not oftener have wiser heads to direct it, and that a government better qualified should not exist in the Mother Country, to choose its viceroy.

In the Plaza des Armas, which is a large handsome square opposite the palace of the viceroy, a band of music plays almost nightly. The performance struck me as good; but the choice of music was not made with good taste, at least the fancy of the captain-general, who selects the airs, must be a lugubrious one, to judge of the dismal sounds that saluted our ears. The preponderance of brass instruments is much too great, and I was soon glad to escape from the uproar, and refresh myself with an ice at a cafe near the Plaza. This custom of eating ices, which are brought to them in their volantes, is a favourite diversion of the Havanna ladies. The gentlemen, meanwhile, offer their assistance, and are rewarded with smiles, and meaning flicks with the ever-ready fan.

On Thursday, Monsieur de Cramayel and Mr. Houstoun dined with the Captain-General Valdez, by whom they were received with the greatest kindness and hospitality. It is not etiquette for the Viceroy to receive ladies at dinner, nor is he himself allowed to dine with any individual, regardless his rank. I was told that the Viceroy did not at all enjoy the forced monotony of his existence. He is unmarried, but Madame Olivar, the wife of the Spanish minister at Mexico, is residing with him and assists in doing the honours of the palace. Though not permitted to invite ladies to dine with him, this prohibition does not extend to evening parties. I attended several soirées there, and was glad to make the acquaintance of Madame Olivar, who is a delightful person.

During some of these visits, I learned a good deal of the present state of Cuba—its products, and the policy of Spain with regard to the colony. My principal informant was a grave, sensible old Spaniard, whose name, however, I have totally forgotten. He took compassion on my evident want of information on the subject, and I felt much obliged to him.

CHAPTER XXIX

CRUEL TREATMENT OF SLAVES IN CUBA
⚓ SUGAR COUNTS ⚓ MINES ⚓ CREOLES
⚓ MATANZAS REVOLT ⚓ SCENERY & CATHEDRAL

Since its discovery by Christopher Columbus, Cuba has frequently been a contested possession between England and Spain. In the year 1760, the island was confirmed as a dependency of the Spanish government, and the Floridas were ceded to Great Britain in exchange. It is a rich and most valuable island. The soil is very productive, and yields two and sometimes three crops of corn a year. Of the extreme fertility of the island, no one can form an idea, till, from some lofty point, he casts his eye over the beautiful view of its fertile plains and wooded hills.

Though early in the year when I was there, the country was covered with sweet-smelling and beautiful plants, while already the shrubs and trees were filling the air with the perfume of their fragrant blossoms. Sugar, rum, tobacco, cocoa, coffee, molasses are some of the principle articles of export. A great quantity of salted meat and fish, as well as grain of many kinds, are imported.

The slave-trade, as is well known, flourishes in this country, and to its existence may, I think, be attributed many of the degrading vices, and peculiar defects which debase the general character of the white inhabitants of Cuba. The Spaniards have the reputation of showing more kindness to their slaves than the white masters in other slave countries. This may be the case with the domestic slaves, as the black population certainly look particularly fat, sleek and well fed. It was at Havanna, however, that I first saw the marks of stripes on the shoulders of a woman, and I cannot describe the effect that the sight produced upon me, and the horror against the unmanly wretches who could thus punish a woman. I once witnessed in the neighbourhood of Havanna, the degradation of a negro slave preparatory to receiving punishment. He was being dragged along with a rope round his neck, like some refractory criminal. Similar and I fear much worse instances of cruelty are, alas, too frequently occurring in the plantations.

The proportion of negroes to white men is greatly in favour of the former. The policy adopted in regard to both Creoles and negroes is injudicious, with no attempts being made to conciliate the good will of either. The iron hand of military and despotic power is the only rule and were it not for that, there is no doubt but that this fine colony would soon pass from the hands of its present masters. No Creoles are ever employed in any high or honourable offices, nor are they allowed any responsibility or share in the affairs of government. Thus this numerous class of the inhabitants are rendered disaffected, and ready to join in any scheme of revolt. Moreover, many of the Creoles are possessed of great wealth, which causes them to be infinitely dangerous as enemies. It is said that the negro population are constantly on the eve of revolt, and the consciousness of this being probably the case keeps the government in perpetual hot water. The regular troops consist of only ten thousand men, while there are six hundred thousand blacks, rendered desperate by oppression and ready at any moment to turn upon their rulers. The Spanish government in Europe seems but little aware of the volcano which is so near bursting beneath their over-strained and injudicious rule.

Not long ago there was a well-ordered and nearly successful insurrection of the Matanzas negroes. They behaved with great courage and resolution, and having obtained some slight advantages, they secured themselves in a strong position, from which they did not emerge till they had obtained conditions extremely favourable to themselves. The authorities of Havanna are now evidently roused to a sense of danger, for even the word "freedom" is suppressed, and the fine national air of "Libertad" is not allowed to be sung. It is vain, however, to suppose that such precautions will prevent the silent longing for freedom from finding a voice among a people goaded to desperation by a sense of their wrongs. The coloured population of Cuba may be subdued and crushed for a time, but the smouldering fire will some day burst forth from the trampled ashes, and not all the power of Spain will be able to stay its fury.

There are a great many natives of the Canary Islands here. They are said to be good, well-disposed people and, as servants, they are valued as faithful and intelligent.

The different classes of society at Havanna are kept, from all I could learn, strictly apart. There are a few still remaining of the real old grandees of Spain. Indeed, I have heard persons well acquainted with the manners and habits of good old Spanish families declare that such are to be found now only at Havanna. In Spain (though the Mother Country) the race is said to be extinct. Great and unqualified contempt is felt and expressed by these aristocratic families for the "*nouveaux riches,*" who, swelling with pomp and pride, lord it over their humbler neighbours. Many of the latter, however, are great landed proprietors and slave-owners. "Sugar Counts" they are called. The epithet is remarkably well-chosen, as it tells, in many instances, the tale of their increase of fortune, and at the same time conveys an idea of the possibility of their titles and riches melting away as speedily as they have arisen.

One of these "sugar noblemen," (his name I have forgotten, but he is said to be the richest man on the island) made his fortune by the importation of slaves—a licensed dealer in human flesh. I looked at him as a sort of monster, when I reflected upon the vast amount of human suffering of which he had been the acting cause.

The alligator, the sea-cow and the turtle are all found in the island of Cuba. The latter, however, are not numerous, and the supply for consumption at Havanna is brought from the island of Nassau.

I saw birds in endless variety—canaries, cardinals, nightingales, linnets, parroquets—in short, everything that can be imagined as most gay and harmonious. I could scarcely help fancying it the pleasant month of June, the air was so sweet and soft, while the song of the birds filled my imagination with memories of past springtimes.

A great drawback to these spring delights were the fearful number of noxious insects and reptiles—snakes of the worst kind, scorpions, centipedes, and I cannot tell what besides. The persevering bloodthirsty mosquitoes were already rife, but happily they did not venture much on board the yacht.

A railroad has been in existence for some time in Cuba, extending to a distance of fifty miles between Havanna and Guines. It traverses a not very level line of country, and there are several considerable cuts through hills, and also a tunnel of tolerable length. These things speak well for the industry and resources of the Cuban people, for even a little appearance of energy shows well among the enervated denizens of the West Indies. Extensive and valuable coal mines, as well as those containing copper and silver, have been discovered in Cuba. These must be a source of immense wealth, and there is no want of ready money to work them. The railroad traverses a beautiful line of country, diversified with cocoa-trees, and innumerable other plants, unknown except within the tropics. We passed, during our railroad excursion, through extensive coffee and other plantations of tobacco, sugar, etc. The coffee shrubs grow very prettily and the green of the leaves is rich and varied. There is great charm to a stranger in seeing the wild growth of the pineapple, the plantain, the custard-apple and the cocoa-tree. The fruit hung on the dark boughs of the orange trees like golden lamps in a green night. There were many other trees, of which I do not know the names, some of which were literally loaded with green fruit. The forests are very thick, and clear rills of water trickle down the mountain sides, refreshing one by the very sight of their coolness.

The climate in the mountains is, I am told, healthy enough, but near the coast we heard enough of its baneful effects. We were warned not to expose ourselves to the influence of the moon's rays. The influence of the gentle planet is supposed to be particularly dangerous, and to bring on attacks of the fell disease.

The principal cities in Cuba are Havanna, St. Jago de Cuba, Principe and Santa Maria de Punto. There are several safe ports and good anchorages, but from the vast extent of rocks and shoals, the navigation outside is difficult and often dangerous. The forts above the city are covered with palm trees. The citadel itself is very strongly armed, as well as the heights above the town, which are bristling with arms. No stranger is allowed to visit the arsenal or to enter the fortifications. Admittance I believe, is limited to the government authorities and the garrison. I heard of a poor artist from a foreign land who, not being aware of the prohibition, strayed with his colours and brushes within the works. He was not even challenged by the sentinel who, without any other notice, fired his musket at the poor man. Fortunately, the wound was not a severe one. Officers of the British navy are especially excluded, not only from visiting the forts, but also from entering the ships of war.

I have already mentioned Tacon, the governor, as one to whom Havanna, and indeed the island of Cuba generally, are indebted for much of their present peace and prosperity. This clever and enterprising viceroy was sent from Spain some years since. He found the colony in a miserable condition. There were but few public works and national buildings, and those in existence were being neglected and abused. Robbery and murder were committed with impunity, and there were neither guardians of the public peace, in the shape of police, nor any laws by which justice could be effectually administered. All these evils, and many others, Tacon took upon himself to redress. He established an efficient police, by which offenders were kept in awe, and quiet was restored to the capital. He enforced obedience to the laws, protected trade, and hunted out and punished the bands of robbers which before infested the country. He also built large prisons and enacted useful laws for their government and regulation. I have before said that the planting and arrangement of the public promenades was his work, but the most conspicuous of the adornments, to which Havanna is indebted to this indefatigable governor, is the *campo militar*, which is called the Square of Tacon. It has four gates, one on each side of the square, to which he gave the name of Columbus, Cortes, Pizarro and Tacon.

El Teatro de Tacon, as its name implies, was likewise erected under the late governor's auspices. It is remarkably handsome and about the size of our Haymarket. The ornamental part is in very good taste. The pit seats, which are usually occupied solely by gentlemen, are comfortably fitted up with armchairs, each one having a number appended to it. There is a good Plaza de Toros, and the bullfights of Havanna used to be celebrated, though at present great complaints are made of the scarcity of good bulls for the arena. The ladies are in despair, "the stupid beasts are so tame." The cathedral is well worth seeing, particularly during the Holy Week, when black kneeling figures are sprinkled over its wide pavement in all directions. The pictures it contains are scarcely tolerable, but there is an urn shown you, which contains, it is said, the remains of Columbus. I looked at the latter with great interest and respect as the only mortal part of the great voyager, ordained by providence to bring into light and truth so large a portion of the globe.

Chapter XXX

Magnificent Private Houses
⚓ Holy Week ⚓ Fruits ⚓ High Prices
Our Last Night in Havanna

The private houses at Havanna, at least a great many of them, are magnificent. It is the custom here to leave all the windows to the street open at night. Living rooms are most commonly on the ground floor, and the passerby is of course at liberty to enjoy the sight of many a gay soirée and tertulia. In other towns, where such things and sights are unknown, a crowd would speedily be collected. But here, the practice is so universal that no one thinks from mere motives of idle curiosity of stopping to look in. Acquaintances of the house, or of some of the guests, may occasionally peep in at the windows, in order to see if any of those they would wish to meet are within. If the results of the survey prove satisfactory, they enter without ceremony. This seems to me a very agreeable style of society. There are no formal reunions and no person need enter a room with the chance of meeting a disagreeable or obnoxious person. Another great advantage, attending this easy mode of visiting, is that you are not compelled to remain a moment longer in any house than you find it agreeable.

Great preparations were being made for the ceremonies of the Holy Week. The gaiety of the previous days was to be replaced by the strictest mourning and gloom. Flags of every nation were floating in the harbour: the gaudy red and yellow of the Spaniard, the French tri-colour, the ensigns of Hamburg, Prussia and Belgium, to say nothing of our own national colours, which in true loyalty to my country, I ought to have placed first in the list. The national colours, if belonging to Catholic countries, are, on Good Friday, lowered half-mast high. The yards are canted, and the effigy of Judas Iscariot, after having been hung at the yard-arm, is, with every mark of ignominy and detestation, thrown headfirst into the sea.

A few days after our arrival, our kind friends Mr. and Mrs. Crawford and their party, besides Captain Barnett of the *Thunder* and a Spaniard or two, dined on board the yacht. Our table was spread (as usual with us in hot weather) on deck, under the shade of the awning. The *Illustrious*, seventy-two, bearing the flag of the Admiral of the station, Sir Charles Adam, was hourly expected. This was, indeed, to my great satisfaction, as I had had very little experience in naval matters, and looked forward quite as a treat to seeing a vessel so large maneuvering her way through the narrow channel. The approach of the expected ship was telegraphed during dinner, and shortly afterwards we saw her tall masts rounding the Moro Castle. The entrance to the harbour is not more than about three hundred yards, and as there was hardly any wind, the entrance of such a ship, her tacking, etc, did not seem by any means an easy affair. Everything else was forgotten in the interest of the sight, and in the anticipated pleasure of seeing more English faces in a foreign land. In spite of difficulties, the flagship came in beautifully, and came to an anchor close to the yacht.

After dinner we went on shore to drive and to shop. I went in quest of sweetmeats, which are excellent here but expensive, as all articles of food are. To us, so lately accustomed to the cheapness of living in Texas, the high prices of necessaries seemed still more remarkable. The price of a very small fowl was half a dollar, and beef was tenpence a pound. The mutton was better flavoured than the beef, which was dry and tasteless. The vegetables were excellent, and in great variety. We had young potatoes, French beans, peas, asparagus, cauliflower—in short every summer vegetable which Europe produces, besides others peculiar to the country. The oranges and pines were delicious, and the watermelons were not to be despised. The Zapote Mamme I did not think a bad fruit, but the natives eat some kinds which are really detestable. The guava, which makes so good a preserve, is, I think, quite unpleasant in a raw state, both in taste and smell. And I am far from approving the mango, though it looks so tempting. There is also a purple fruit, the name of which I forgot, but it is anything but delicious, and another equally bad, of an ugly brown colour, resembling in appearance a potato half-baked, with its skin on. In my opinion, none of the fruits here are to be compared to those we eat in England, as I confess I prefer an apricot greatly to a banana, and a good pear to a custard-apple. Indeed, many of the fruits which are considered good in Havanna would be given only to the pigs in our country. Wearing apparel costs more here than it does in any place I ever was in. The price of long white kid gloves are two dollars, more than eight shillings a pair. It will be seen that the expenses of living in this city are not small, and I must wind up my items with mentioning the rent of houses—one of even tolerable size cannot be hired at less than from four to five hundred pounds a year. The washing of clothes costs three dollars a dozen.

The following day we paid a visit to the Admiral on board the *Illustrious*. I was conducted over the ship and, as it was my first time undergoing the ceremony, I was much surprised at all I saw. I thought the heat, when I arrived at the midshipmen's quarters, something fearful, but I suppose they soon become accustomed to it. We dined on board the flagship, and afterwards accompanied the Admiral on shore to a soirée at the Captain-General's. From the morning of the Thursday before Good Friday till the evening of the Saturday following, the most perfect stillness reigned in the streets. Not a carriage was allowed to pass through any part of the town, and we were consequently obliged to go on foot to the vice-regal residence. The distance from the landing is not considerable, but in this climate all exertion is disagreeable and I felt inclined to quarrel with anything that forced me to take exercise, let it be in what shape it would.

The military band was playing in the square, and mournful and tiresome airs seemed the order of the day. The square was crowded with people, but principally by negroes, to whom it appeared a kind of fête day. They were all dressed in white, and the contrast it afforded to their black hands and faces was very striking.

The Spanish ladies, however, are dressed in the gayest colours, as if they wished to make themselves amends for the deep mourning in which it was *de rigueur* to clothe themselves on the morrow. As we left the palace, the city watchmen, who are reckoned particularly good and efficient, told the hour from time to time. With the exception of their warning voices, not a sound was heard to break the stillness of the night.

During all this time, I spent my mornings on deck under the awning. My sofa was spread where I could obtain the most of the refreshing breezes, of which, however, you feel but little in the harbour. I occasionally, in the course of the day, received visits from my neighbours and thus, in a most indolent, enervating mode of life the scorching hours passed by.

Good Friday arrived. The guns were fired, with a dull heavy sound, and muffled drums with all sorts and signs of gloom and lamentation were in full display. Everyone was in black, and the churches were thronged by penitential visitants.

About midday, Sir Charles Adam gave us much pleasure by paying the *Dolphin* a visit, and I greatly regretted, that owing to its being Good Friday, we were prevented from receiving him with a salute and all due honours.

Many strict rules in regard to the regulation of moral conduct are laid down by society here, and a great outcry is raised if any unfortunate individual is so rash or so misguided as to break through them. As an instance of this—no lady is permitted by the rules of decorum to drive in her volante on the Passeo without being protected either by a female companion or by her own husband. Even her brother is not considered a proper chaperon.

I suspect that there is more of outward show, than of real decorum, in all this vigorous straining after gnat-like trivialities, and I have often heard it remarked that neither the education of the young Spanish women, nor their habitual conversation, were in keeping with this overstrained prudery. Mothers and elder sisters are, it is said, in the habit of paying far too little attention to the moral education of the more juvenile and female branches of their families. It not unfrequently happens that topics of scandal are discussed and reputations canvassed before them, the details of which are sufficient to blunt their moral perceptions. When it is remembered that in this country, girls become wives and the mothers of families at an age when in England they would be still in the schoolroom, the evil of this fatal system of education was seen in all its magnitude.

Saturday we took a drive on the railroad through shrubberies of coffee bushes. The rate at which we travelled was not greater than ten miles an hour, and I could not help rejoicing that we went no faster, as otherwise we should have seen much less of the country, which is extremely picturesque. There is a height above the town, which it is well worth taking the trouble to ascend. The hill, which is very steep, is crowned by a fort and the view from it, looking down on the city, and the surrounding country, is panoramic, and very striking. The race-course is within a couple of miles of the town. In the course of our late drive we paid a visit to this spot, dedicated to the gambling propensities of the "gentlemen sportsmen" of Havanna. It is a good and convenient course, and we saw several fine looking American horses in training.

The Bishop's garden, which we next visited, is well worth seeing. It is crowded with oleanders, roses, verbenas, convolvuluses, and every sort of beautiful flower, growing in wild and tangled disorder, and all in full and luxuriant blossom. The fireflies at night were brilliant. The road to this paradise of flowers is thickly planted on both sides with guava and sour-sop trees, besides coconut trees, and palms, many of them loaded with green fruit. In addition to the trees I have mentioned, there are ebony, cedar, mahogany, and lignum vitae. Indian corn too is much cultivated, and adds not a little to the beauty of the country.

In the evening we dined with the British Consul, and met the Admiral and a large party of naval officers. I ought not to omit to mention that the individual of the party who made the greatest impression on me was one of the prettiest English girls I ever saw. Her roses had not yet paled under the influence of a tropical sun, and she was a pleasing contrast to the sallow beauties of the island. We remained late on shore.

The following day being Sunday, we had hoped to have heard divine service performed on board the flagship, and most of the English and Protestant inhabitants of Havanna had assembled on board with the same expectation. The chaplain, however, was too unwell to officiate. Most of the party remained on board till the evening, when we again paid the Passeo a moonlight visit. This was the grand night for theatrical performances at Havanna, and we went with a large party to the pretty theatre at Tacon. The house was crowded, and the performance, which I thought tedious enough, was much applauded. There was a great deal of pantomimic acting, and the scenery was remarkably good. The two boxes which had been secured for us would scarcely hold our party, and we would have rejoiced, and I doubt not would many others of his acquaintance, to have taken possession of the Captain-General's empty box. It is not etiquette for ladies to be seen in it, which seemed to me very strange, nor do I understand the motives for keeping this poor man so apart from the common enjoyments of life.

There exists here a great jealousy of the English, among naval men. As I have before remarked, none of our officers are allowed on board Spanish ships, which are certainly too ill-equipped, dirty, and ill-conditioned to bear inspection. On the evening of this day we had a delightful dance on board the flagship. There was a great deal of beauty present, particularly among the English. The Misses M., who are half Spanish, unite in their own persons the charms of both countries. The dark brilliant eyes, betray their Spanish descent, while the soft, clear complexion reminds us of our countrywomen.

It seems a strange thing to assert that good cigars are as difficult to procure in Havanna, as in any part of the world. The state of the case is this—it is impossible to have good cigars unless you order them, and that also at a considerable period of time before they are required for use. It is well known how much time improves the flavour, and no smoker here uses them as fresh as they do in Europe. It is notorious, also, that the slaves steal the best tobacco and make it into cigars, unknown to their employers. The cigars, thus manufactured, are excellent, but high-priced and extremely difficult to procure.

On the Wednesday previous to our departure we accepted an invitation to the house of the "belles of Havanna," whom I have before mentioned. It was a pleasant tertulia, the windows opening into a delightful garden full of jessamine and the perfumed dhatura. Dancing was going on for those who liked it, while others, who in this fervid climate preferred a state of quiescence, were at liberty to enjoy sweet sounds and perhaps sweeter thoughts, in indolent repose.

It was our last evening at Havanna, and a last evening is always more or less painful and trying to one's feelings. We had to bid adieu to friends most kind, though lately found, and to leave a happy spot, which it is more than probable we should never see again. I do not like saying goodbye. It "sets me on end-like" as Sam Slick says.

On our return from this scene of brilliant gaiety, I noticed, as our volante drove slowly through the suburbs, a house, the front of which was brightly lighted up. The lower windows, which were so large that they in point of fact formed the front of the house, were wide open, and afforded a perfect and distinct view of the objects within. My curiosity was excited by the sight of a raised platform within the room, at the lower end of which sat two men, in mute silence. To my surprise, for who would have supposed that the remains of the dead would thus exposed to view, I saw on the platform the pale face of a corpse. The stiffened limbs were stretched beneath a thin white covering, and in the next hour, the form, which in the morning was endued with life, was to be lowered into the earth. I cannot describe the effect that this spectacle had upon me, and how much I was struck by the contrast it afforded to the scene of dancing and merriment I had so lately quitted. Verily in the midst of life, we are in death! I went on board, and tried to forget it all—the whirling dance and the blank face of the dead—but they haunted me all night, and I was glad when the morning came, when I was to change this place of varied recollections for our own wild changing element once more.

CHAPTER XXXI

BERMUDA ⚓ WHALE FISHING ⚓
GARDENS ⚓ THE BISHOP'S HOUSE ⚓
DEPARTURE FOR ENGLAND

Friday, April 20th, 1843—Light breeze from the eastward. We left Havanna harbour and passed Moro Castle at nine o'clock in the morning. The flagship weighed anchor at the same time and we promised ourselves her company on the voyage. The sea breeze at Havanna begins about ten in the morning, and dies away about three or four p.m. It is, therefore, impossible for vessels to leave the harbour in the intermediate time. For two days and a night, we went on well together, though in order to do so we were frequently obliged to shorten sail. We amused ourselves during these two days by talking, unintelligibly enough, I must confess, by signals, and we frequently found ourselves within hailing distance. On the third morning, I looked in vain for our tall friend. We had burnt a blue light during the night, which had been duly answered. But now, not a vestige of her towering masts were to be seen, and we had to go on our way alone.

April 28th—We had some strong breezes. Reefing, especially in the afternoon, when the whirling and tumultuous state of the sea gave us some idea of the dangers of the coast.

April 29th—Sighted Bermuda, and vexed enough was the sea that surrounds her hundreds of islands. After making pilot-signals for a long time, a black man at length put off from the shore in one of the beautiful 'Mudian boats and told us he was a Queen's pilot. It was, however, so late in the afternoon, that he refused to take us into the harbour till next morning. Accordingly, we kept him on board, tacking about all night. At five o'clock the next morning he took us in, and we anchored off the admiral's house. Our first inquiry was for the flagship. She had not arrived, and I rather triumphed, I acknowledge, at our having won the race, particularly in the stormy weather we had encountered, and having latterly been running before the wind. We found ourselves very much exposed, in St. George's Harbour, to the force of the wind. As we intended to remain some days at the Bermudas, we shifted our quarters, almost immediately to Hamilton, the principal town.

The navigation, through hundreds of rocks and islands, is difficult, but very beautiful. It really seemed like some dream of beauty, the water being so clear that you could see the pebbly bottom, and then the coral rocks and the cedar groves! It was, indeed, a bright and fairy scene. And when I think of it now, in this cold climate and matter-of-fact country, how I long to be there with those I love about me, again to realize the visions of the past and spend my existence in that bright land of poetry and romance.

Hamilton is a pretty, clean town situated close to the water. The houses are all white, and there are hills rising behind them, dotted with villas and interspersed with cedar trees. We went on shore almost immediately after our arrival and hired a carriage to take us up to the admiral's house, in order to acquaint Lady Adam of our having so recently parted company with the flagship. There is a very pretty view from the house and the garden, which is kept with great care, is full of flowers.

During our visit, the *Illustrious* came in sight. It was Sunday and, in the course of our drive, we had a good opportunity of forming our opinion of the appearance of the Bermudian population. The churches were very numerous, and everyone we met was on his or her way to some place of worship. The blacks are, in general, quite as well-dressed as the whites, and are particularly civil and well-conducted, touching their hats in a courteous way, which reminded one of old England. The supply of fresh water is very limited. I was told that the reason for painting the houses white was so that the rainwater, of which every drop is of value, may not, in its descent from the roofs, come in contact with any dirty or discolouring substance.

The roads are excellent, and well-kept. They are made chiefly of granite, taken from the many picturesque rocks which are interspersed among the cedar woods.

I should say that the inhabitants of Bermuda were inveterately idle. By far the greater proportion are very poor and live mostly on fish. Boat-building is the most common trade, and that seems very much overstocked. A great many whales are taken at Bermuda during the season, and several were caught during our stay.

On Monday we took a pleasant drive about the island, during which I saw, among other curious things, a large natural tank, hollowed out in the granite rocks, and filled with salt water. It was full of fish of different kinds, some of a very large size. The fish called groupers were the most numerous. There were others of brilliant and beautiful colours, particularly the angel-fish, covered with blue and silver. We saw them fed, and it was wonderful to mark so closely the habits of these monsters of the deep. They came up to the surface of the water, opening their enormous jaws, and then rolled over again, making room for some huge companion to take his turn.

On Tuesday morning we went on shore to pay a visit to Mr. and Mrs. Kennedy. Mr. Kennedy is the government secretary, and his house and gardens would really, in any country, be a model of good taste, comfort and beauty. Such a profusion of flowers I never saw! Gorgeous flowers from between the tropics, roses from France, all Knight's and Colville's choicest houses ransacked for sweets and beauty. I know little about flowers, their scientific names or their natures, but I do know that none ever seemed to me so beautiful as those I saw in Mrs. Kennedy's exquisite garden. Imagine hedges of rich double pomegranate; roses, in whose thick foliage and glowing blossoms you might lose yourself; and such geraniums! The sweet-rose and the scarlet intermingled with heliotropes and verbenas, and all wild and uncultured.

The kitchen-gardens are no less worthy of notice. Every sort of vegetable, growing to a perfection I rarely have seen before. Though it was so early in the year, there were beans, peas, cauliflowers and young potatoes.

All these things are pleasant, but a kind welcome is pleasanter by far, and that is a luxury one is sure to meet with at Rose Bank. We took a long drive today, first to the house of the Bishop of Newfoundland, who had previously honoured the *Dolphin* with a visit, and who promised to show me the view from his house, as well as the famed sea-grape which flourishes near it. The day was hot, but not so much as to be disagreeable. Though the carriage indeed was rough and the horse stumbled, I nevertheless enjoyed the excursion, for it was a new country, and novelty has always its charm. There is a very steep ascent before arriving at the residence of the Bishop, but the prospect from it amply repays one for the toil.

After a walk of about half a mile from the house to the sea-beach, we seated ourselves beneath the shade of one of those peculiar trees, the sea-grape. In growth, they resemble ancient fig trees, having the same rough, bold branches and broad leaves, far apart from each other. When I visited the spot, the leaves, which are very thick, large and broad, were shaded into red of different hues, and only the remains of the berries were hanging from the branches. I sat down beneath them with my agreeable companion, and our imaginations naturally wandered to the magical creation of nature's "favourite son." We made up our minds that it was at this particular spot that Prospero sojourned, and Miranda first saw the "brave form," she thought a spirit. We fixed upon the place where "quaint Ariel" gently did his "spiriting," and even discovered the tree from which his master freed him. It was but the imagination of an idea, yet still it seemed tangible and clear.

I never felt any climate so enjoyable as that of these lovely islands, at the period of our visit. There were many beautiful plants and shrubs which I have seen nowhere else. The inhabitants, however, seem, most of them, to be too indolent and too tasteless to care much about these sweet favourites of nature.

The time had now arrived when we were to leave these wooded islands. Enchanting indeed were the days we spent among their sunny waves, and bowery and breezy hills, and now we are afloat again on the old majestic sea. On the occasion of our coming to Hamilton, I had seen nothing of the scenery through which the schooner had passed, it being so early in the morning. But now, to make me amends, I saw it all in perfection. Winding through the narrow channels, formed by coral rocks and cedar-wooded banks, through water so clear and so shallow that you could distinctly make out the shells and shining gravel at the bottom, the yacht glided on towards Ireland harbour.

After a voyage far too short, we found ourselves at Ireland Island. It is very pretty here and, as we intended to remain a day, the gig was ordered to be manned, and we set out on a long cruising expedition about the islands. Somerset was our first point, and there we landed and roamed about the rocks, picking up shells and coral. We passed the "Haunted Island," which no 'Mudian will go within sight of after dark, and then paid a visit to the dockyard, which did not seem to me much worth seeing. There were a great many convicts, several of whom, I was told, were comparatively rich men. Indeed they can all earn a comfortable existence by the manufacture of pretty little toys and ornaments of coral.

The *Electra*, man-of-war corvette, had arrived at Ireland Island the day before, and we went on board. It was impossible for even a landswoman not to be struck by her extreme beauty, and the care and evident attention which were paid to the most trifling minutiae of her personal appearance. The *Dolphin* was lying alongside the flagship, and was kindly permitted to take in a supply of water from the latter. This long operation, which was performed during our absence, for we did not return till after dusk.

Some of the officers of the flagship dined with us onboard—a parting visit, for we intended to sail at daybreak. The evening was enlivened by cheerful music from our giant neighbour, and we separated at a late hour.

A pilot was taken on board, and I was awoke at five o'clock in the morning by the sounds attendant on departure. I rose, and dressed immediately. Having in my mind the many wonderful anecdotes I had heard of Bermudian pilots, and of their taking ships through narrow rocky channels, I was eager to have my curiosity gratified. The wind was directly ahead, and it was consequently necessary to beat out of the narrow channel. The pilot said he had never taken a vessel, anything like the size of the yacht, out of the harbour with a head wind and she had thus an opportunity of display-ing some of her good qualities. It frequently occurred, that when the forepart of the schooner was almost touching a buoy, her stern was within a foot of the myriads of rocks which mark the channel. The difficulty of surmounting all these dangers must be very great, and the power of doing so only to be acquired by long practice and experience. Soon after we had discharged our pilot, we saw a whale at some distance from us. On looking towards the shore, we perceived that the presence of one of these monsters of the deep was known there also, for a whaleboat was putting off with all despatch.

On rolled the creature, his great black sides turning up and over, in his awkward disportings, while every now and then he rose up in the air and a spout of water darted up from his nose. I was, I confess, anxious to witness a strife between the whalers and their prey, but I was destined to be disappointed. The whale got into deep water, too far off for the whalers, who never go to any distance to sea to overtake them. The weather was fine and moderate, and once out of the harbour, the wind was tolerably favourable.

And now, we were fairly off for England!

Chapter XXXII

Azores ⚓ Terceira ⚓ Scilly Islands ⚓ Eddystone Lighthouse ⚓ North Foreland ⚓ Conclusion

May 17th—Sighted the Azores. The island of Pico on the leeward bow, and in the afternoon we passed close to Terceira. The coast seemed pretty, I thought, the most distinguishing feature being an immense conical-shaped mountain. The hills are in very picturesque arrangement and are ornamented with many white, and good-sized houses. We were becalmed for some time off these islands, and had thus an opportunity of seeing as much of Fayal as could be seen from the sea. With the help of a good glass we could make out both animate and inanimate objects very distinctly. After this calm, we had some rather strong winds, but they were in our favour, and we dashed home at the rate of nine and ten knots an hour.

On the 24th of May, after a wonderfully short passage from Bermuda, we sighted that Scilly Islands, and greeted a misty view of English land. There was a very heavy swell, and a cold drizzling rain falling.

The next day in the forenoon, we passed the Eddystone lighthouse, and fell in with many "outward bounders." Ungraceful merchant ships, laden doubtless with rich stores for all parts of the known world, were to be seen in all directions. More than once we were hailed by those asking to know our name, and whence we came.

The weather was essentially English—an English May! The sea, cold and dark, reflected the cheerless clouds. Through the thick, wet air, dismal-looking gulls were flying heavily. It was a discouraging view, and nothing but the thoughts of home could prevent one continually drawing comparisons very unfavourable to our country's climate. In the afternoon we passed Portland Lighthouse, and saw green fields and pleasant hedgerows. Here we met the "lone fisher on the lonely sea, who, in the wild waters had been labouring, far from home, for some bleak pittance." For a dollar, the only species of coin we possessed, we purchased as much fish as would have supplied a meal to a ship's company, and greatly did we enjoy it. Soon after this we passed a fleet of fishing boats, and sent letters on shore, too happy in the thought that we were sparing a few hours of anxiety to those who had so long been looking out for us.

May 25th—We passed the North Foreland, and felt that we were at home. The little schooner, after her long and distant career, had returned in safety. Though we had encountered more than our due share of severe gales and stormy weather, scarcely a sail or a spar had been carried away, and not a single sea had been shipped. That this had been so, may be attributed as much to the excellent seaworthy qualities of the yacht, as to the skill and unwearying attention of her officers and crew. But now how quietly we glided up the river! Our troubled, but joyous course over the wild waves was over, and the dull stream bore us on its sullen waters!

I could have grieved for the blue seas and the bluer skies that we had left behind us, but that I looked forward to happy meetings with long-parted friends. I thought, with still deeper gratitude, on the Power which had preserved us through the many dangers which threaten those "that go down to the sea in ships and occupy their business in great waters."

But our voyage up the river is ended, and preparations are making for leaving the yacht. I look round upon the hardy crew, who have shared our dangers and, foolish as it may seem, feel something very like a heaviness of heart. I shall never see the shipmates of so many months collected together on that dock again. But still more do I regret to part from my home upon the waters—from the gallant vessel that has borne us in triumph through so many storms and dangers.

RETURN ENGAGEMENT:
DECEMBER 1845

RETURN TO GALVESTON ⚓ STATEHOOD ⚓
PRESIDENT ANSON JONES ⚓ GERMAN EMIGRANTS ⚓
COL. MORGAN'S NEW WASHINGTON ⚓
DR. FERDINAND ROEMER ⚓ MR. ASHBEL SMITH

[*EDITOR'S NOTE: The following is taken from Mrs. Houstoun's second book,* Hesperos, *which details a second trip to North America in 1845-46 in the form of letters sent home to England periodically. Mr. and Mrs. Houstoun arrived in Texas in December of 1845.*]

Among the foreigners, German and French, counts and barons, who from time to time take up their temporary quarters at the St. Louis Hotel, I must not forget to make honourable mention of the old Marquis de T., a member of the Montmorenci family, and withal a Legitimist, and an advocate for all that savours of the old mode of living in France. It may seem matter of wonder how the old man (for he is nearly fourscore years of age) could have chanced to find himself a sojourner in the United States. But Monsieur de T., unlike the generality of French Marquises, is a man of very large fortune, and having, as he said, met with severe family misfortunes, he had rightly concluded that the greater the change produced by travelling in his habits and mode of life, the more likely it was to prove beneficial in chasing away the memory of his sorrows.

He did not travel alone, being accompanied by his private secretary, and attended by several servants. All his ideas and habits (except that he took snuff in tremendous quantities) were aristocratic, and as a real, living and tangible nobleman, he was welcomed with open arms by the kind-hearted Americans. I sometimes fancied that the poor old gentleman was writing a book, so much perseverance did he display, not only in making notes in his commonplace book, but in asking the most searching questions of everyone he met. It is a favourite joke of the Americans and not a very judicious one, to make the most extraordinary and extravagant replies to the queries of strangers. In the case of the old marquess, there was nothing too wonderful for them to say, or for him, in the simplicity of his heart, to believe. Whether from this, or from other causes, I certainly perceived that he grew more bitter against the 'greatest country on earth' every day he remained in it. Monsieur de T. was our constant guest, for he sent in his card every evening with such an irresistible appeal to our compassion, in the shape of an inquiry as to whether he might not have *l'honneur de faire ses compliments à Madame*, that we almost always admitted him.

As the time drew near for our Texan trip, I confess I looked forward with great pleasure to seeing again the country in which we had before made so interesting a sojourn. Moreover, I was glad to find that we were to go in the *Galveston*, quite a new steamer, and not one of those which, three years ago, I had not thought by any means in their prime. In this new steamer, therefore, we secured our berths. No sooner had we done so, than our friend, the marquess, did the same. So away we steamed, one bright December evening, down the thickly flowing Mississippi— ourselves, Monsieur de T., Monsieur le Secretaire and suite—for the 'happy hunting grounds.'

Our steamer was a very fine boat to look at, particularly inside. But she was long, narrow, and shallow—much better suited to the navigation of rivers than to encounter the fierce northers of the Gulf of Mexico. She was fitted up with the choicest woods, birdseye maple and rose, and the decorations of the saloon were really beautiful. There was, however, (as we soon found) a great deal too much above water, and far too little below, for either safety or comfort. The steamer literally consisted of three stories, one more than the ordinary riverboats. I preferred sleeping in the attic, as did most of the passengers, but the weather was so mild and warm, that as long as we continued in the river, almost everyone remained in the open air.

There is rather a fine building on a very large scale, about six miles from New Orleans, which, I was told, is the convent of Sacre Coeur. Some miles below it is the ground where the Battle of New Orleans was fought. I looked at the latter with painful interest, I assure you. We arrived at the Southwest Pass late in the evening, and had to wait for several hours before we could get over the bar at the mouth of the river. I never beheld anything more dreary than that low, reedy, marshy shore, as (under the fitful light of a cold December moon) we gazed upon it from the hurricane deck. It looked so desolate, so blown upon, and so defenceless!

When once fairly over the bar and in the open sea, we found that it was blowing pretty fresh, and also that the good ship *Galveston* rode by no means easily in heavy weather. I never heard a vessel make such a noise as she did through that remarkably disagreeable night, for the southerly wind turned suddenly into a norther. It continued to freshen, so that before morning there was more than half a gale of wind. Every timber and bulkhead creaked and complained in a most painful manner. The motion, too, was most disagreeable, and the sense of insecurity very great, owing as much to the above causes as to the drunkenness of the captain, who was in a state of intoxication the whole time we were on board. I soon missed our friends, the Frenchmen. Their faces ceased to be present, but I suspected that some bundles of cloaks, heaped on the two sofas of the upper saloon, were the coverings of their suffering frames.

At length, day dawned upon our miseries and brought to light some ugly spectacles. It was such a bright, joyous looking sunrise that it made us all look still more cross and frightful than we should perhaps otherwise have done. Galveston was nearly in sight, so all the passengers woke themselves up, as well as they could, and commenced their preparations for departure.

One or two rather rough-looking individuals were soon busily employed in sharpening their Bowie knives, an operation, as it appeared to me, of rather an ill-omened nature. A few passengers, more peaceably disposed, were thinking of breakfast, but breakfast on board any steamer is an odious thing. As we had seen enough of the corn bread, salt butter, 'Boston crackers' and sticky molasses, we resolved to wait till we had crossed the bar, and to 'make it breakfast' when we should arrive at the Tremont Hotel. As we approached the low sandy shore of Galveston Island, we perceived a great many merchant vessels lying outside the bar, the captains, or supercargos, preferring to unload their freight there, than to running the hazard of crossing the formidable impediment at the mouth of the harbour. We were soon agreeably surprised by the visible improvement which had taken place in the appearance of the place since our former visit. As we gently steamed over the bar at half-speed, we saw how much the city had increased in size, and what a busy air pervaded the harbour of Galveston.

As we touched the pier, I saw some familiar faces among the crowd standing on the quay, and amongst others was Captain Cary, the negro livery stablekeeper, with his black woolly head shaped like a sugar-loaf, and his countenance of singular rascality and cunning. He lost no time in asking for custom, and was very anxious to know, if "Massa Cap'em didn't want some berry fine 'osses, or carriages fixed first-rate." There, too, was our pilot of former days and the polite pier-master, all unfeignedly glad to see us, and eager, after the fashion of the country, to shake hands with my companion, and bid us welcome to Galveston.

Captain Shaw, the landlord of the Tremont, lost no time in conducting us to his hotel, which has greatly increased in size, and is now an immense building. Having cheered us with many glad greetings and solicitations, on our return to Texas, he installed us in our new apartments.

We, that is to say, the *Galveston* passengers, and ourselves met at breakfast in the *table d'hote* room, an apartment of gigantic proportions, in which two hundred persons might easily have sat down to dinner. I never saw anyone appear more thoroughly disgusted with his situation than the old Marquis on that occasion, except perhaps the hapless secretary, whose sensations of misery might almost be said to rival those of his companion. The former took his place near me, looked daggers at a great flat piece of beef, as large and nearly as hard as an ancient shield, and after contriving to swallow a soft-boiled egg, confided to me that he felt convinced of the impossibility of longer endurance, and that he had taken his passage back to New Orleans in the *Galveston,* which gallant ship was to return to that port the same evening. "Ma foi" said he, "c'est vraiment trop fort ce Galveston—comment diable! Il n'y a rien ici, pas même une cuisine française, rien que la mer, et des messieurs en Poncio Mexicain." In vain I strove to convince my aged friend that it was a charming country, and that an excursion into the prairies would fill his mind with new sensations of delight and wonder, and that French cuisine was not quite indispensable to existence. It would not do, the aggrieved and disappointed man took a walk round the town, inserted some very fractious notes in his commonplace book, made us some very low bows, and then took his leave of Galveston forever.

We received a visit soon after our arrival from a very agreeable acquaintance, Monsieur de Cramayel, who had formerly been (during the time that Texas was an independent Republic) Charge d'Affaires from that power to France. We received him with much pleasure, not only on account of his universally acknowledged talents, but as one who, from his peculiar position, was enabled to tell us something of the present state of Texan affairs.

This country is now in a state of transition, it having been for some months virtually a State of the Union, though the formalities of annexation have not yet been consummated. The President, Mr. Anson Jones, has not yet been "dethroned." He is a most excellent, straightforward, talented and honourable man, and is at present in Galveston, awaiting with perfect composure the course of events, which are to lead to his dismissal into private life. He spent one most pleasant evening with us at the Tremont, as did also

Monsieur de Cramayel, and the English minister, Captain Elliott, whose unexpected arrival we had hailed with great delight.

We could boast of but two rush-bottomed chairs in our little apartment, so the President of the country was obliged to content himself with a travelling trunk for a seat, and I could not help thinking, that if there is "a divinity which doth hedge a king," it was a shame there should be so little of it for a *President*. The late honourable Charge d'Affaires chose the foot of the bed as the most comfortable seat, and as for England's gallant representative, he had, of course, the place of honour, namely, a chair with three legs of a very insecure description.

The conversation turned principally on the policy or impolicy of the measure (now nearly concluded) of swamping the Republic of Texas in that of the United States. A good deal of doubt was expressed as to whether annexation would be likely of permanent benefit the interests of the former country. The fact is, however, undeniable that since the idea has been seriously entertained, the increase of emigration to Texas has been very considerable, and also, that (for the moment at least) the affairs of this country are apparently in a very flourishing condition. How long, under the new order of things, this prosperity may last, remains to be proved. In the meantime, the pride of many of the original contenders for the independent freedom of the young Republic is deeply wounded. They do not at all seem to be of opinion that the privilege of living under the protection of "Uncle Sam" can possibly compensate for the mortification of bearing his yoke.

[*EDITOR'S NOTE: Because of the requisite politeness and adherence to etiquette incumbent upon a well-married Englishwoman of the 19th century, or perhaps because of a true lack of interest in Texas politics, Mrs. Houstoun says in a very subtle way, above, much about what had been happening in Texas in recent days. The contenders, indeed, were wounded. About a month after her meeting with the diplomats and President Jones, the Republic would be no more.*

Mrs. Houstoun was obliged to pass her time with some of the key players in the annexation saga. When the Houstouns sailed from Texas in March 1843, De Cramayel accompanied them back to Europe. Surely the topic of Texas came up on occasion while crossing the wide Atlantic! Her friends, Captain Charles Elliott and Monsieur de Cramayel, were intimates of Sam Houston and Anson Jones. The two Europeans had done much to try to stabilize relations between Texas and Mexico prior to annexation. England was decidedly against Texas joining the Union and intervened, via Captain Elliott, to prevent it. Mexico owed England money and an "independent" Texas which might lean on the British Empire for stability put the British in courting mode. Captain Elliott offered the Crown's assistance to an independent Texas, on the condition of abolition of slavery.

Ultimately, in 1845, the two diplomats persuaded President Anson Jones to hold off on calling the annexation vote for ninety days so that they might treat with Mexico. Santa Anna finally consented to recognize Texas as a nation, so long as she never join with another nation. But the people of Texas were already sold on the idea of becoming a State and demanded Jones' head on a platter for delaying the proceedings. The Texas congress considered ousting Jones for the delay, but instead voted, of course, to reject the Mexican treaty and in favor of annexation.

Surely Mrs. Houstoun heard some remarkable things during the visit mentioned here and on many other occasions during her travels. While it may not have been considered the height of refinement for a lady to tell the secrets of diplomats in a travelogue, we'd all be richer for it today if she had. The following exemplifies my point. It might not have been wise for her to eschew decorum to repeat Sam Houston's pillowtalk, but don't you now wish she had?]

It must not be supposed that the proceedings of the late President Houston escaped our notice. On the contrary, we spent a good deal of time in discussing the merits of the conqueror of Santa Anna, and learned, in the course of conversation, that he is senator-elect for the State of Texas in the American senate. Many interesting anecdotes were told of him. They would, I dare say, have impressed me with a greater degree of respect for the dignity of the man, as president of an independent republic, had not the ex-Parisian Charge d'Affaires allowed us to penetrate a little *too far* behind the scenes.

It was after dinner, otherwise the diplomatist would not, in all probability, have been thrown so much off his guard. After repeating to us some really remarkable expressions used, and opinions delivered, by General Houston, he destroyed the effect of all, by adding "I shared his bed with him you know, and as he was fond of talking, the president often told me, at night, a good many of his secrets, and kept me awake sometimes for hours, when I wanted to go to sleep."

A great many changes have taken place since our last visit to Galveston. The number of German emigrants who have poured in, and are still coming in whole shiploads to the country is immense. They are existing—poor creatures!— in wretched, suffering crowds, crammed into temporary wooden houses built on the damp prairie in the immediate neighbourhood of Galveston, and undergoing all the miseries arising from sickness, and the want of wholesome, and sufficient food. The river steamers take them up the country, with as little delay as possible, but many die where they are landed, and thus escape the prolongation of the misery which would otherwise await them. It is melancholy to reflect that their inability to lay in the necessary supplies of provisions, and their certainty of finding no home prepared to shelter them from the inclemency of the weather, should make their death appear a positive blessing.

Who would not grieve over the sorrowful sight that we daily have to witness! The poor women, still retaining their national costume, bareheaded, and ill-clothed, are surrounded by shivering children, and are almost destitute of the means of subsistence. The men are always out shooting, endeavouring in this manner to procure some slight repast for their hungry families; but as human beings have increased in the little island, the wild animals have become proportionately scarce. The daily search of the German emigrants for food, fully accounts to us for the diminution of game on the island.

We were woefully disappointed on our first sporting excursion to find how very little there was left to shoot. Everything has been destroyed or scared away by the hungry Germans. No living creature is now to be seen but a pelican or two on the shore, watching the approach of its prey, and some little white sandpipers tapping their beaks into the wet sand, and scudding along with redoubled activity at our approach.

The bayous, or arms of the sea, which formerly stretched far into the interior of the island, are no longer in existence. Either the sands of the seashore have shifted, or some other cause has operated to effect this transformation. Whereas, three years ago, our rides were circumscribed by these natural boundaries, we can now canter for miles in every direction without being stopped by any such impediments.

Business has evidently greatly increased here. The stores are now numerous and display articles of luxury before unknown in this wild spot. The 'restaurants' are neither few nor untempting in appearance. All this speaks well for Galveston, but still wise and far-seeing people shake their heads, and say it is too good to last, and that New Orleans will very soon swallow up all the trade of this now prosperous city.

We found that here, as at New Orleans, the ordinary meal was at so inconvenient an hour that we often gladly availed ourselves of the possibility of having our dinner in our own apartments. The public dinner at the Tremont is a curious scene to witness, for many of the men are dressed in what are called blanket coats of every colour under the sun—scarlet, pea-green, and sky-blue—while others again make their appearance wrapped in the graceful folds of the many-coloured Mexican poncho, which is flung with apparent carelessness over the shoulder. I have no doubt that the fine host of the Tremont would gladly dispense with the presence of some of these gentlemen, as he frequently has considerable difficulty in persuading them to pay their score. Of all his bad customers, the one he most dreads is the "hard-up Yankee," one of those smart penniless gentlemen, who make a merit of shaving anyone who is weak enough to be taken in by them.

Our landlord told us of an individual of this description, who had one morning, long before the breakfast hour, poked his knife-like countenance into the large dining-room of the Tremont, and called over a 'Boy.' He was a traveller, evidently from the Northern States, and was attired in a green blanket-coat, and an unmistakably Yankee hat.

"I say," he called out, "what's to pay here for breakfast?" The waiter named the sum.

"And how much for dinner?"

"Half a dollar."

"And supper, how much do you expect to get for that?" Having received the reply, and ascertained that the meal called "supper" was the cheapest to be had for money, the provident Yankee laid down his hat, seated himself at the table, and delivered his orders.

"Well, I expect that's what I want. I say, you 'coon-faced fellow," he said to the Irishman who stood awaiting his decision, "bring me some supper, and look alive!"

If it is curious to see the somewhat fanciful costumes in the public room of the hotel. It is still more remarkable when they are collected together in the Episcopal church, where they show by their respectful and quiet demeanour that, notwithstanding the usual recklessness of manner of these struggling people, they can testify deep veneration when in the house of God. The service in that wooden church, which is built on a sand-bank and in a place so recently peopled by anything like civilized beings, is beautifully and reverentially performed. The clergyman is an Irishman by birth, and is an eloquent preacher, and the church, one of considerable size, is well filled. The singing is really beautiful and here, as at New Orleans, the ladies have decorated the church with evergreen, formed into appropriate texts from Scripture.

After the service, we entered the Roman Catholic chapel, where mass was being performed, of which circumstance we were warned as we approached by the tinkling of the little bell in the interior of the building. It is a very small and unadorned chapel, but within it stood the white robed and tonsured priest before the altar, which, lowly as it appeared, was raised with humble trust to the honour of the Creator. There were two candles burning before a small picture of the Crucifixion. A good many of the poor Germans were meekly kneeling before the altar, and worshipping God after their own faith, in the strange (and as it must appear to them inhospitable) land to which they have fled from the increasing poverty of their own.

The responses of the exiles rose in hushed and tremulous sounds to the roof of the storm-rocked chapel, and near me knelt a fair German girl, with large tears falling silently down her cheeks. Just beyond her was a group which excited still more my sympathy and commiseration. A mother, careworn, sad, and weeping, was on her knees praying fervently, whilst around her were her children, who seemed almost as fully alive to the desolateness of their position as herself. It was, indeed, a painful sight to witness. They looked so poor, so friendless, and so forlorn.

I was far too much overcome by the feelings, which the sight of those poor emigrants called up, to remain where I was, so I left the chapel. But I could not escape the sight of human suffering, for there, exposed to the cold north wind and the now-commencing sleety rain, stood the temporary sheds of the poor emigrants. The thin planks of which they were built afforded but little shelter from the tempest, and the pools of standing water before their doors heralded the fever which, when warm weather should come, would be certain to break out among them!

These unfortunate emigrants have come out with the intention of settling in the German colony, called "New Braunfells," which is being established in the northwest part of Texas. The section of the country in which this colony is situated, cannot, I believe, be surpassed, in regard to climate, by any country in the world. It is very much out of the way, the first settlers having placed themselves as far from a market as possible. There is, as I am told, no means of conveying their produce, either by land or water, to any place where purchasers are likely to be found, and this is a very serious drawback to prosperity. If they manage to struggle through their difficulties for a year or two, they will, in all probability, after that, enjoy the necessaries of life in abundance. But, in the wilderness in which they have pitched their tents, their labour will never make them rich.

There can be no doubt that at some future time Texas will become one of the wealthiest states of the union. It has upwards of three hundred miles of coast bordering on the Gulf of Mexico, and it extends in a northwesterly direction for nearly seven hundred miles till it is bounded by the lower ranges of the Rocky Mountains. From that elevated region down to the Gulf of Mexico, the surface of the country presents a gradually inclined plane, which is watered by several large rivers, running parallel to each other, and about sixty miles apart. The state of Texas covers an area of nearly five hundred thousand square miles, and there is every reason to believe that no other country in the world can surpass it in the productiveness of its soil, and in the salubrity of its climate. It contains three distinct sections of country, each of which differs singularly from the others, in regard to climate, soil, and surface. They are the low, the rolling, and the hilly countries.

The first of these is the country bordering on the Gulf of Mexico, and extending inland to a distance of from fifty to seventy miles. Its surface is perfectly level, and its soil generally is a rich alluvial deposit of the most productive nature. The climate of this part of the country is decidedly unhealthy for Europeans, and its lands can be cultivated by slave labour alone. This level tract is succeeded by the rolling prairies, so called from the surface being gently undulating, like the waves of the sea. This section extends from one hundred and fifty to three hundred miles, as far as the Red River on the north, and on the northwest to the spurs of the Rocky Mountains, which constitute the third, or hilly region.

It is the middle division, or rolling country, which (as I have before said) unites within itself the mighty advantages of richness of soil and healthiness of climate. Moreover, the beauty of its scenery is very worthy of remark. The general appearance of the prairies is that of a fine English park, beautifully diversified with wood and pasture land, the latter being embellished by an endless variety of flowering plants. But you will be tired of hearing so much of the wild unsettled state of Texas. The greater part of this interesting and beautiful country is still uninhabited, and it will, doubtless, be many years before the riches which are contained in what is now a wilderness and a desert, shall be brought to light by the hand of man, and properly and duly appreciated.

Among the many kind invitations which we have received, was one from Colonel Morgan, the proprietor of a large estate up the country, called New Washington. Our friend has taken an active and distinguished part in the Texan struggle for independence, and is not a little mortified by the turn which affairs have taken, and by the merging of the Lone Star into the stars and stripes of the Union. Colonel Morgan was on his way up to his own place, which is situated at the head of the bay of Galveston, and about thirty-five miles from the island. Our journey there was to be performed by water, and we were also to have among our party both the ex-Charge d'Affaires, and the English Minister. The latter was bound for Washington, and had hired a light carriage and a pair of horses to convey him across the dreary swamps of the Brazos Bottom.

We were all on board at sunset, and happily the weather was fine, so that we were enabled to take up our station on the balcony, in the stern of the vessel. A river steamer in Texas is never a very pleasant thing to inhabit, nor were the charms of ours increased by her being forced to contain a good many more passengers than, when originally constructed, she was intended to carry.

Still, all we saw was amusing from its novelty, so, as the bright moon shone clearly out on the frosty night, we wrapped ourselves up in our cloaks, and defied discomfort of any kind either to depress our spirits or to affect our tempers. I must admit, however, that on such occasions as these there are some things rather trying to the best constituted minds, and among them I shall mention first the loud breathing (I use a mild term) of the sleeping passengers around us, and, secondly, the evils entailed upon unfortunate travellers by the use of two, and even of one, pronged forks. To the indigenous inhabitants of the country this last evil is a matter of perfect indifference, as they generally use a knife *par préference*. But to us, who are less ingenious in the art of using the latter article, the inconvenience is very great. Salt spoons were also a luxury as yet unknown in Texas, they having hitherto travelled no further south than New Orleans, and even there they are not in very general demand.

It was two o'clock in the morning when we reached New Washington. The moon had sunk far behind the forest trees, and it was quite dark when we touched the landing, which is about a quarter of a mile from the house. Notwithstanding the inky obscurity of the night, we were soon safely landed, and the six of us made our way to the house of our entertainer.

Our host is a widower, but his son and his son's wife, live with him. Of this I had been totally unaware till I was casually informed of it on approaching the house, and also of the fact that we were taking the home party completely by surprise. It was too late to retrace our steps, and not being as yet initiated into the warm-hearted character of settler hospitality, I could only regret very much what we were doing, and determine to mollify the anticipated displeasure of the lady of the house to the best of my power.

It was far too dark, as we approached, to see anything of the exterior of the wooden houses (for there were two of them) but it was a great comfort to find in the large but scantily furnished room into which we were ushered, a blazing wood fire burning on the hearth—the best possible welcome on such an intensely cold night as we had spent in the open air on the steamer's deck. It was now between three and four in the morning, and the lady, whom I confess I dreaded to see, had long ago retired to rest, but she sent me word that she would get up immediately. Though I earnestly begged that she would remain where she was, the only words I could extract from the little sleepy black attendant were, "Miss ull come in right away." Five minutes afterwards, she glided into the room, wrapped in a white morning gown, with her jet black hair carelessly tucked behind her ears, and words of the warmest welcome on her lips.

She was a very pretty creature, under twenty I should say, but her countenance bore traces of early care, and the languor which was visible in every movement, betrayed ill health and suffering. It did not take long to make the discovery that our young hostess was possessed of one of the many kindly hearts which are encountered with such joy and gratitude in distant and half-civilized countries. She was a northern American, and one who, born and bred among the comforts and luxuries of more polished society, was but ill-calculated, either from nature or education, to rub successfully through the trials and difficulties of a prairie life. She had married (as they all do in America) when a perfect child in years, and at seventeen was brought into the wilds of Texas to superintend a slave household, and to live upon corn dodgers. The consequences of this early initiation into the trials and troubles of life were, as may be supposed, sad enough. But the instance of the fair young creature at New Washington, is only one among the many who lose their health and their spirits in the strange mode of life to which they are, without preparation and so very prematurely, condemned.

Mrs. Kosciusko Morgan lost no time in conducting us to our sleeping apartment, which, if not luxuriously furnished, was very comfortable; and, having left us with a kind "Goodnight," a little 'darky' of about twelve years of age (Tempe by name) alone remained, waiting about, partly from motives of curiosity, and partly in obedience to an order from her mistress to attend to all our wants and wishes. Now, Tempe was very black and shining indeed, with a woolly head, small, and extremely round, like that of a large black pin, and she had withal a thin, lathy body, covered with, a scanty garment of what is technically called 'negro clothing.' Tempe's principal employment was that of endeavouring to keep the little grandchild of our host out of mischief, and this, as the said grandchild, by name Kosciusko, had a decided leaning towards freedom, and was of no account whatever, as far as quietness and obedience went, was no easy task. The two accordingly played from morning till night, and as there were plenty more dark-coloured domestics, all equally indulged with the little black slave and all fully as indolent, it may well be believed that the order of the household was not very strictly kept. [*EDITOR'S NOTE: Kosciusko "Kos" Morgan and his wife, Caroline Cox, did not produce a son named Kosciusko. Mrs. Houstoun, here, likely has the father's memorable name confused with the more common name of the only child in their household in early 1846. This child was named Louis M. Morgan and, sadly, died later in 1846 at New Washington.*]

We had the satisfaction of finding our beds excellent, and, indeed, this is almost invariably the case in America, as well in private houses as in the hotels, and even the steamboats. It was late in the day before we awoke from our slumbers, and as from our window we could but just catch a glimpse of the bay, we soon hurried out to ascertain what we could of the locale. The situation which has been chosen for the chateau is a charming one, being within fifty yards of the summit of the bluffs, which rise perpendicularly from the waters of the bay, and which are here upwards of a hundred feet in height. New Washington is, as I said before, at the head of the bay, and these bluffs may be said to indicate the commencement of the St. Jacinto River, although, in front of the house, the water is at least a mile in width. The house itself is surrounded by fine trees, and some of the magnolias are really magnificent. After passing for about a quarter of a mile through a belt of wood, you come to the open prairie, which is very prettily diversified by clumps of trees, but the surface is as level as the ocean in a dead calm.

Our mode of life is as follows: We breakfast at nine on hot cornbread and pork dressed in various ways. There is, moreover, good milk and eggs, tea and coffee. We dine at two, on roast pork, boiled ditto, and cornbread, and at seven o'clock in the evening we sup on the same. The food is spread before us in profusion and, as I before said, our welcome has been the very warmest possible. Moreover, we have horses caught for us whenever we wish to ride, rifles provided for shooting, and fishing rods at our disposal if we should feel inclined to try our luck in catching any of the numerous fish with which the bay abounds. Our host keeps a regular hunter in his establishment, not the quadruped so called in England, but a human half-bred, who is renowned for his skill in all field sports, and whose only ostensible business is to lasso the wild horses when they are required, and to kill game when it is wanted. Within a short distance of the house, and all over Colonel Morgan's extensive estate, game of many kinds is found—deer, prairie birds, hares, etc. Yet with all these varieties of excellent food within their reach (besides the produce of the poultry yard) will it be believed that our hosts are content to live upon fat pork, and fat pork alone, every day of their lives?

They are all ill, all out of spirits, and apparently weary of their existence, and this entirely from the unhealthy mode of life which is common, more or less, all over America. In vain do I endeavour to instil into their minds that the indulging three times a day in the luxury of fat, greasy pork and molasses, with the overpowering accompaniment of hot "dough doings" is enough to lay low the strongest man that ever breathed the breath of life.

My arguments are of no avail, for the 'niggers' are greatly too much indulged, and the masters too indolent either to plant vegetables, shoot game, or catch fish, so the demon of dyspepsia having at New Washington taken seven other spirits more wicked than himself, dwells here unrestrained. The unhappy Kosciusko the elder sits on one side the chimney-corner, wrapped in his blanket-coat, for hours together, and groaning with the possession of the familiar but malignant spirit, whilst the still more suffering, but patient wife rocks herself on the opposite side throughout the livelong day, and, as she says, "cries for company."

Among the numerous guests assembled here (for it is to all intents and purposes an open house) is a young German geologist. I forget his name, but he is a Prussian by birth, and is sent out by his government to report upon the mineral resources of the tract of land selected for the German colony. I have an idea that he is some relation of Baron Humboldt's, and it appears he enjoys a considerable reputation for scientific skill and attainments. We find him gentlemanlike and well-informed, and indefatigable in his endeavours to further the cause of the particular branch of study to which he has devoted himself. [*EDITOR'S NOTE: This is, of course, Dr. Ferdinand Roemer, the Father of Texas Geology who arrived in Texas in 1845 and published his own travelogue, Texas, in 1849.*]

He has not a tooth in his head, poor man, but that is not his fault, excepting, perhaps, that (inasmuch as I have remarked this peculiarity as a common one among German students) the inordinate use of tobacco may have had some effect in depriving him of his organs of mastication. Dr. Roemer is never without a cigar in his mouth (which feature is by no means of even moderate dimensions) but he is far too good-natured to mind a laugh or a joke, and often makes them himself at the expense of his own personal appearance. The use of soap and water is apparently unknown to our scientific acquaintance, and any change of raiment is a possession which he appears to consider quite unnecessary. His researches amongst the mud of the Texan rivers, and his diggings after geological specimens in the deep alluvial soil of the country cause great amusement to us all. It especially amuses the negroes, who take intense delight in watching his proceedings, and in recording the signal mistakes which he (in common with all men of science) is liable sometimes to make.

Our host, like all his countrymen, has an ardent, and inherent love for speculation, and he grew quite excited, when one morning the savant, taking one from a heap of small shells, which were lying before the door, announced to us that such a specimen would be worth half-a-dollar at Berlin. I verily believe that the worthy colonel was already making a mental calculation of the expense and expediency of sending off a cargo of the precious conchological specimens to Prussia, when his hitherto blind confidence in the geologist was severely shaken by another assertion which he rashly, and most unfortunately, made. In front of the house are two large slabs of stone, and our geologist, in the fullness of his zeal for science, at once, and most unhesitatingly, pronounced that the said stones must have been imported from Bonn on the Rhine, for that in no other part of the world was this exact description of rock to be found.

Now it must be observed, that except in the mountainous regions of Texas, some hundred miles from Galveston Bay, there is no such thing as stone of any kind. Most unfortunately for the credit of the savant (who did not appear at all to relish the refutation of his theory) Colonel Morgan had seen with his own eyes the stones in question quarried near the city of Mexico, and had himself transported them to Galveston.

The doctor, poking in the mud, is nothing in comparison to the doctor on horseback! And it is the best fun in the world to see him mounted on a little spirited half-broken mustang, with his stirrups far too short, and his breath coming thick and fast with excitement and fear. He never quite calls out for assistance, but I am convinced that it is pride alone which prevents his doing so. His face grows more and more cadaverous, as he splutters forth convulsive and guttural sounds, and prolonged ejaculations of "Ach, a-c-h gott!" "O o-h, o-o-h," till, if I did not feel that even a geological philosopher has no excuse for being afraid, I could find it in my heart to pity his distress.

It is difficult to form an adequate idea of the extent of our host's improvidence, or, I might say, blindness, to his own interests. He has here an estate of several thousand acres of the finest land, and a sufficient number of negroes to cultivate a considerable quantity of it. He has made all sorts of experiments, and can tell exactly how many bushels of Indian corn or pounds of cotton every acre may be made to produce. He has also shown us a small plantation of sugar cane, which is now nearly seven feet in height, and which has rattooned (it is generally necessary to plant fresh canes after they have ratooned, or sprung up, and been cut three years in succession) for five years successively, and contains an unusual quantity of saccharine matter. Yet, with all this, not an acre of land is cultivated, nor are even the common garden vegetables raised by the idle hangers-on of the place. There are large herds of cattle and droves of horses on the estate, but of the number of animals he possesses, I believe Colonel Morgan to be in a state of entire ignorance.

Our stay at New Washington (which, by the way, is not a town nor even a village, but merely four or five wooden houses, belonging to the 'lord of the manor') has been diversified by a dinner party! The lady who kindly sent us an invitation is the wife of General Shaw, who is at present away with the army. She is the sister of our pretty friend, Mrs. Kosciusko Morgan. The scene of festivity was about three miles from the place, and higher up the Bay. We were all to go, even Tempe being dispatched to the scene of action in the fulfilment of her functions namely, the superintending of 'Kossy,' the infant hope of the house. The waters being very much out in the prairie in consequence of the continued rains, it was agreed that we should all ride on such animals as we might prefer. The horses being caught, we set off in high spirits. [*EDITOR'S NOTE: Mrs. Houstoun made a simple name error here. Caroline Cox Morgan's sister, Katherine Isabelle Cox, didn't marry a Shaw. She, in fact, married General Sidney Sherman.*]

I had an active Mexican pony allotted to me, while the doctor was mounted on a tall, rawboned beast, with a mouth as hard as its own bit, and a trot high and rough enough to shake even a better rider than the gentle German out of his saddle. He bore his trials, however, better than I had expected, and happily for him, the prairie, besides being very much under water, was thickly covered with stunted trees, so that we were obliged to proceed both slowly and cautiously, to avoid the risks of either being knocked off our horses, or of being plunged above their girths in the water through which we splashed.

At about four o'clock (the dinner hour) we arrived at our destination. It is a log house, like the one we had quitted, but it is constructed with great architectural taste, and covered (porch and all) with creeping-plants, which, in summer weather, must have a charming effect. But in the winter one has certainly a prejudice in favour of glazed windows, carpets, and curtains, and the house is too decidedly a summer residence to be quite enjoyable in the month of January. Though the house was cold, the welcome was not, and we were charmed with Mrs. Shaw, who is a most agreeable and intellectual person, full of energy and decision, and just the character to make even a prairie life an endurable, if not a happy one. She is handsome and highly accomplished, and conducts the education of her children with admirable skill. While with her, I could not help feeling that were such women as numerous in America, as they are perfect, the censure so often bestowed upon the manners and habits of American ladies might well be spared.

The dinner party in this unpeopled prairie, though totally (and partly perhaps because it was so totally) unlike any at which I had ever before been present, was most enjoyable. The *tout-ensemble* was well calculated to make an impression upon European minds, drilled by the mighty forces of fashion and habit into a subserviency to the conventional rules of society, and habituated to its monotony. You must not, however, suppose that there was any want of refinement either in the conversation or the dinner itself. On the contrary the wines were so excellent and the table talk so varied and so intelligent that we could hardly realize the fact that we were in a wooden house, with nothing better than a wilderness around its rough and unpretending walls.

It was twelve o'clock before the horses were ordered for our return. The rain was beginning to fall, and the moon (on which we had reckoned to light us home) was taken with one of her sudden fits of caprice, and had hidden her face behind the clouds. Our kind entertainers (the lady had a brother, nearly as intelligent as herself) were urgent in their entreaties that we would spend the night where we were. To this, however, we would by no means consent, so they followed us out into the prairie, and after many injunctions not to lose our way and a strong hope expressed by all sides of meeting again at some future period, they wished us a cordial "Goodnight," and we proceeded on our way.

We had not gone a quarter of a mile from the house, before our difficulties began in earnest, for it was only by calling aloud to each other that we could keep together, so pitchy was the darkness of the night, and landmarks (even if we could have seen them) there were none. There is, at all times, a despairing sameness in the aspect of a prairie, but with us, the difficulties of "plumbing the track" (for road there is none) were increased tenfold by darkness, and the watery state of the country. It was impossible to divest oneself of a bewildering fear that each step might plunge one into a bog, or into the far more appalling dangers of the Bay, which rolled somewhere at the depth of a hundred feet beneath us, though of its exact locality the obscurity rendered us entirely ignorant. And so we blundered along at one moment finding ourselves fixed against a young tree, and at another perceiving, by the fitful gleams of the moon, that we were surrounded by the shining waters of the prairie flood.

I thought that midnight march would never come to an end, so interminable were our turnings and doublings, and so little the progress that we made. I was beginning, in consequence, to think rather gloomily of our prospects for the night, when I was aroused by a sound near me, which bore some faint resemblance to a human voice, in supplication and entreaty. It was the Doctor, in the act of beseeching his refractory steed to move on. So we listened, and presently, in guttural and most unmusical phraseology, these plaintive words were heard "I karn nicht get on mit mine horse at arl! What can I do mit him? He is so idle, and when I want him to go squick, he will here stay to eat!" At that moment, the moon peeped out between two driving clouds, and there was the poor foreigner, and his obstinate *monture*, fixed as it seemed till eternity. The animal's Roman nose was buried in the long grass, and the unhappy doctor was pulling hard, but hopelessly at the rein, with both hands, in the vain expectation of persuading the creature to desist from his ill-timed repast.

This touching appeal to the compassion of his companions was not made in vain, and by dint of their united efforts the mule-like animal was once more in motion. We all eventually, but not till it was three o'clock in the morning and we were wet through with the heavy night dew, reached our temporary home at New Washington.

The day following our memorable party in the prairie we agreed to cross the river, on a visit to a still wilder country, and also to the estate and country house of Mr. Ashbel Smith, the ex-diplomatist, and also our fellow guest at Colonel Morgan's. We were to cross the water, a long mile in width, in two remarkably rickety boats, nearly as unsafe in their build as canoes, and rendered particularly so at this precise period from the extent to which they were known to leak. The party consisted—besides our two selves—of Mr. Smith, the German doctor, and two negroes, experi-

enced in river navigation, one of whom was to seat himself
in each boat and paddle her across.

The instant that Mr. Smith and I, with our black companion, stepped into the boat appropriated to our use,
we perceived that it would require our united efforts to
be employed in incessant baling, if we expected to reach
the opposite shore alive. The other boat was, if possible,
in a still worse condition, and the doctor (who proved to
be a very inefficient auxiliary in case of danger) was with
difficulty persuaded to take his seat, and his baling machine, which machine was neither more nor less than a tin
saucepan, devoted *pro tempore* to this useful and humane
purpose.

It was a mysterious-looking morning, for, though the
heat of the sun was great, there was a thick river mist which
threw a veil over it and every other object, and sometimes
prevented us from seeing a yard ahead of our boat. From
the difficulty which we found in keeping our boat even tolerably clear of water, we could judge of the exertions which
were being made by our consort to effect the same end.
Many was the anxious look I cast astern, but all to no purpose. The mist was too thick and I could make out nothing
of the whereabouts of the other boat. The water is in most
places of great depth, but every here and there are shallows
which extend for many yards, and which at low water it is
necessary to avoid. We continued to bale incessantly, but
still the water gradually gained upon us, and it was with no
little joy that we at last found ourselves stranded (though
neither high nor dry) on a shallow within a few yards of the
desired shore. It was more than three quarters of an hour
before the other boat arrived, and in the meantime we had
contrived, not without considerable difficulty, to struggle
through the mud and water to dry land.

The troubles of the rest of the party had been manifold.
The doctor had been thrown into such a state of alarm that
he either could not or would not exert himself for the general good and as to joining in the necessary duty of baling
out the water, his hands shook greatly too much for any

such exertion. The poor creature really looked like a spectre as he scrambled up the bank, and he vowed a vow that no earthly consideration should induce him to return the way he had come, though what was to become of him if abandoned on the side of the river we had reached, was a mystery to all parties.

We had no sooner landed than we perceived a small settler's house not far from where we stood, and to this it was agreed that we should betake ourselves, while our white companion and the negroes should walk to Mr. Smith's clearing, and return with mules for our use. We then introduced ourselves to the party in this dog house, which consisted of a mother and daughter, and three neglected looking children, who were playing about the floor. The age of the daughter did not appear to exceed eighteen, but she must have been older, being, as I soon discovered, the mother of the three young settlers in the corner.

The whole domestic establishment were fresh importations from one of the northern cities of the Union, where they had enjoyed balls and theatres, and the pleasures of fine clothing. But here they were, apparently greatly to their own surprise, transported with their city habits, their summer clothing, and their thin shoes (for I never yet have seen an American female, in any weather, in thick ones) into the heart of the Texan prairies! I never saw two people look more thoroughly miserable or more hopelessly discontented. The way in which they described their landing at New Washington in the keen wind of a winter's night, and the misery they had endured from having to wait there in the open air till morning without either food or warm clothing, plainly showed how deeply they considered themselves aggrieved, and convinced me that the husbands of the two dissatisfied women had been obliged to undergo not a few reproaches from their companions in misfortune.

All these calamities were dwelt upon, as they sat shivering in the verandah, drawing round them their light summer shawls, and bitterly lamenting the hour when they first heard the name of Texas. We spent more than an hour with them—not willingly, I confess for they were not good specimens of Yankee character, and, moreover, we had exhausted all our topics of conversation and began greatly to long for the reappearance of our companions. At this juncture I unfortunately caught sight of two men, whose heads were peeping over a new fence some distance off, and whose employment and dress were those of field labourers. Their costume was so different from that of the females, that there was perhaps some excuse, though not much, for the awkward and blundering remark which I was drawn into making regarding them.

Stimulated by a complete dearth of any subject for conversation, and wearied to death of our situation, I, in an unguarded moment, complimented the elder lady on her good fortune in having been able to procure white labour, suggesting at the same time, how very superior the work done by white men is, to any which the negroes are in the habit of "getting through." The look she gave me was one which it was intended should convey volumes of independent pride and Yankee scorn of strangers. "Those gentlemen happen to be my sons and my brothers," was the indignant reply of the republican matron, greatly to my distress and discomfiture. As you may imagine, I had no more intention of hurting her feelings or her self-love, than I had of walking back across the river to New Washington. I did my best to recover my lost ground, and to do away the impression which she evidently entertained—that I had wantonly and designedly insulted her in the persons of the male branches of her family. But it was in vain that I remarked upon the praiseworthy conduct of those who by honest industry gain a comfortable livelihood for themselves and their families. I even went so far as to disparage the gentlemanly vagabondism which prevails in our country, and to extol the working habits of hers in contradistinction to it. But it would not do, and I felt that the "English woman" was being mentally accused of the worst description of pride and overbearingness.

From under the cloud of ill-feeling which we felt was gathering around us, we were, as you may imagine, most happy to escape. I cannot describe to you the feelings of satisfaction with which I at length mounted my mule and rode away, feeling, however, that the "set-up female" from the old country was being subject to very severe remarks from the party in the shanty. Our party were all mounted on very lazy mules, and all being armed with rifles, we were going (as it is called in this country) "a'hunting." We saw a good many deer, both singly and in herds, and several prairie birds. The scenery, too, was very varied and pretty. The heat of the sun in the middle of the day was intense, and we were glad to linger under the shade of the far-spreading ilexes, and spend the chief part of the day in the woods.

It was late in the afternoon when we reached Mr. Smith's habitation, a neat bachelor's establishment, far enough from either the pleasures or the disturbances of social life. A good many small wooden tenements for "my black servants," as the slaves are generally called by their owners, were dotted about, and there were some young stock frolicking about, in the shape both of negro children and horses. There was poultry in great plenty and variety, and the farm and farm buildings looked well-kept and thriving. As for the house itself, there is no denying that it was small; neither am I at all prepared to say that it contained more than one room of very limited extent. I heard a dark hint given about another apartment, but if it were a real, and not an imaginary chamber, I must be allowed to wonder why the ostensible room was made to do duty for "bedroom and parlour, and hell-all," for such was, in fact, the state of the case.

No one was, apparently, more heartily amused at the entertaining deficiency of plates and places than our host himself. With too much good taste to oppress us with apologies for the absence of luxuries, which, in that wild scene, would have been quite misplaced, he allowed us to enjoy ourselves in our own way, and we were, in consequence, quite happy. The doctor was as hungry as a hound, and devoured boiled fowls and fried eggs enough for a dozen men at least. Though the wood fire did smoke, so that we were forced to sit with the door open, and though one took his plate upon the bed and another was obliged to content himself with a wooden box, I never recollect passing a more agreeable day. Our host, enlivened by some excellent French brandy, shone particularly in anecdote and repartee, and when the shades of evening began to close around the prairie home, it was with real regret that we made our preparations for returning.

I never saw more happy, laughing faces than those of the negroes on that location. They were ready to give their opinion on all subjects without a shadow of fear, and in their joy at seeing their master's face again, exerted themselves to the utmost for the comfort of his guests. One of them, a stout, jet black young negro was an admirable rifle shot, and carried away the palm from the gentlemen who, one and all, tried their skill while the dinner was in preparation.

We mounted our horses when the evening was far advanced, and in company with our hospitable entertainer prepared to ride once more towards the Bay. But nothing could move the Dr. Roemer. He had been far too much frightened when it was broad daylight to be willing again to risk his precious person in those horrid boats. Seeing that his fears placed him beyond the reach of persuasion, the ex-charge had nothing to do but to express a courteous hope that he would make himself quite at home where he was, and then we wished him farewell. The last glimpse I caught of the scientific German, was the dim outline of a man seated on the wooden bench before the door of the shanty, with his hammer and bag of specimens in his hand, and a considerable quantity of Cognac in his head. What became of him after that we never heard.

Our voyage home was performed in safety, though with much discomfort, and on our return we found that a bear hunt had been arranged for the following day. The weather, however, proved so unpropitious that, as the *Houston* steamer was expected down, we agreed to return to Galveston without any further delay. We could not part from our new friends without much regret, and there was so much genuine kindness and real simplicity in all their feelings and actions, that we felt as if we had known them for years instead of days. We regretted to think how little chance there seemed to be of our ever meeting again, either in the wild prairie or in the busy hum of crowded cities.

It is almost impossible to say too much in praise of the spirit of hospitality which is found in these new countries. Every house on the wide-spreading and dreary prairie is open to the traveller, and no one is ever turned from the door of a dweller in the wilderness without a shelter and a meal. It is true that far up the country there are said to be persons who have been suspected of playing most unfair and cruel tricks upon unweary travellers. One gigantic backwoodsman in particular, Shadowan by name, who inhabits a sort of lonely inn in the Washington direction, is suspected of having (in concert with his wife, a lady of equally formidable dimensions) brought not a few wandering settlers to an untimely end. His house is, in consequence of these reports, looked upon with a good deal of suspicion, and there are not many gentlemen traveling alone found bold enough to take up their quarters in it, even for a single night. This bad character, however, may not be entirely deserved, for there is no doubt that great injustice is often done to these wild men of the woods.

There is certainly enough in their appearance to justify the worst conclusions, and one cannot fancy anything but strife and bloodshed as connected with all the pistols and bowie-knives with which they are generally covered. Still, notwithstanding their repellent looks, I have been assured that very many of these gentlemen of the border are meek and gentle as lambs, and only get themselves up in so fierce a guise because it is the prevailing fashion of their set. Our friend, Mr. R., who has seen a great deal of frontier life, informs us that he has generally found that those who looked to be the greatest desperadoes were, in reality, the meekest men in nature, and that he considered it very unfair to judge of a man in the backwoods by either his appearance or reputation.

In support of this opinion, he gave us an amusing account of an adventure which happened to himself at the abode of the very Shadowan whom I have mentioned above, and who must have been as ruffianly a looking fellow as could well be seen. Mr. R. was journeying along the pathless prairie in a sulky—a vehicle most appropriately named, as by no possible contrivance can it be made to carry more than one person, and that sufficiently uncomfortably to account for the traveller's becoming rapidly in a frame of mind suitable to the epithet bestowed on his conveyance.

Our friend had passed a solitary day. No human form had he seen, and the only variety through the long and weary hours was, when passing among the clumps of trees that are occasionally seen in the prairie country, he caught a glimpse of an opossum on an overhanging branch, or of a graceful mockingbird balancing itself aloft, and carolling forth its pleasant noonday song. And so he "got along" bound upon business, and leaving it quite a matter of uncertainty where he should spend the night. It was growing dusk, the air was cold, and our Yankee friend began to think it was time to look out ahead in search of a place where he could procure a night's lodging for himself and his exhausted steed. He was well aware that the vague and indistinct track which he had been plumbing, led somewhere in the direction of the hostelry of the dreaded and far-famed Shadowan. There was no other house for many a mile, so the traveller was forced to put up with what he could find, and steered straight for some smoke which he saw rising at a short distance, and which he rightly enough conjectured to be the spot he was in search of. It was not without some trepidation that he thought how probable it was that he should have to lay his bones there, and that long before the morning light his sulky, and all that it contained, would become a prey to the rapacious Shadowan and his unfeminine lady.

At length, the inn (a small log-house) appeared in sight. Mr. R. urged on his horse and soon found himself at the door of the inhospitable looking abode. A gaunt and very unprepossesing looking female having appeared to answer his summons, the newcomer requested to know if he could be accommodated with board and lodging for the night. The woman, who was no other than the redoubted Mrs. Shadowan herself, hesitated very much, but at last said, she really didn't think she could. Mr. Shadowan, she said, was out hunting, and he wasn't over-fond of having strangers loafing about when he wasn't at home himself. The good lady ended by distinctly saying that she strongly recommended the weary man to go about his business.

Now, the idea of doing so by no means suited the views of the Yankee. He was fatigued, and his horse was fairly used up. He mustered up all his eloquence, and what with that, and no little expenditure of soft sawder, he fairly got the better of the lady's scruples, and gained a footing within the house. His hostess, after throwing another log or two on the fire, took down a rifle and left the house, in order, as she said, to get him some supper. A short time only had elapsed before a shot was heard and Mrs. Shadowan appeared, bearing on her back a fine buck, which she had just killed, and a part of which was immediately prepared for the hungry Yankee.

The hours passed on. It was a dark night, and yet no Shadowan had made his appearance. Mr. R. soon began to feel like sleeping, he had devoured a good many fixings in the shape of venison, eggs and cornbread. Fatigued with his gastronomic exertions, he requested his hostess to show him the place where he was to pass the night. He was, accordingly, conducted to a little inner room, or rather closet, where he found a low sort of pallet bed on which, he was informed, that he was to stretch his weary limbs. The bed was not an inviting one in appearance. In fact, no one but a tired Yankee would have ventured to trust his person on such a miserable and unseemly couch. The traveller, however, was not inclined at that moment to be fastidious. So, having placed his bowie knife by his side, and a loaded pistol near his right hand, he soon sunk into a profound slumber.

How long he had slept he knew not, when he was awakened by a stir in the adjoining apartment. It was not much of a noise, but men who have gone to sleep with a consciousness of personal danger, slumber lightly, and the Yankee's ears were on the full cock in a moment. His eyes were fixed on the door, but he feigned slumber to watch with greater security the movements of a man, whom he perceived through the half-opened door, and whom he sensibly enough concluded to be no less a person than Shadowan himself. He had not long to watch, for soon the door opened, widely though softly, and betrayed to his agitated glance the figure of a man of unusual height and breadth, who, with a large knife in his hand, was moving stealthily to the bed on which lay the Yankee traveller. His situation was an awful one, and, almost giving himself up for lost, he gently cocked his pistol. The thought flashed across his mind that he might fire, and possibly kill his man, but then came the recollection that if he missed, his weapon would be unloaded. Then he would have to encounter, almost unarmed, a no less redoubtable foe in the shape of Mrs. Shadowan.

These thoughts passed rapidly through the mind of the agitated Yankee, as with his hand firmly grasping his pistol, he saw the giant Shadowan advancing on tip-toe to his bedside. He neared the bed, the bare knife in his hand, whilst his victim lay nearly paralysed by fear and the variety of emotions which he was enduring. One more! A last step, was taken, and Shadowan was at the bedside!

Mr. R. had his pistol ready, and his finger was even laid on the trigger, when Shadowan stretched over the bed, and raised the long blade of a knife above his head! Now was the critical moment! The eyes of the desperated Yankee, who was on the very point of firing his weapon, were turned full upon his blood-thirsty host, when he fortunately perceived that above his head hung a side of bacon. It was with the intention of cutting a rasher for his own supper, and not with any murderous design that the hungry Shadowan had intruded on his slumbers. True to his human nature, the first sensations of the traveller were those of joy at his own safety, but his second were those of unfeigned satisfaction that he had not been led by his ridiculous suspicions (however justified under the circumstances) to sacrifice the life of a fellow creature.

The remainder of the night was spent in quiet and in sleep. On the following morning the only circumstance which could be supposed to have any reference to the adventure, was a remark of Shadowan's, that he was afraid his guest had been alarmed at something in the night, for that he fancied he had heard the click of a pistol. Whether this little click saved our friend's life can never be known, but certain it is, that Messrs. Shadowan and R. shook hands and parted the best friends in the world. How many midnight murders have been committed by this worthy gentleman remains a mystery, but there he still remains, to entrap unwary travellers, and afford the settlers a subject for many a harrowing tale of treachery and spoliation.

The steamers are in the habit of making such a momentary stay at the New Washington landing, that we were obliged to hold ourselves in readiness to go on board, by taking up our position by the water's side for a considerable time before the vessel was telegraphed as being in sight. Happily for us, the steamer was heard snorting towards us before we had had time to grow very weary of our somewhat cold and comfortless situation. In a very short space of time we were all on board, and steaming rapidly down towards Galveston.

When we returned to the Tremont, we were greeted with the melancholy intelligence that, from the great influx of guests, our comfortable little sitting room could no longer be called our own. So for the short remainder of our stay, we were obliged to content ourselves with the "ladies' parlour" by way of drawing-room. There was only one thing to make us much regret our change of quarters, and that was, that in the component parts of the society, the juvenile branches were in far too great a majority. An American child is not generally a favourable specimen of that period of life, and a Yankee boy of ten or twelve years of age, is one of the least pleasant creatures in existence. When scarcely past the age of infancy, one of these young republicans will, if he be not prevented (and they are very tenacious of their rights as free citizens) puff his cigar in your face, without the slightest regard to the decencies of life.

The wealth of many of the locomotive Americans, who halt at Galveston on their way up the country, seems frequently to consist in the number of their offspring. Babies are a staple commodity, and their cries frequently rendered our nights sleepless and our days wearisome. There was one large family who had spent a noisy night close to us, and whose parents, to my dismay, forgot the baby on their departure. I have no doubt it was a girl, and a sickly one to boot, or their memories would have served them better.

The ladies were all busily engaged during the day in needlework of some kind or other, but I was surprised to find that the now universal art of crochet work was unknown at Galveston. They fell in love with the accomplishment when directly it was explained to them, and were all eager to begin a purse immediately. Unfortunately, the means did not keep pace with the intention, for Galveston could not boast of a single skein of the requisite silk, nor could the blacksmith whom they summoned to their assistance, contrive to make even the humblest imitation of a delicate crochet needle. I left them still struggling with their difficulties when I commenced our preparations for departure.

We did not return to New Orleans in the same steamer which brought us to Galveston, greatly preferring the *Alabama*, a vessel lately taken off the Havanna station, where she had been running for some years. The influx of emigrants into Texas was at this time so great, that it had become quite a profitable speculation to charter vessels for their conveyance. Thus it was that the *Alabama* a good and safe boat with an excellent captain, found herself running between New Orleans and Galveston, to the comfort and convenience of many who, like ourselves, neither considered the steamers already on the station quite seaworthy, nor the conduct of those on board altogether blameless.

We had made several pleasant acquaintances at Galveston, with whom we were sorry to part, and had also to regret a delightful young English horse, nearly thoroughbred, which had been hired for me during our stay, and which I could not of course take away with me. We left Galveston with the conviction that she was "going ahead" fast, and we felt happy in her prospects. The weather was calm and delightful, and we had a charming passage back to the city. We approached the gay scene after an absence of a few weeks, with real satisfaction, for it certainly looked infinitely more cheerful than the lonely island we had left. As I passed the convent of the Sacre Coeur, I could not help thinking how much less the fair nuns who inhabited that lightsome building were to be pitied than those who vegetate in a similar establishment at Galveston. Since our former visit to that place, the largest house in the island has been converted into a convent for the sisters of the Sacre Coeur, and I always thought it the most gloomy looking refuge for single ladies that I ever saw. We have now been returned two days, so I shall bid you farewell for the present.